RETHINKING
SCHOOL IMPROVEMENT
Research, Craft, and Concept

RETHINKING
SCHOOL IMPROVEMENT
Research, Craft, and Concept

ANN LIEBERMAN, Editor

Teachers College, Columbia University
New York and London

Published by Teachers College Press, 1234 Amsterdam Avenue, New York, N.Y. 10027

Originally published as *Teachers College Record*, v. 86, no. 1, Fall 1984.

Library of Congress Cataloging in Publication Data

Main entry under title:

Rethinking school improvement.

   "Originally published as Teachers college record,
v. 86, no. 1, fall 1984"—Verso of t.p.
   Includes index.
   1. School improvement programs—United States—Addresses, essays, lectures.   I.   Lieberman, Ann.
LB2822.82.R47   1986   371.2'07   85-26173

ISBN 0-8077-2807-1

Manufactured in the United States of America

91   90   89   88   87   86   1   2   3   4   5   6

Contents

Introduction

ANN LIEBERMAN
Teachers College, Columbia University

After all the national reports on education have been read, analyzed, praised, and critiqued, there will still be the crying need to figure out *how* to improve schools to make them better places for both the adults who come to teach and the young who come to learn. Schools are complex organizations; we therefore need complex ways of thinking about them. The authors in this book have participated in a variety of studies attempting to better understand schools. They have been involved in large-scale national studies as well as ethnographies of single schools. Some are veterans of reform movements of several decades ago, while others are associated with the current reform debate; some have created policies about school improvement that others have implemented, while others have been responsible for creating new ways of thinking about schools. They have all been asked to write about ideas that go beyond their formal reports, to expand their original notions, to speculate, to create new images, or rework some old ones.

The chapters are under two major headings — "Extending and Refining Old Ideas" and "New Images and Metaphors." In the former category, the authors go back to their own work and think critically about how to understand in a more complete way what they or others have dealt with in the past. In the latter, the authors offer us several fresh ways to think about school improvement. All the contributors recognize that the world they are looking at is both linear and nonlinear, artistic and scientific, private and public, planned and unplanned — in short, a complicated human organization. None are guilty of making the world small or simple.

The book opens with Seymour Sarason as he raises the complex issues of educational reform. In revisiting his own work and reflecting on current work, he takes us to task, encouraging us to look at the issues that must inform the school improvement discussion. He reminds us once again that the preparation of teachers and the reform of schools are not two separate issues but are intimately related to one another.

Maxine Greene calls on us to pay attention to the actions we undertake, to the interventions we make, to our own life histories. She extends both the vision and the value of teaching.

Judith Warren Little goes back to her earlier study of school success and staff development and closely examines the conditions necessary to sustain "collegial" professional relationships, with particular focus on the dilemmas inherent in these relationships.

Tom Bird's analysis of a delinquency prevention research and development program extends the earlier notion of "mutual adaptation" by adding the concept of "mutual accomplishment." He describes what success looks like from the perspective of both the developers and the participants.

Michael Huberman and Matthew Miles look deeper into their field study, which was part of the larger *Study of the Dissemination Efforts Supporting School Improvement.* They discuss what they come to call an "ecumenical" approach to both the rational and conflict theories of social change.

Lou Smith, John Prunty, David Dwyer, and Paul Kleine as a team go back to Kensington, a school Lou Smith studied fifteen years earlier with Pat Keith. While doing a follow-up study, the team struggles with a conceptualization that helps explain their work. They blend natural history and the life histories of the people under study to enlarge their own perspectives on educational reform over time.

Lynne Miller and I go back to our 1978 article in the *Teachers College Record* on the social realities of teaching and add to our findings some themes on school improvement based on further research and experience. These themes look like common sense but are not yet common knowledge or common practice.

Terry Deal convincingly argues for changing our thinking about organizational change in education by looking at the political and symbolic side of the way people act in schools. Using many examples, he argues for a conceptual pluralism that allows for a richer understanding of the culture of organizations.

Karen Zumwalt compares the new mother with the new teacher and finds striking similarities and differences. She concludes with implications for changing the conditions of support for the new teacher and offers some suggestions for involving more young people in teaching.

Phil Schlechty and Anne Joslin suggest that the present image of the school as a factory (as well as several other metaphors) is insufficient. They offer in its place the metaphor of the school as a knowledge work organization and explain the roles of student and teacher with this image in mind.

Milbrey McLaughlin argues for the use of teacher evaluation as a tool in school improvement. She analyzes all the current and potential difficulties in teacher evaluation, and then, using a research base, builds a case for a complex view of evaluation as a means of professional development.

Joann Jacullo-Noto reports on strategies of staff development through collaborative research, an enterprise that teams in-service teachers with universities. In doing so, she works for a new understanding of the possibilities of a partnership between schools and universities.

Judith Schwartz describes an in-service education institute that is run by teachers within a school district. Her chapter describes aspects of a different image of school improvement, including the organization of the institute, content and evaluation of the in-service program, and the collaboration between parents, teachers, and the administration.

A. Harry Passow ends the book with a look backward and a look forward. He urges us to work for "meaningful change," which must include changes in "the knowledge, skills, attitudes, understandings, and values of staff; in the organizational relationships of the school; in the climate and the environment of the school; and in the transactions between teachers and learners."

Part I
Extending and Refining Old Ideas

The Preparation
of Teachers Revisited

SEYMOUR B. SARASON
Yale University

Initially the focus of this paper was to be on discipline: a ubiquitous, bedeviling problem for everyone in schools, especially teachers. Discipline has always been a problem, but its frequency and management have in recent decades taken on a note of urgency, particularly in our urban schools. I resisted this focus for several reasons. For one thing, the problem is not peculiar to the school setting; it has also become a major issue in family life. If we have learned anything about discipline in family life, it is that it is not understandable in terms of the single individual. Discipline is comprehensible only in terms of the family as a social system embedded in larger systems. Similarly, when a child is a disciplinary problem in the classroom, our understanding is grossly incomplete if we rivet our attention on the characteristics of that child independent of the teacher, if we do not fathom the constitution (formal or informal) by which that classroom is governed, if we neglect the relationship between the characteristics of that classroom and those of the school in general, and, of course, if we pay no attention to the ways in which what happens in that classroom and school reflects features of families and the surrounding community. A third reason derives from the fact that when we talk about disciplinary problems, we usually refer to the failure of school personnel to manage these problems so that they do not recur or, better yet, to prevent such problems from even arising. In my experience, as soon as we use the word "failure," we have narrowed the problem to an encounter between a child and a teacher—a narrowing that effectively blinds us to the need for a broader perspective. It goes without saying that a teacher must take action in the here and now, that some ways are better than others in managing rule-breaking children and defusing potentially explosive situations, that no teacher is equally effective with all types of children, and that situations of stress are not conducive to reflective thinking and dispassionate action (on the part of child or teacher). But two other things are no less obvious.

First, the prospective teacher is ill prepared, both in terms of theory and practice, to think about and deal with issues surrounding discipline. As I shall stress later, teachers are clinicians in that they diagnose and

3

treat, but their preparation for the clinical role is woefully inadequate. Second, as I describe in *Schooling in America: Scapegoat and Salvation,* the disinterest and boredom felt by many students are major contributions to the increase and severity of discipline problems.[1] In short, as long as we discuss discipline in terms of the classroom, we will miss seeing that the larger context in which schools exist, and whose features they reflect, are ultimately more fateful for what schools are or will be than focusing on the disciplined and the disciplinarian. This explains why I had such resistance to focusing on discipline. I had come to the conclusion that however important discipline is for teacher and student, the fact that it has become an object of obsessive concern—for educators, the mass media, policymakers, parents, and (often) the police— should warn us that we are dealing with issues that go far beyond the classroom and the school. What this suggests, at least to me, is that something about our educational systems and our contemporary society, our imprisonment in traditional ways of thinking about and organizing the encapsulated classroom in the encapsulated school, and our inability to confront squarely the gulf that children experience between life in and out of schools not only create discipline problems but will also continue to erode support for public schooling. Put in another way, discipline, however important it may be is only one of a number of interrelated issues that engender incomprehension, hostility, and criticism in the general public. Therefore, given my resistance to a focus on discipline, I have devoted the following pages to explaining why the outlook for educational reform, including any efforts to reduce the frequency and severity of disciplinary problems, is not a pleasant one.

The return of public education to the national agenda has occurred not because new ideas or proposals are creating controversy. Writing as I am after the recent presidential election, it would be safe to bet that education will receive increasingly less attention and that the unimaginative, traditional proposals of recent years will continue to receive most of what little of the fleeting attention policymakers and the general public are forced to give to the issue. And if test scores increase by a couple points—or if they do not take a downward course—policymakers will not have to be forced to take the blame for the failure of their "shape up or ship out" psychology. I can understand why many want to believe that quality of education is highly correlated with quantity of education. That quantity and quality of education are correlated I will view as an article of faith; that they are highly correlated is a belief that requires delusionary tendencies that I think (hope) I have outgrown. I am not being flip or nihilistic. Within the past two years I have spoken to scores of educational colleagues (teachers, administrators, policymakers) regarding my recent book *Schooling in America.* It is in this book that I take up and reject the axiom that education should and best takes place inside encapsulated classrooms in encapsulated schools. I do not have space here to repeat or even summarize the argument I advance in that book. But what I need to tell you are the major reactions I have gotten from those who have heard or read my argument that schools are not interesting places for students and teachers. One nearly unanimous reaction is that engendering and maintaining student interest that is intellectually powered and self-generating is inordinately difficult and *most of the time, it is impossible.* I would like to stress that point, which was made by teachers of vastly different student populations, not only because it was a nearly unanimous reaction, but also because it was shared by teachers who were regarded by others as very good teachers. They were saying more than that the task is difficult; they were saying that it is virtually impossible. Others thought that the consequences of the rejection of the encapsulated classroom were too unclear, too impractical given the size of the student population. In short, they accepted the argument I developed up until its final conclusion. So, again, we agreed that engendering and sustaining student intellectual curiosity and powers was a sometime thing, and that if the near past was a harbinger of the near future, the classroom would become even more boring, slight rises in test scores not withstanding. Teachers, of course, are delighted if test scores rise, but few delude themselves with the belief that those higher scores reflect a desirably altered intellectual and personal orientation. When we speak of the quality of education (be it in regard to elementary, secondary, undergraduate, or graduate schools), we refer to the degree to which the varied strands of the learning process are woven, so to speak, into a welcome mat that invites the learner to willingly traverse it into an indefinite future, that is, it is a mat from which the student does not wish to stray. A third reaction to my argument is agreement that the "unmotivated and disinterested" student looks remarkably motivated and interested when you follow him or her around outside of school.

Added up, these reactions say that my diagnosis is valid but my prescription is unacceptable. But the fact is, I offered no prescription. Indeed, I made it clear in the book that if I were given the power to implement my proposals, I would not do so. My sole aim, which I explicitly asserted, was to gain currency for these ideas: to get them into the marketplace of ideas where they could be discussed, shaped, and reshaped, and to stimulate imaginative minds to try them out on a modest scale. If we have learned anything about the change process, it is the bedrock importance of gaining the understanding and support of those who "own" the problem, because directly or indirectly they will be affected by what happens. But I use the pronoun "we" inadvisedly, because, to my knowledge, every new policy that has been articulated by policymakers and implemented by administrators—on the federal, state, and local levels—has violated what *we* have learned about institutional change.

With the above as prologue, I now turn to a set of issues that, regardless of one's perspective, is of crucial importance to the future of public education. (If you feel any kinship with my perspective, it represents a set of issues that hits you in the face because it is obvious that radical change in regard to where education takes place will require a similar degree of change in the preparation of educators.) These are issues I take up in a forthcoming book, *Caring and Compassion in Clinical Practice: Issues in the Selection, Training and Behavior of Helping Professionals.*[2] The following are assertions upon which I will subsequently base certain proposals:

- The hallmark of the clinical role is that on the basis of formal training and experience, someone endeavors to help another person who has a problem. The label clinician conjures up imagery of a hospital, a clinic, or a practitioner's office, but there are in fact many nonmedical professionals who in their daily work find themselves in the clinical role. Educators, teachers especially, are clinicians. If the word teacher conjures up an image of someone standing in front of a class of children—informing them, stimulating them, guiding them, evaluating them—it is an image as valid as it is incomplete. As any teacher will attest, no day passes that does not require the teacher to deal with a troubled child or parent, that is, to diagnose for the purpose of being helpful. And as many teachers will go on to attest, the number of such academically and/or personally troubled children is frequently not miniscule. No less than an internist, pediatrician, or cardiologist, the teacher is faced with individuals in distress.
- The preparation of teachers is blatantly inadequate in light of the realities of classrooms and schools, and this is particularly true in regard to the clinical role. This inadequacy has long been recognized (especially by teachers), and yet in the plethora of reports that have appeared in the past four years, there has been literally no recognition of this inadequacy. I find this omission astounding. It is an omission that over the decades has contributed to the perception that teachers are less effective than they should be and, in regard to children in distress, that they are not as caring or compassionate as they should be.
- In comparison to other professions whose practitioners are clinicians (e.g., physicians, psychiatrists, clinical psychologists), education requires the least and most narrow preemployment experience. Even in terms of the traditional conception of what a teacher needs to know

and be able to do, the duration and substance of practice teaching is, at best, inexplicable and, at worst, irresponsible. Needless to say, if one views the teacher as a clinician—as a fateful intervener in the lives of students—the situation can be characterized as intolerable. That competent and excellent teachers do develop goes without saying, but they are what they are despite their training, not because of it.

- The criteria by which practitioners are admitted to the educational profession are irrelevant to the kinds of characteristics we wish them to have. For example, if we believe that teachers should be caring and compassionate people, why are those characteristics not reflected at all in the criteria for selection? In this regard education is no better or worse than other clinical professions. Within the past few years the medical community has been criticized, from within and without, because physicians seem to be less caring and compassionate than they should be. When we look at the criteria by which people are admitted to medical school, they have nothing, but nothing, to do with the characteristics of caring and compassion.

These assertions probably sound harsh, but I see no point in glossing over, or taking the edge off, unpleasantries our field has been unable or unwilling to face. The harshness of my response derives from both anger and despair over the irrelevance of the reports on educational reform— reports that are amazingly and unforgiveably ahistorical, and that implicitly (sometimes even explicitly) set up educators in general and teachers in particular as scapegoats, as if they "willed" the current malaise. But what I most damn in those reports is the reinforcement they provide for the traditional images of what a teacher and a classroom are. More than two decades ago Burton Blatt, Kenneth Davidson, and I wrote *The Preparation of Teachers: An Unstudied Problem in Education*.[3] One of the themes in that book was that the preparation of teachers bore little or no relationship to the realities of the classroom. The book had no impact whatsoever and it went out of print very quickly. Yet, though the book died a silent death, the same cannot be said for the issues we raised. They have come back to haunt us again and again. It is a source of satisfaction to the three of us that as the years have passed, the major themes of our book have been confirmed, not by explicit recognition of the validity of the themes, but by the failure of every effort toward improvement that rested in principle on acceptance of traditional practice.

The situation in education today is similar to that which existed in medicine at the turn of the century. The preparation of physicians then, like that of educators then and since, was inimical, rather than conducive, to the goals of repair and prevention. Indeed, the majority of medi-

cal schools were not only unaffiliated with a university but even unaffiliated with a hospital! Put in another way, the clinical preparation of the
physician was flimsy, occasional, and even harmful in its consequences
for sick people.

In *Caring in America,* I devote a longish chapter to Abraham Flexner's 1910 report on medical education in the United States and Canada.[4] Rarely has a report had such quick and long-lasting consequences.
We cannot truly understand medical education today without reading
Flexner's report. Why did it have such an impact? First, Flexner described in unvarnished terms what passed for medical education, leaving
no room for doubt that the clinical preparation of physicians was scan-
dalously inadequate. Second, he made it clear that preparation for practice required a step-by-step and continuous exposure to the demands on
and obligations of the clinical endeavor. Practice was not to be divorced
from theory, and theory could only be comprehended in light of the
realities of application. Third, he emphasized that those responsible for
the training of physicians had to be, among other things, experienced
clinicians — role models for the students. Fourth, he not only called for a
revolutionary overhaul of medical education, but he also outlined and
justified lengthening medical education. In doing so, he reminded his
readers, he was being eminently practical, not utopian, in regard to
serving the public welfare. Finally Flexner was the right man at the right
time with the right kind of foundation support. What most people do
not know is that Flexner's report was commissioned by the Carnegie
Endowment for the Improvement of Teaching. Flexner was not a physician, he was an educator. And he had a cast of mind that did not permit
him to resort to generalities, to confuse what is with what should be, or
to resort to scapegoating. There was too much at stake to spend time
fruitlessly assigning blame as if people had consciously willed the deplor-
able conditions he described.

That education today needs a Flexner is all too apparent when we
read the reports of the past few years on what is wrong with our schools
and what needs to be done. We are not faced with problems *in* schools,
we are faced with problems that reflect the processes by which people
self-select themselves into education, the criteria by which people are
selected by our educational institutions, the style and substance of
teacher education, and the nature of the relationship between school
and community. Colleges and universities, schools, communities — the
problems that plague us will be intractable as long as our efforts at
change deal with them separately or, worse yet, betray an inability to
confront the need for radical change.

It is far beyond the scope of this article to outline what I believe needs
to be considered if public education is to be given a new direction, to be

infused with a renewed sense of mission. In the following proposals I have restricted myself to the issue of teacher education, if only because teacher education is the litmus test of how seriously we take our knowledge of the realities of the role of the teacher in the culture of the school and its community.

- First of all, during the undergraduate years there should be available to *any* student a year's field experience in schools. The major aim of this field experience is to expose the student to the culture of the school: the types of roles within the school; how these roles vary with grade level; the rationale for and problems of administrative structure; the formal and informal sources of power; the processes and styles of decision making; the roles of parents, and the issues surrounding community attitudes and participation; the budget-making process, and the economic context (local, state, federal) within which it occurs; the origins and role of unions, and the nature of and steps in collective bargaining; and the myriad ways in which schools are political organizations in that they are not understandable without attention to the ways in which power and authority (within and without the system) are defined and distributed.
- This year in the field would *not* be for the purpose of training teachers, although some exposure to the teaching role would be desirable. Its major purpose would be in principle identical to that of the anthropologist who seeks to understand a particular culture. The student would attempt to grasp the wholeness of the culture by studying its political, economic, historical, and sociological features and how these features create the conditions for, and explain the variations among, the individuals and groups in that culture. Put most briefly, it is a year in which the student is helped to attain a social science perspective on our schools and society. It is not an experience that would be the responsibility of a department, or of a school of education, or of any one of the social sciences. Wherever responsibility would be placed, it would reflect the commitment of a multidisciplinary team. This year would be a demanding experience both intellectually and educationally.
- In addition, the year would be an attractive experience for any student desiring to gain an understanding of one of the crucial institutions in our society. As a result of the experience, some students who had not considered a career in education may decide to pursue such a career. And those who had given thought to a career in education would have a far more secure basis for making a decision than is now the case. At the very least, the availability of the year's field experience would provide a rationale for and give a status to education that it does not have

now in the undergraduate curriculum. Let me emphasize that this year in the field would not be a professional experience, or an experience devoted narrowly to educational methods. It would be an attempt to integrate perspectives that broaden and deepen the student's knowledge and conceptualization of the school culture.

- Following this field experience those who seek a career in education would be required to have a year-long practice teaching experience. This could be during an undergraduate or a graduate year. I would expect that precisely because the practice teaching would be preceded by the field experience, it would involve more than simply spending time in one classroom in one school. In other words, the substance and goals of practice teaching would, in different ways, be changed if only because the student would already have an experiential base upon which to draw.

These proposals will doubtlessly encounter numerous objections. For one thing, carrying them out would require an undergraduate faculty in education and the social sciences that some colleges do not have or, where such faculties do exist, they often have no interest or expertise in regard to the culture of the school. This is less an objection than a statement of the problem: How do we begin to bring education into the mainstream of the social sciences, failure to do so in the past having contributed to the low status of education in the university? It is an issue that John Dewey raised and discussed in his presidential address in 1899 to the American Psychological Association.

In coming before you I had hoped to deal with the problem of the relationship of psychology to the social sciences and through them to social practice, to life itself. Naturally, in anticipation, I had conceived a systematic exploration of fundamental principles covering the whole ground, and giving every factor its due rating and position. That discussion is not ready to-day. I am loath, however, completely to withdraw from the subject, especially as there happens to be a certain phase of it with which I have been more or less practically occupied with the last few years. I have in mind the relation of Psychology to Education. Since education is primarily a social affair, and since educational science is first of all a social science, we have here a section of the whole field. In some respects there may be an advantage in approaching the more comprehensive question through the medium of one of its special cases. The absence of elaborated and coherent view may be made up for by a background of experience, which shall check the projective power of reflective abstraction, and secure a translation of large words and ideas into specific images. This special territory, moreover, may be such as to afford both sign-posts and broad avenues to the larger sphere, the place of psychology among the social sciences. Because I anticipate such an outcome, and because I shall make a survey of the broad field from the special standpoint taken, I make no apology for presenting this discussion to an Association of Psychologists rather than to a gathering of educators.[5]

Education is or should be a social science; it cannot go it alone in any intellectual sense. Assigning blame for the isolation of education in colleges and universities is fruitless; the task is less one of explaining than of changing the situation.

A second objection, somewhat related to the first, is that my proposals require a degree of change—in the curriculum, in faculty commitment, and in interdepartmental cooperation—that is not "realistic." In short, introducing change into our colleges and universities means running an obstacle course identical in all respects to the one encountered in introducing meaningful change into our public schools. My proposals imply that without radical change in our colleges and universities, we make the process of changing schools an exercise in futility—inexcusable, ineffective, wasteful, and self-defeating. This is a point that Flexner faced squarely in 1910 when he surveyed medical schools; that is, in order to change medical *practice,* we would have to change medical *education,* and that would mean changing undergraduate and professional schools.

A third objection is that given the low salaries of educators, my proposals would decrease rather than increase the number of students who would seek a career in education because the preparation time for independent practice would be lengthened. There are two responses to this objection. First, when the requirements to enter a profession have been made more intellectually demanding and respectable, quantity and quality of the applicant pool have, more often than not, been increased. My second response would be to point to the development at Queens College in New York of a one-year graduate internship in teaching to follow the undergraduate teacher training sequence. This internship reflects the spirit of my proposals even though it has a much more narrow conceptual and experiential focus. In any event, there has been no difficulty in attracting students. And in fact, as word of the program has gotten around, school systems have requested the opportunity to interview interns for teaching positions because, having increased the salaries they offer, these systems are seeking unusually well prepared teachers.

To say that these and other objections are groundless would be ridiculous. But it would not be ridiculous to say that we have no alternative but to put our own house in order—better yet, to radically restructure our house. We can and should continue to proclaim that the educational enterprise is poorly understood and poorly supported by society, that for too long education has been viewed unrealistically and unfairly either as salvation (secular style) or as scapegoat. But we as educators have played a role in that enterprise; we are not blameless. In the past few years the stimulus for change has not come from the educational community but rather from interested, puzzled, angry policymakers in both the public and private sectors. If, however well-intentioned, their proposals are laughably superficial, let us at least recognize that the stimulus for change has been absent from the educational community for too long. As long as we continue to direct our anger outward and to proceed as if we do not have to radically alter our customary practices and their rationales, we remain part of the problem. If we have met the enemies and recognized that one of them is us, we have at least started the process of meaningful change. If, however, we are incapable of such a recognition, the future is indeed bleak.

Notes

1 S. B. Sarason, *Schooling in America: Scapegoat and Salvation* (New York: Free Press, 1983).

2 S. B. Sarason, *Caring and Compassion in Clinical Practice: Issues in the Selection, Training and Behavior of Helping Professionals* (San Francisco: Jossey-Bass, 1985).

3 S. B. Sarason, K. Davidson, and B. Blatt, *The Preparation of Teachers: An Unstudied Problem in Education* (New York: John Wiley, 1962).

4 A. Flexner, *Medical Education in the United States of America: A Report to the Carnegie Foundation for the Advancement of Teaching* (Washington, D.C.: Carnegie Foundation for the Advancement of Teaching, 1960. Originally published in 1910).

5 John Dewey, "Psychology and Social Practice," in *American Psychology in Historical Perspective,* ed. E. Hilgard (Washington, D.C.: American Psychological Association, 1978), 65–66.

How Do We Think about Our Craft?

MAXINE GREENE

Teachers College, Columbia University

To speak of craft is to presume a knowledge of a certain range of skills and proficiencies. It is to imagine an educated capacity to attain a desired end-in-view or to bring about a desired result. Where teachers are concerned, the end-in-view has to do with student learning; the desired result has to do with the "match" between what students have learned and what their teachers believe they have taught. We differ considerably among ourselves, of course, on the ends we actually have in mind and on the degree to which they can be predefined. Some of us focus on measurable competencies; others, on the process of coming to know, or on "knowing how" rather than "knowing that." Some of us confine our attention to the cognitive domain; others try to cultivate imaginative capacities as well as cognitive ones; still others place equal stress on the affective domain. Many of us are uncertain about how much of our craft we have learned and about how much "comes naturally." We wonder how much of our understanding can be put into words. How much of what we do is purely habitual and routinized? To what degree are choice and imagination involved? Is there a frame of reference to which most of us refer, what has been called "procedural lore"?[1] How often, in any case, do we reflect on what we are doing, given our incessant involvement in the activity of teaching, maintaining order, meeting needs, making plans?

To ask how we think about our craft is not to ask what we know about it. Following Hannah Arendt, I would describe thinking as a "soundless dialogue,"[2] an internalized dialogue through which (as it were) we talk things over with ourselves. In order to engage in it, we have to "stop and think"; and, inevitably, it interrupts ordinary activities. To proceed unthinkingly is to be caught in the flux of things, to be "caught up" in dailyness, in the sequences of tasks and routines. Of course we have to proceed that way a good deal of the time, but there should be moments when we deliberately try to draw meaning out of particular incidents and experiences. This requires a pause, a conscious effort to shake free of what Virginia Woolf called "the nondescript cotton wool" of daily life.[3] She associated such moments of awareness with "moments of being"; and she knew how rare they are in any given day and how necessary for the development of a sense of potency, of vital being in the world.

Thinking about our craft often brings conscience to bear on the actions we

13

undertake in the course of our work. This is not surprising, since the capacity to think about what we are doing involves an attentiveness that overcomes distancing and neutrality. John Dewey once described mind as a way of paying attention, as "care in the sense of solicitude—as well as active looking after things that need to be tended."[4] To take care in this sense is to consider the value of what we are trying to accomplish in our classrooms. It may be to try to justify our interventions in the lives of our students, especially those whose lived experience is markedly different from our own. It may be to reconcile our desires to free them to pursue meanings with our equally strong desires to mold them, to shape them in accord with some mainstream or "middle-class" model of what we conceive to be personhood. How *do* we argue the worth of separating students from their backgrounds, what we may consider their "enclaves"? How do we justify stimulating and encouraging certain individuals, while providing only minimal support for others? How do we justify provoking some to move beyond where they are, while approving others who just about reach their grade level in the work assigned? To bring conscience to bear is not only to ponder the purposes of what we do, although surely it is that as well. It is not only to ponder the meanings of the "worthwhile" encounters we are expected to make possible for the young.[5] It is to take the time for reflectiveness about ourselves and our relation to that segment of the human world in which we do our work.

For all the fact that we pursue our projects within what sometimes appear as concentric circles of influence and opinion (the cultures of the school, the school district, the surrounding public, the state and federal governments), we live most of our working lives in particular situations, understood in large part by means of what Clifford Geertz calls "local knowledge."[6] We are persons with identifiable vantage points and modes of being, simply because we engage in the action called teaching; and, although we can hope for some reciprocity between ourselves and persons in different worlds, with different projects, what we do profoundly affects what we see and how we are. Our consciousness of craft (our singular craft) may be most acute, for example, when we are endeavoring to enable students to decode a short story in a way that will release them into new ways of apprehending and, at once, equip them to do justice to fictionality and other literary norms. This is one of multiple occasions of trying to empower young persons to make their own kinds of sense and, at once, live up to standards of "correctness" or efficacy. We need but think of preparing students to devise and test hypotheses in a chemistry laboratory, or to read the historical record in a manner that gives rise to an explanation of some past event. Any person who teaches understands what it means to feel oneself to be an "authority" with respect to what one is trying to teach. For Peters, this means communicating the idea that the teacher is engaged in something worth doing, something exciting having to do with certain spheres of knowledge and skill. Behind them, Peters writes, "stands the notion that there is a right and a wrong way of doing things, that some things are true and others false, and that it matters desperately what is done and said."[7] Most of us realize, however, that our authority or authoritativeness is likely to be acknowledged by our students only when they need help in becoming, in pursuing what they desire to pursue. "The child," says Donald Vandenberg, "constitutes the authority of the teacher."[8] When our words open up possibilities for the child, he means, when they are felt to contribute somehow to the child's ongoing explorations (or inquiries, or investigations), they are accepted as authoritative. Those of us who view ourselves as teachers rather than trainers know in a very particular way that what we offer—and even what we demand—has to connect with student interest and need and concern. Students have, in some sense, to consent to what we are communicating; they have to *choose* to acknowledge it as somehow relevant to their own sense-making. And then they have to try it out, with all the risk of error that entails, for themselves.

"The craft of teaching has a number of aspects," writes Herbert Kohl. "It relates to the organization of content and the structuring of space and time so that learning will be fostered."[9] He speaks of the need to understand students' levels of sophistication and learning styles; and he associates with "teaching sensibility" a knowledge of how to help diverse students "focus their energy on learning and growth." This may involve a variety of ways of addressing them, of provoking them to attend to the matter at hand. Where young children are concerned, it may require us to play with, indeed to reorganize our knowledge of the subject matter so as to increase the area of contact between that subject matter and the children's minds. "And you reorganize it," David Hawkins once wrote, "according to a different principle than that of textbook. . . . By spreading way out, by making many parts of the logically organized subject matter accessible to the already established means of knowing, and interests and commitments of the learner, you greatly increase the probability and the rate of learning in that subject matter."[10] In the case of older students, we are more likely to stay close to what we believe to be a logical organization of the subject matter, to lay stress on the principles fundamental to the discipline. Here, too, however, there is the possibility of seeking alternative processes for marshaling what Howard Gardner calls "intelligences"[11] in the pursuit of educational goals. He has been describing the multiple intelligences or the range of know-hows of which human beings are capable; and it may be that ways can be found, even in the course of initiating students into the same discipline or symbol system, of establishing contact through the activation of different sorts of potential. Most people, of course, come to know the fundamentals of history through the use of linguistic and logical intelligences; but it is at least conceivable that some can be brought to understanding through the exercise of personal or literary or even spatial intelligence. The same may be true of literature or sociology or even physics. The crucial point is to focus energies in such a fashion that different students, taking different paths, are enabled to learn the appropriate language or notation or symbol system. Each is a perspective, after all; each provides a new opportunity for structuring experience; each offers a distinctive lens through which to attend to the lived, intersubjective world. Equally significant is the fact that, the more languages or notations persons learn, the richer and more varied will be their conversation, and the more likely they will be to participate (from their own standpoints) in the ongoing cultural conversation.[12] We are just beginning to discover what it means for a minority person or a young woman to come to learn, for example, the language of history and to express dimensions of experience in that language that have never been attended to before.

Thinking about what is involved in initiating persons in this way, we cannot but summon up some of our own memories of sense-making, of being enabled to thematize or to symbolize our own lived landscapes when we were young. Some of us are still vaguely aware that the world we originally inhabited was a *perceived* world, not (as in our adulthood) conceived. It was a world of presences, shapes, colors, sounds, tactile surfaces. Only gradually did we begin to name it and, by naming, discover how things were known and understood, how those around us interpreted their lives. Paulo Freire, known as a liberating teacher for his work in literacy programs,[13] has provided an example of what it means to recapture childhood and recreate the experience lived before being able to read words. "I see myself then in the average Recife house where I was born, encircled by trees," he wrote. He told of learning the names of birds, trees, animals; he described how he entered "the language universe of my elders, expressing their beliefs, tastes, fears, values . . . which linked my world to wider contexts whose existence I could not even suspect." And then he went on to describe how it felt to learn to read with a Portuguese teacher's help, to engage in "critical interpretation of texts . . . offered to our restless searching." Finally, he linked that experience to his own beginnings as a young teacher who "lived intensely the importance of the act of reading and writing" with his own students. He was trying to make clear, as any of us might do, the consonance between the procedures he later chose to use and "my way of being and . . . what I am capable of doing."[14]

To reach back, even for a moment, into our life stories may be to find the sources of our craft. Also, it may enable us to regain an awareness of what it actually means to be enabled to learn, to reach beyond where one is. Like Freire, we all began to break through the limits of the perceived world when we moved into the life of language; little by little, we came to know the commonsense reality of everyday that our elders and other people shared:[15] grocery stores, neighbors' kitchens, play yards, work habits, religious beliefs, attitudes toward strangers. We began structuring our own worlds by means of the concepts, the patterns, the schemata associated with those around us and those who came before us. If we can recall our first days in school, we may even recapture the "shock"[16] we felt on moving into a social domain where things were arranged in unfamiliar ways, where activities were scheduled according to regulations we did not quite understand, where we had to live by rules that remote "others" had somehow made. I say all this because whatever "teaching sensibility" we possess must be affected by early experiences, especially experiences of initiation and disclosure. The way we think about our craft must be influenced to some degree at least by the models with whom we came in contact, the teachers who taught us to read and write (or who trained us, drilled us, tested us for our "competencies"). Some of us, clearly, recall teachers who were primarily concerned with communicating ways of proceeding, particular knacks and proficiencies they expected us to try out for ourselves. We realize now that they believed we would learn from our own mistakes, if we became reflective enough about our practice when it came to writing or using Bunsen burners or trying to find out the importance of the cotton gin before the Civil War. They were able to communicate, by the way they handled their materials or gave assignments or spoke with us, the idea that people actually begin to learn when they begin to teach themselves.[17] Others of us have other memories: of teachers whose idea of learning seemed to be limited to what we did on classroom tests, how we behaved, how we performed; of teachers committed to prescribed exercises in the "basics," to unalterably sequential moves, to the transmission of manageable fragments or pieces of "knowledge," to knowing that rather than knowing how.

If, out of weariness or disinterest or indifference, we neglect to think about our craft, we are often likely to repeat certain behaviors recalled from the past. As I have suggested, the point of thinking about what we are doing is to avoid mindlessness and totally routine behavior. I am not suggesting that there is one right way of thinking about our craft, nor that there is one technology or tool kit of procedures. It does appear, however, that our profession is continually learning more about patterns of human development, the growth of meaning structures, the ecology of education, the impact of everyday experience, the modes of communication taking place in classrooms; and, whether or not what we know as educational research is reliable in every instance or even understandable, there does exist a frame of reference to which we are able to refer. Our thinking, in other words, can be mediated by what we have come to know about, say, the ways in which children structure their own experiences or the ways in which various literacies are taught in their homes, of the influences of status or language or class. It is not a matter of storing up notes from classes we have taken; it is a matter of attending to our lived situations in our classrooms with the aid of (or through the lenses of) what we have come to know over time.

It is one thing, we all realize, to encounter a roomful of young people and begin classifying them intuitively in terms of the way different ones look, what they are wearing, how they place their desks. It is another thing to allow what we have learned about cultural diversity and the dramas of development to shape our judgments about the young strangers gathered before us. Instead of seeing a stratified group, we may find ourselves meeting a plurality of individuals, each one posing a distinctive challenge. Instead of viewing them as a kind of hierarchy—with the best-looking and the cleanest and the most eager ones at the top—we might (after thinking about it for a moment) view them as a gathering of persons about to create something like a "public space"[18] between themselves, a space in which they may come together to speak (each in his or her own voice) and read and write and learn. This is one of many conceivable examples of the ways in which what we have learned from the human sciences might direct our attention and help us be reflective about what we are doing. Obviously, if we have been taught by empiricists, we will be more likely to structure our class in a more experimental mode: to see ourselves as testing certain hypotheses with respect to cognition, say, or memory, or micro- and macro-learning. If we have been taught by Skinnerian behaviorists, we will be more likely to perceive our students as organisms whose behavior can be differentially reinforced as they respond to the stimuli we provide.

Much depends on the degree to which the concepts we have learned over the course of time help to illuminate the actual situation. But there is also the question of how what we have learned to conceptualize or formulate relates to what Michael Polanyi called our "tacit knowledge,"[19] our unformulated knowledge, "such as we have of something we are in the act of doing." For all the scope and richness and testability of formal or articulated knowledge, Polanyi believed, the tacit component is the decisive one. Where we ourselves are concerned, our tacit powers are the ones that provided our original understanding of experience, of words and other symbols; and, when we are teaching or attempting to move someone else to learn, we have to rely on the tacit contribution the other person makes if we are to be understood. We can say, then, that the systematic knowledge about the psychological and sociological aspects of teaching and learning gradually made accessible to us actually served (if it was meaningful to us at all) to clarify or verify what we already understood uncritically, by means of our tacit awareness. This is not unlike what has already been said about our lived landscapes. It seems reasonable to say, therefore, that the ways in which we conceptualize or construct or articulate classroom reality ought (if we are thoughtful about them) to be congruent with our original understanding of learning and the world. Thinking about our craft, we cannot but recognize how much more we know than we can ever say; and this is testimony to the tacit awareness that underlies what we have learned. It is also testimony to a sense of personal engagement with what we have come to *understand,* a consciousness of our human desire to keep knowing more, to extend what Polanyi called "personal knowledge."[20]

It is not, then, a matter of making logical deductions from things we as teachers have been taught; it is not a matter of opening old notebooks, textbooks, and lesson plans to find out what specifically applies. Rather, it is a matter of funding the meanings we achieve as we attend to our experiences with the aid of the various things we have come to understand and the various things we have learned. If we choose to see ourselves as pursuing a craft, we may see ourselves as gradually ordering our experience and refining our skills or our capacities against the background of those funded meanings. New understanding and new knowledge, after all, are encountered *against* what was understood and known before. Dewey once made the point that experience itself is most conscious at the moment meanings enter in that they are derived from previous experiences. He said, "Imagination is the only gateway through which these meanings can find their way. . . the conscious adjustment of the new and old *is* imagination."[21] Any one of us can conceive himself or herself in a wholly novel teaching situation, in another place or in an unfamiliar context. We may be acquainted with the exigencies of suburban schools and suddenly find ourselves in an urban ghetto; we may be used to urban ghettos and suddenly find ourselves in a rural school. The alternative to purely reactive behavior is to think about what we are confronting; and it may indeed be the case that we feel peculiarly "conscious," peculiarly alive when we realize that some of what we already knew about preadolescent learning, say, does apply to an unfamiliar group of ten- and eleven-year-olds. What we actually *do* may have to differ from what we did in the old classroom. Farm children, for instance, inhabit a world that is paced differently from that of city children; their family lives may be firmer; their value landscapes may be more constrained. We may find ourselves reconstructing familiar techniques, honing a set of unused skills, and—significantly—using our imaginations in what turns out to be an effort to improve our craft.

This is in many ways an example of personal knowledge at work; it is also a reminder that mastering a craft goes far beyond repetitions and routines. Also, there is some carryover between our own efforts to adjust what we know to new situations and what we hope to empower our students to learn. We are not likely to empower them, however, if we cannot posit them as free agents, persons with the capacity to choose to learn. We speak of classes occasionally in collective terms, but we realize at the same time that, even as it is necessary to make distinctions between the "fifth grade" and the "seventh grade," fifth gradeness and seventh gradeness do not define those we are trying to provoke to learn. Nor, we now realize, is it appropriate to view potential learners as deficit systems, empty vessels awaiting our ministrations. Most of us have come to understand that children and young people, whoever they are, are not merely deficient adults. They have their own legitimate (and sometimes illuminating) ways of constructing their realities. Their lived situations, different from ours as they may be, are many-faceted and (like ours) forever in the making. They possess strengths, aptitudes, skills, sensitivities, interests—

sometimes latent, sometimes manifest—that our tests do not measure. They exist in cultures and participate in symbol systems our ordinary taken-for-grantedness too frequently ignores.[22] Many of us remember all too well how we imposed "invisibility" or "nobodyness" on black children over the years. We are, in fact, only just beginning to take heed of the diverse backgrounds of Hispanic children and the great and varied traditions from which many of them spring.

Gradually becoming aware of all this, we are beginning to recognize that every young person must be encountered as a center of consciousness, even as he or she is understood to be a participant in an identifiable social world. Each one may be encountered as a being who is at once a distinctive individual and someone whose consciousness opens out to the common, an intersubjective world in which he or she is inextricably involved. R. S. Peters has written about how much depends on the importance a society (or a school) attaches to "the determining role of individual points of view."[23] And indeed, in many senses, we are obligated to create situations in which such points of view can emerge and *become* determining or significant. Lacking this recognition, we cannot easily move students to fund their own meanings, to adjust what they know to new situations. We need only think for a moment about girls and women, long convinced that their "different" voices had no determining role.[24] Peters did *not* have them in mind; but what he said about people taking pride in their achievements, choosing for themselves what they ought to do, developing their own styles of emotional response, and about the relevance of all this for their thinking of themselves as persons can be suggestive for those of us concerned about creating educative atmospheres.

Only if we do create them are we likely to move various persons to take the responsibility for trying out the proficiencies, the knacks, the modes of procedure we as teachers may try to make available. Some of us are eager to have our students take their own initiatives, take their own risks. We know, on some level, that they will learn best if they consciously recognize their own errors; make recursive moves; correct, reorder, reconceive, in pursuit of their own possibilities. We know that learning goes beyond what is taught; and some of us have the courage to recognize that individual (like cooperative) learning transcends teacher planning and control. If we are "successful" or "effective," then, there will be no visible product for which we can take the credit. There will be diverse individuals in diverse contexts, engaging in continually new beginnings as they work to make sense of their worlds.

Of course, it probably will have helped if we have been able to engage them in what Israel Scheffler described as a "critical dialogue" aimed at the achievement of learning of the development of needed proficiencies. The teacher, in such a relation, gives honest reasons and welcomes radical questions. "The person engaged in teaching does not merely want to bring about belief," wrote Scheffler, "but to bring it about through the exercise of free rational judgment by the student."[25] What we want, he suggested, is to have teachers submit their own judgments to the "critical scrutiny and evaluation" of their students. To do this, of course, is to avoid manipulation, conditioning, infantilization, and imposition. It is to empower persons to do what John Passmore has called "critico-creative thinking," even to the point of challenging existing rules. Passmore made the point that this is likely to be embarrassing to the teacher: "Anybody who sets out to teach his pupils to be critical must expect constantly to be embarrassed. He can also expect to be harassed, by his class, by his headmaster, by parents. If he gives up the idea of teaching his students to be critical and salves his conscience by training them in skills, this is not at all surprising. But he should at least be clear about what he is doing, and even more important, what he is *not* doing."[26] Clearly, this is another challenge to think about our craft.

Neither Scheffler nor Passmore, however, confront a problematic aspect of all this that requires additional thought. Both, ostensibly, want to create classroom situations that impose the same constraints as any situations governed by the norms of rational discussion. There must be a particular "manner" of carrying on the teaching-learning dialogue. This entails regard for the other, respect for each other's freedom and integrity, consideration, and commitment to a largely cognitive teaching-learning domain. On the surface, there is little wrong with this. Most of us are willing to accept the notion that our teaching activities are largely oriented toward enabling persons to take cognitive action, to become less ignorant, to make properly supported knowledge claims, to distinguish truth from falsity. At a moment in our history when censorship is rife in schools and libraries around the country, when demands are made for teaching "creationism" along with or instead of evolutionary theory, when people are bombarded with all sorts of mystifications by the media, when it becomes increasingly difficult to sort out "fact" from propaganda, grounded assertions from lies, numbers of us see very good reasons for an increasingly cognitive (and critical) emphasis in schools. But then we are reminded by Jane Roland Martin, for instance, that an education oriented to liberating human beings as persons ought to include a broader range of things than the acquisition of knowledge. There are, she wrote, "skills and activities, feelings and emotions" that need to be attended to; there is the sense of community to be fostered, along with the "recognition of our solidarity with other living beings"; there is the natural context to be heeded and understood.[27] She was saying, in other words, that the creation of a rational atmosphere and the encouragement of personal autonomy in the effort to learn were simply not enough.

Other critics and observers raise equally significant issues when they remind us, first of all, that knowledge is ordinarily distributed unequally in existing schools.[28] In the ongoing processes of "cultural reproduction,"[29] we are told, only a relatively few are likely to benefit from the encouragement of free rational judgment. Most students will be trained to take their allotted roles in a stratified society. The languages they speak and their cultural experiences will be consistently disconfirmed;[30] they will be taught that they are in important ways inferior, ineffectual, and powerless. No matter how well-meaning their teachers, they will be condemned, as it were, to mastering the basic skills and little more, because they are conceived of as people bound for futures in which only basic skills will be required. We are being reminded—or informed—by such thinkers that, since the schools inevitably mirror the socioeconomic system, little education will take place within them. We who are teachers, in spite of all we remember and understand and know will be expected to keep order and to train; however we identify ourselves, we may be functionaries.

To think about our craft, then, also involves thinking about schools in their complex social and political frameworks. It may even involve attending to patterns of belief and conduct in the surrounding community—phenomena that cannot but mediate what we do, what we are permitted to do, what we can expect of the young. As I have been suggesting throughout these pages, the very charge to think about what we are doing is a charge to rebel against mere acquiescence, the project of functionaries and clerks. There is probably little the schools per se can do to alter the socioeconomic system, reduce unemployment, halt worker dislocation, transform cost-benefit arguments into humane dialogue and debate. But there remains a great deal teachers can do to empower the young to reflect critically on what happens to them and around them, to identify what is possible for them and move to make it real. It may even be that those of us who can awaken the young to go beyond in their sense-making and their risk-taking may make some contribution to the transformation of their worlds.

It appears beyond question that we must do more to imagine ourselves into the lived worlds of our students. We can, for example, provide opportunities for the telling of life stories, the display of family customs and family histories. If, indeed, a public space is to open in our classrooms, it must be one where young people can come together in terms of who they are and be granted respect and regard. Yes, there are likely to be Hispanic voices and black voices and Chinese voices and Haitian voices, along with the voices of the traditional ethnic minorities. All of them offer potentially new perspectives on what is intersubjective, what is shared; at once, all are in some manner partial, as all perspectives are partial. There are always boundaries to be broken through, new horizons to be revealed.

There is also the always impinging world of popular culture—television, video, video games, rock music, and the rest—the "curriculum" of which is easily as influential as any we fabricate in our schools. In some degree, it is popular culture that unifies the young throughout the country, in suburbs and big cities, in rural towns and mountain villages; it may even play the role the "common school" was once supposed to play. Many of the meanings young people sediment and fund derive as much from their experiences with film and rock concerts as they do from family lives; and it seems important that we acknowledge all this and try not to disconfirm it. If we ignore it or show contempt for it, students will (and do) invent their own "hidden curriculum" to counter the hidden curriculum we are continually informed exists in schools.[31] This in no sense means that we become aficionados of popular culture, or even connoisseurs. It does mean that we understand enough about it and about our students' response to it to make it one of several occasions for reflectiveness. No matter how we evaluate soap operas, say, or news programs, or MTV, or talk shows, or rock performances, we cannot but come to realize the staccato and fragmented experiences to which they lead. Empowering young people to think about what *they* are doing (and listening to and watching and applauding), we may be able to communicate the idea that there are possibilities, not solely of an expansion of their landscapes, but of a new coherence, an order they have the capacity to create themselves.

Yes, many of us desire to acquaint the young with the large possibilities of vision and feeling we associate with Shakespeare, Herman Melville, the Impressionist painters, Martha Graham, Mozart, Schumann, filmmakers like Truffaut and Bergman and Altman, dramatists like Pinter and Stoppard and Miller and O'Neill. These may be exemplary; they may be paradigm cases of openings into alternative realities and more extensive worlds. If we can remove what Walter Benjamin called the "aura" from such forms,[32] if we can release the young to engage with a degree of informed awareness and against the background of their own experience, they may come to encounter such forms as enlargements of their lived lives, extensions of what rock and video and sitcom do in their worlds. But we ourselves have to care. We ourselves have to be literate enough to comprehend the media and the shaping of media that produce the forms of popular culture, even as we have to be literate enough to know what it is like to move into a pictorial space and discover a Cézanne mountain, to allow our imagination to achieve the illusioned world of *The Glass Menagerie*, the symmetries and diagonals of Balanchine's *Jewels*, the textures and melodies of a Mozart quartet. It is not that we are morally "better" or possess more status when we know these things. It is that, through our own attending and the going out of our own energies, we are able to break the bonds of the ordinary and the taken-for-granted, to move into spaces never known before. And that is what some of us, considering our craft, want for those we teach: the opportunity and the capacity to reach beyond, to move toward what is not yet.

I think of Virginia Woolf and of Celie in Alice Walker's *The Color Purple* and the Lady in Brown in Ntozake Shange's *For Colored Girls Who Considered Suicide When the Rainbow Was Enuf* and the narrator in Walker Percy's *The Moviegoer* and Wallace Stevens's man with the blue guitar who would not "play things as they are." I think of numerous figures in literature, yes, and in history who overcame their own powerlessness through "shocks of awareness," through increasingly rich and impassioned letter writing and "naming" of the world, through leaps to the "Adult Reading Room" to find their "own reality," through embarking on a search—because "not to be onto something is to be in despair." These are images of transcendence, images of resistance. Thinking about our craft, thinking about what it might mean to release the newcomers, the diverse young to learn how to learn, we can think of ourselves as empowering. And the desired end-in-view? To enable persons to reach beyond, to seek in distinctiveness and membership for what is not yet.

Notes

1 Vernon R. Howard, *Artistry: The Work of Artists* (Indianapolis: Hackett Publishing, 1982), p. 189.

2 Hannah Arendt, *The Life of the Mind: Thinking* (New York: Harcourt Brace Jovanovich, 1978), pp. 31, 122.

3 Virginia Woolf, *Moments of Being* (New York: Harcourt Brace Jovanovich, 1976), p. 70.

4 John Dewey, *Art as Experience* (New York: Minton, Balch & Co., 1934), p. 263.

5 R. S. Peters, *Ethics and Education* (London: George Allen & Unwin, 1979), pp. 144–66.

6 Clifford Geertz, *Local Knowledge* (New York: Basic Books, 1983).

7 Peters, *Ethics and Education*, p. 259.

8 Donald Vandenberg, *Being and Education* (Englewood Cliffs, N.J.: Prentice-Hall, 1971), p. 67.

9 Herbert Kohl, *Growing Minds: On Becoming a Teacher* (New York: Harper & Row, 1984), p. 57.

10 Quoted in Anne M. Bussis, Edward A. Chittenden, and Marianne Amarel, *Beyond Surface Curriculum* (Boulder, Colo.: Westview Press, 1975), p. 24.

11 Howard Gardner, *Frames of Mind: The Theory of Multiple Intelligences* (New York: Basic Books, 1983), p. 391.

12 Richard Rorty, *Philosophy and the Mirror of Nature* (Princeton: Princeton University Press, 1979), pp. 371–72, 389–90.

13 Paulo Freire, *Pedagogy of the Oppressed* (New York: Herder and Herder, 1970).

14 Paulo Freire, "The Importance of the Act of Reading" (Read at Brazilian Congress of Reading, November 1981), *Boston University Journal of Education*, Spring 1982, pp. 5–11.

15 Alfred Schutz, *The Problem of Social Reality*, vol. I, Collected Papers (The Hague: Martinus Nijhoff, 1967), pp. 57f.

16 Ibid., pp. 231f.

17 Gilbert Ryle, "Teaching and Training," in *The Concept of Education*, ed. R. S. Peters (New York: Humanities Press, 1967), pp. 117–19.

18 Hannah Arendt, *The Human Condition* (Chicago: The University of Chicago Press, 1958), pp. 50–52.

19 Michael Polanyi, *The Study of Man* (Chicago: Phoenix Books, 1958), pp. 12–14.

20 Michael Polanyi, *Personal Knowledge* (New York: Harper Torchbooks, 1962), p. 155.

21 Dewey, *Art as Experience*, p. 272.

22 See, e.g., Paul Willis, *Learning to Labor* (Westmead, Eng.: Saxon House, 1977).

23 Peters, *Ethics and Education*, p. 211.

24 Carol Gilligan, *In a Different Voice* (Cambridge: Harvard University Press, 1981).

25 Israel Scheffler, *The Language of Education* (Springfield, Ill.: Charles C. Thomas, 1960), p. 57.

26   John Passmore, "On Teaching to be Critical," in *Education and Reason*, ed. R. F. Dearden, P. H. Hirst, and R. S. Peters (London: Routledge & Kegan Paul, 1975), pp. 33, 41.

27   Jane Roland Martin, "Needed: A New Paradigm for Liberal Education," in *Philosophy and Education*, ed. Jonas F. Soltis (Chicago: The University of Chicago Press, 1981), pp. 56-57.

28   Henry A. Giroux, *Ideology Culture & the Process of Schooling* (Philadelphia: Temple University Press, 1981).

29   Michael W. Apple, ed., *Cultural and Economic Reproduction in Education* (London: Routledge & Kegan Paul, 1982).

30   Michael F. D. Young, ed., *Knowledge and Control* (New York: Collier Books-Macmillan, 1971).

31   Henry Giroux and David Purpel, eds., *The Hidden Curriculum and Moral Education* (Berkeley: McCutchan Publishing, 1983).

32   Walter Benjamin, "The Work of Art in the Age of Mechanical Reproduction," in his *Illuminations* (New York: Schocken Books, 1978), pp. 217-52.

Seductive Images and Organizational Realities in Professional Development

JUDITH WARREN LITTLE

*Far West Laboratory for Educational Research and
Development, San Francisco*

This article is an exercise in healthy skepticism. Findings on effective staff-development programs, reported with some enthusiasm and confidence,[1] have been subjected to a closer look. The enthusiasm survives; the confidence has been tempered.

Studies of effective professional-development programs have proliferated in recent years, spawning a host of compelling images: collaboration, cooperation, partnership, mutual adaptation or accomplishment, collegiality, and interactive development among them.[2] Such images are seductive, creating a vision of professional work and professional relations at once intellectually stimulating, educationally rigorous, and professionally rewarding. On closer examination, however, conditions that are powerful enough to introduce new ideas and practices in classrooms and to sustain "collegial" relations among teachers require a degree of organization, energy, skill, and endurance often underestimated in summary reports. A closer look reveals the challenges of organization and leadership and uncovers the strains that accompany (and perhaps yield) the triumphs.[3]

This article is adapted from "Designs, Contexts and Consequences in the Real World of Staff Development," a paper presented at the annual meeting of the American Educational Research Association, New Orleans, 1984. The work on which this article is based was supported by contract no. 400–79–0049 from the National Institute of Education to the Center for Action Research, Inc., Boulder, Colorado. The views reflected herein do not necessarily reflect the views of the National Institute of Education, and no official endorsement should be inferred. This article draws on interview and observation data collected in three elementary and three secondary schools in a large urban school district. The study was conducted in collaboration with the district's Office of Staff Development. Schools were selected on a combination of success criteria and involvement in district-sponsored staff development. Taped interviews, informal conversations, and direct observations were conducted with more than one hundred teachers, all administrators and all (assigned) district staff developers.

TWO PROGRAMS: A TALE OF TORTOISE AND HARE

A comparison of two staff-development programs illustrates the organization, initiative, and skill required to achieve collaborative, rigorous programs of effective professional development. The two programs had certain characteristics in common. Both were designed with care, thought, and imagination by the same district specialists, all of whom had reputations as masterful classroom teachers. Both programs began with a focus on ideas derived from research on effective teaching that were considered to be worth testing in practice. (Basically the programs combined principles of mastery learning and interactive teaching, with an element of proactive classroom management.) Both programs were introduced by well-conceived and well-conducted training sessions in which staff developers themselves employed the practices they expected teachers to use. Both provided teachers with a notebook of reference materials that paralleled the training sessions. Both required participation by faculty groups or teams and both provided time during training for group discussion, planning, and problem solving. Finally, both programs received enthusiastic evaluations from participants.

Three years after the programs were launched, one had produced widespread implementation of new practices, renewed professional commitment among experienced teachers, enduring habits of professional development in participating schools, and changes in the routine organization of school life ranging from time schedules to job postings. The other program continued to get good marks from its participants long after they had *ceased* to think about the ideas to which they were introduced or to use the recommended classroom practices. As an in-service program, the latter program was better than most in the eyes of teachers. As a meaningful contributor to a professional repertoire, it was virtually inconsequential. The similarities in the two programs are substantial, but the differences are critical and merit close attention (see Figure 1).

COLLECTIVE PARTICIPATION: WHAT'S A GROUP FOR?

Acting on the premise that influential programs of staff development require the interest and participation of a "critical mass" of staff, designers of both programs set a criterion level for school participation: one-third of a secondary school faculty and three-quarters of an elementary faculty. In the less successful program, teachers were asked to participate in *training* as a group. In the more successful one, teachers and principals were asked to participate in *training and implementation* as a group; in effect, the school staff made a commitment to work with the district in a test of promising ideas that involved training as one of several activities. Teachers at one elementary school placed considerable weight on their collective commitment to the pilot program in accounting for its success:

Figure 1. Designs and Consequences in Two Professional Development Programs

Program Characteristics	"Pull-out" Program with Classroom Follow-up	Long-term School-based Pilot Program
Designs:		
Focus	"Mastery learning" and interactive teaching	"Mastery learning" and interactive teaching
Skills Training	Training modeled expected practices, supplied clear materials, provided for group discussion	Training modeled recommended practices, supplied clear materials, provided "application" time each session
Collective Participation	School-based groups recruited for training only	School-based groups recruited for training and implementation
Collaboration	Trainers receptive to teachers' suggestions for revising training	Invitational process for site selection, collegial team work for implementation. Staff developers and teachers discover together how to implement ideas in practice
Time	Five-day and eight-day training cycles, with one or two classroom visits	Three-year commitment; weekly in-service and curriculum planning sessions
Leadership	Principals agree to teacher release time	Principals take direct, active leadership role in implementation
Consequences:		
Evaluation of training	Positive	Positive
Implementation	Low, uneven	High

I think that it would be a disadvantage not to have the whole school behind the project. . . . I don't see how a few people . . . in one school can have much impact on the whole school. (Teacher)

Admitting that there were some variations in interest and enthusiasm, the participants describe a situation in which persons have some latitude to recruit others in the name of professional growth and school improvement.

I'm not enough of a dreamer to think you're going to get a whole faculty behind something without a little coercion, a little polite coercion. And if you don't do that you don't ever have any growth in your faculty. (Teacher)

The argument can be made, of course, that professional growth is principally a matter of individual preference and skill, and that school improvement is the cumulative effect of many individual efforts. Certainly that is an argument advanced by many teachers, backed by their own stories of learning to teach through a combination of trial and error, luck and persistence. Teachers in all six schools described their isolated experiments with ideas "picked up" in classes, from reading, from other teachers, or by dint of their own imagination.

Nonetheless, teachers' accounts and our observations also suggest some limits to that argument. First, teachers have few opportunities to watch each other at work, and tend to form impressions of each other's competence from students' comments and from casual glances through classroom doorways. The criterion for "good teaching" is often no more than the sense that things are "going well" in the classroom. If trying a new approach requires a disruption in established routines, if it will thereby create the appearance of floundering and place teachers at risk of being judged negatively by colleagues, teachers may be less likely to make the attempt. The more complex and unfamiliar a practice, and the greater a departure it requires from past practice, the more likely it is that teachers will indeed struggle with it. Teachers in one school reported that "it's hard to keep a theory in your head" when embroiled in the day-to-day press of classroom life, even if one admires the theory and wants to test it in practice. A group of implementers may offer a combination of technical advice (problem solving), moral support, and tolerance for mistakes.

Second, new practices may require time-consuming study and preparation even before they can be tested in the classroom. A teacher left to rely on individual preference and skill many reasonably choose to avoid a new practice rather than take the chance that a substantial investment of time and thought will not pan out. If the experiences in these schools serve as evidence, practices that have resulted in greater student achievement and classroom order have required precisely that kind of extensive thought and preparation; without denying the attractiveness and occasional utility of "tricks," "little hints," and ready-made materials, these teachers trace their most impressive accomplishments to more complex undertakings that stretched the limits of their knowledge and experience. Collective participation on some scale (even four members of a single department or two-person grade level teams) eased the burden. Teachers describe group discussions of ideas, shared work in preparing written materials and designing lessons, and collaborative review of progress.

Finally, some practices that teachers have found to be effective over time may show those effects only when used on a large enough scale to alter the entire pattern of teaching and learning in a building; sporadic, isolated attempts in individual classrooms may seem not to "work" when they simply have not been tested on a scale large enough for their virtues to become evident.

Practices of this sort are beyond the power of a single teacher either to sustain or to alter; they draw their influence from collective participation.

COLLABORATION: THE INTERACTION OF PEOPLE AND IDEAS

Three provisions for collaboration among staff developers, principals, and teachers helped to ensure that a collection of bodies would become a group whose members shared equally in the obligations and the risks, invested equally in the hard work of applying ideas in practice, and were credited equally with the accomplishment.

A Four-stage Negotiation with Pilot Schools

In preparing for a pilot program, district personnel constructed a four-step negotiation with schools to ensure clear agreement that the ideas were promising and plausible (worth implementing), that teachers would implement the ideas collectively over a long enough period to see effects, and that a working partnership would be forged among teachers, principal, and district personnel. The terms of participation in the project reflected certain "working hypotheses" on the part of staff developers about the conditions (time, collective support) required to understand, test, and institutionalize ideas that were both unfamiliar and complex.

In a first step, the program's designer and coordinator presented the project in broad outline to a meeting of all elementary school principals, with an invitation to declare interest. Principals who were interested on the basis of that first presentation were invited to a second meeting, where the terms of participation were elaborated further. One condition was an agreement by principals to participate in training and eventually to displace the district consultant as instructor and resource person in the building. That provision was designed to improve the prospects that any changes in teaching practice would endure; it nevertheless had the effect of narrowing the field drastically.[4]

> Well, as I remember, when we met with the coordinator four years ago and she talked about this, she mentioned the fact that when the principal gets involved, it isn't just a matter of sitting through the in-service with the faculty and participating that way. Your involvement had to be a lot deeper and . . . there was lot of training and background that went into it, even, before you began working with the faculty. . . . There were a number of principals that showed an interest until she made that statement and then it kind of cleared the field, really and truly. She was looking for five schools and she almost didn't get five schools because there were not five people who were willing. Because she was very, very clear about the amount of time it was going to take. As I look back on that first year, it did.   (Principal, Westlake Elementary)

A third step required the principal to confirm agreement with at least 75 percent of the faculty before committing the school to participation. Teachers and principal at one elementary school trace their decision to participate to a combination of the principal's stand on the program and the faculty's own disposition to explore promising new ideas:

I told the faculty that I'm willing to be involved if you are. I'm willing to spend the time, I'm willing to commit myself. (Principal)

Four years ago, when we were deciding about this, the whole staff sat down and talked about it. It was put to a vote. . . . We voted as a faculty and it's been great. Not everyone goes along wholeheartedly but everyone would have to admit they've learned something. (Teacher)

In a fourth step, entire faculties of the proposed pilot schools met to hear a description by district personnel of what would be expected over the three-year tenure of the program:

We had an opportunity . . . the five schools that were selected had an opportunity to meet one entire afternoon with the coordinator. And she discussed with them in detail the proposal, the amount of time and commitment that it would take. And they had a chance again at that time, at that point, if they wanted to, to withdraw. And there was one school that did withdraw . . . because they didn't have the support of the faculty. (Principal)

As might be expected, no negotiation procedure, no matter how stringent, is sufficient to anticipate the actual time required, the actual dilemmas faced, the nature and pace of observable progress. Still, the original negotiation forestalled the kind of resistance or indifference that might have emerged had the district left the terms of participation unclear in the hopes of attracting schools more readily.

The persuasiveness of this negotiation rests on shared agreements (clarity) of three sorts: agreement about the promise of the program ideas, agreement on the nature of the roles and relationships required of teachers and principals, and the adequacy of the description to reflect an actual sequence of implementation. For the mastery learning project, the ideas were powerful enough on their face to attract nearly half the elementary school principals. The role envisioned for principals, however, was apparently enough of a departure from the role that was being then enacted by most principals to discourage their participation. Good intentions and "receptivity" apart, teachers and principals may resist program opportunities that represent radical departures from their view of what being a teacher or being a principal permits or requires.

Professional Relations

At stake in staff development are basic rights to the description, analysis, interpretation, and evaluation of classroom practice. Teachers' favorable and unfavorable judgments about staff development revolve precisely around the issue of teachers' rights to propose or share in such analyses and around their obligation to accept the analyses (and advice) of others. The salient point here is not whether a description is recognizable (i.e., demonstrates familiarity with the real world of classrooms), or an analysis accurate or plausible, or particular advice pleasing to the teacher. Those are separate, if important, matters. The point here is whether the interaction called "staff development" is conducted in ways that are properly reciprocal, calling for shared aims and collaborative effort among fellow professionals.

In this program, teachers and staff developers alike found their views mutually valued, sought, credited, and tested. The issue for teachers and for programs of staff development is how such reciprocity was established as the basis for shared work, and was confirmed in the course of routine interaction. Several contributors seem likely.

First, all parties were explicitly invited to act as knowledgeable contributors. The district consultant was expected to combine classroom experience with "theory" to provide an initial introduction to new ideas, and to advise teachers as they prepared curriculum units and materials. Teachers were expected to contribute knowledge gained from close observation of present practice and from efforts to apply new ideas to actual classroom situations. The principal was expected to contribute knowledge gained from observation of classroom practice and from additional readings of theory and research. Working as a group, they discovered and resolved the problems of instrumentality, congruence, and "cost" that Doyle and Ponder[5] and others have associated with teachers' decisions whether to introduce new principles and practices into the classroom.[6] The task was sufficiently complex to make collaboration sensible and fruitful.[7]

Program implementation became an enterprise in which teachers, principals, and staff developers discovered what it meant to move from general ideas on paper to specific applications in classrooms. Over time, the ideas evolved and took shape in numerous concrete ways in an instance of what Bird (in his article in this issue) characterizes as "mutual accomplishment."

Thus, collaborative arrangements between staff development and schools offer the opportunity to demonstrate reciprocity among fellow professionals, to develop clearly known and shared aims, and to establish trust by building a history of predictable performance.

Second, time for shared work was allotted in the weekly schedule. The district consultant visited the school at least once a week. Periods of "instruction" were structured to introduce new elements of theory; to permit questions, comments, observations, and problems raised by teachers; and to organize a period of group work to connect theory to practice. Knowing that the principal was devoting yet another morning each week to studying with other principals, teachers willingly spent additional afternoons after school working on materials.

Third, decisions about the focus and scale of curriculum units emerged out of teachers' analysis of core topics and critical skills at each grade level.

Finally, criteria for classroom observation emerged out of the shared discussion of theory and practice, were agreed upon in advance, and were specified at a level of detail that made all parties comfortable about what might be important to notice. Observers used anecdotal records to capture as faithfully as possible all that was said by teachers and students; these notes served as evidence around which teachers and principal or consultant would organize conference discussions. Support for implementation included an element of what has since come to be termed "coaching."[8]

Time

Learning to teach is, according to one teacher, like learning to play a musical instrument. Beyond the wish to make music, it takes time, a grasp of essential patterns, much practice, tolerance for mistakes, and a way of marking progress along the way. In the more successful of the two programs, a major contributor was the organization of time. While the less successful program relied on a "pullout" training session of several days, followed by one or two classroom visits, the more successful program organized before-school sessions every Wednesday morning for more than two years. Each session consisted partly of new material introduced by the resource consultant, the principal, or—in later stages—teachers, followed by group work on curriculum in grade-level teams. *Frequency* of involvement was high: the sheer number of opportunities that teachers had to work on ideas and their application in classrooms. Extended *duration* provided for gradual and incremental command over a set of ideas and cumulative discovery of the ways that they could be applied in classrooms:

> Whenever a basic idea was presented, people would ask, "Now, how are we going to apply this?" (Teacher)

The first six months, according to teachers, were slow and clumsy on all sides. Teachers were uncertain of how to make sense of what they were hearing; staff developers and principals were learning from and with teachers which advice was sound and which was off the mark. Teachers commented:

> You couldn't do it otherwise. . . . You have to get far enough into it to see the advantage.

Units were horrendous headaches to prepare at first. Everyone was new. . . . It was a little easier in the second year and even easier in the third.

It's difficult at first because it's complex.

We spent the first year proving it to ourselves. It took a while . . . not that they moved too fast but that it was all new material.

Give yourself time to see it work. You'll be frustrated at first because it will seem overwhelming. If you'll go step by step and give it at least six months, give it a chance and don't take shortcuts . . . then you'll be convinced.

Such comments, together with other observations of both programs, call into question approaches characterized as "minimal intervention," even when supported by well-designed materials and thoughtfully conducted training sessions.[9]

PROJECT LEADERSHIP AND THE PRINCIPAL'S ROLE

The crucial role of building principals was acknowledged by both programs. Principals were approached first for discussions of the underlying ideas, and their cooperation was sought in recruiting interested faculty members. In only one of the two programs, however, were the principals explicitly required to assume a more direct leadership role in regard to the project, and supported in doing so. In the pilot, principals were expected to learn the theory and practice of mastery learning. They attended weekly in-service sessions conducted by the district consultant. These weekly sessions, as described by teachers and principals, served several purposes. First, the principal became increasingly knowledgeable about a specific set of concepts and practices. Because he was knowledgeable, he was a fair and helpful judge of classroom instruction. He was able to recognize progress in teachers' efforts to implement new ideas, and was a reasonable judge of requests for materials, released time, or other assistance. In the words of one teacher: "The principal has been the mainstay here—he knows the program and can answer teachers' questions."

Acting as a resource person to teachers over a three-year period, the principal:

Attended in-service sessions and read relevant materials that equipped him to assist teachers in implementing the recommended ideas and methods.

Conducted in-service sessions for teachers in a fashion that combined theory, research, and practice.

Gave advice on curriculum units and ideas for course materials.

Observed in classrooms often enough to make feedback useful and to recognize and credit teachers' accomplishments.

Spent time in a weekly workshop conducted by teachers.

From the point of view of one elementary school principal, direct involvement in the program exemplified a shift from a "gatekeeper" stance to a "change-agent" stance; he attributed the change in part to his reading of the results of the Rand Corporation's "change-agent" study.[10] In the five years prior to the pilot project, this principal increasingly engaged in actions that could be viewed as assisting or promoting change (rather than merely permitting or approving it). The gradual development of that role is reflected in Figure 2. In secondary schools, school size and curriculum complexity may make this scale of direct involvement difficult; principals are confronted with establishing a structure of leadership in which selected teachers, as department heads or team leaders, can take the initiative in matters of curriculum and instruction.[11]

CONCLUSIONS, DILEMMAS, AND CHALLENGES

On the evidence, some strategies more than others appeared promising over a range of relevant goals (improvement of teachers' competence, confidence, and commitment; implementation of school-based improvements in instruction or curriculum; balancing the need for stability against the demand for change; and the like). Researchers concluded that staff development is most influential where it: (1) ensures collaboration adequate to produce shared understanding, shared investment, thoughtful development, and the fair, rigorous test of selected ideas; (2) requires collective participation in training *and* implementation; (3) is focused on crucial problems of curriculum and instruction; (4) is conducted often enough and long enough to ensure progressive gains in knowledge, skill, and confidence; and (5) is congruent with and contributes to professional habits and norms described elsewhere as norms of collegiality and experimentation.[12]

Together, these program elements constitute a set of design characteristics. These are complex conditions; each contributing factor also poses certain dilemmas for those who design, conduct, and participate in such efforts. Some of the dilemmas associated with program elements have been displayed in Figure 3. Others, associated with the place of such programs in district initiatives, include these:

Staffing

The successful program required a disproportionate concentration of staff resources on a five-school pilot program. Although the budget for the program was hardly exhorbitant ($40,000 in federal funds during the year of

Continued on page 41

Figure 2. An Emerging Role of Principal in Staff Development

Time Period	Nature of Principal's Behavior	Role "Image"
1960s	"Coordination" of Title I projects —approve ideas —proposal preparation —negotiation of funds —general supervision of project directors	Principal as "gatekeeper"
1973–1974	Participant in collective in-service in response to state legislation —approve ideas —prepare proposal —participate in (sit in on) teacher training	
1974–1975	Participant in in-service; observer of teachers CARE program —approve idea —approve teacher release time —sit in on teacher training —attend principal training —observe teachers in classroom —hold conferences with teachers	
1975–1976	Precision teaching —approve teacher-initiated idea —approve released time for team of teachers —encourage trained teachers to train others —sit in on training ("sharing") session conducted by returning teachers	
1976–1980	Mastery learning: instructor/consultant/ "resource person" —approve and promote idea —seek group commitment to in-service —attend principal training —attend teacher training —conduct teacher training —attend teacher-conducted training as participant —observe and critique classroom performance —rearrange schedules to permit joint work among teachers —arrange released time for teachers —report relevant research to teachers —encourage teachers to serve as consultants to other schools	Principal as change agent

Adapted from J. W. Little, *School Success and Staff Development* (Boulder, Colo.: Center for Action Research, Inc., 1981), Appendix A, p. 40.

Figure 3. Dimensions of Influential Staff Development

DIMENSIONS	CONTRIBUTIONS	DILEMMAS
FOCUS	Permits concreteness and "practicality" that in turn permit useful assistance	Practicality may win out over relevance or defensibility
	Contributes to a shared language for describing, analyzing, and refining teaching practices	Guiding principles may be compromised too casually in the search for practical "adaptations"
	Permits teachers or schools to try out a set of ideas on a large enough scale, with enough concentrated effort, to test their effects	Choice of promising focus may be limited by ambiguous or conflicting research, by prevailing district priorities or circumstances, by existing patterns of practice
	Permits more rigorous evaluation of the relative influence of staff development	Good ideas may go unmatched by powerful program or evaluation design, leading people to say, "We tried it and it didn't work."
ORGANIZATION OF INSTRUCTION		
Model in training the practices you expect teachers or principals to use on the job	Increased credibility of claims that the ideas are effective and practical	Persons will not notice modeling unless it is explicitly stated
	Increased confidence through experience and observation	A performance that is too smooth and polished may discourage persons and may erode rather than build confidence
	Participants offer more thoughtful and precise evaluations of training	All aspects of intended practice must be modeled— demands for preparation time, skill, imagination, and good will

Figure 3. Dimensions of Influential Staff Development (*continued*)

DIMENSIONS	CONTRIBUTIONS	DILEMMAS
Introduce new ideas in sequence Demonstrate, illustrate what ideas look like in practice Provide opportuties for actual practice Provide feedback on performance	Cumulative, progressive command over new ideas and practices; increased willingness to try new ideas in practice	Time constraints, and the temptation to "cover" more than can be mastered through practice in a single session The prevailing view that how one teaches is a matter of "just style" Overcoming the relative isolation of the day-to-day work situation, in which exposing one's ideas and practices to others is rare and "threatening"

TIME
  Frequency
 	
  Duration
	Greater command and confidence with more opportunities to discuss, practice, observe, reflect
	Opportunity for progressive gains over time—cumulative, incremental increases in knowledge, skill, and confidence
		If not seen as useful, more contact likely to erode commitment rather than build it
		Effect relies on increasing expectations over time—escalating stringency and comprehensiveness
		
		Problems of bringing new people in as experienced innovators gain understanding and skill—"creeping exclusivity"
		Limited resources—people "spread thin"

Figure 3. Dimensions of Influential Staff Development (*continued*)

DIMENSIONS	CONTRIBUTIONS	DILEMMAS
ROLES AND RELATION-SHIPS		
Collective involvement	Relevance more assured when "we're all in it together" Opportunity for moral support and technical advice from colleagues Tolerance for struggle with new ideas and practice New ideas tested on a large enough scale to witness effects and to work through problems of implementation Strengthens habits of shared work and problem solving—builds a faculty that is capable of designing and managing improvement	A collection of bodies is not a group: mere exposure to training as a group is insufficient. Effect requires group identity (and interaction) for purposes of implementation Terms of group involvement in early stages must be negotiated in a manner that preserves underlying principles, establishes role expectations, and accommodates local realities without "pulling punches." The temptation will be to emphasize the attractions and downplay the hard work in an effort to attract participants Schools that have had previously successful group involvement with staff development are more likely to accept the terms—the problem of creeping exclusivity
Collaboration	Opportunity to build known and shared aims Opportunity to build trust by demonstrating reciprocity, deference	"Imposed" programs limit the opportunities for collaboration Existing norms limit persons' skill and willingness to act reciprocally (e.g., by giving specific feedback on performance)
	Opportunity to develop a shared lauguage for describing, analyzing, and refining practice (i.e., opportunity to be useful to one another)	The closer people move to the building and the classroom, the higher the risk to self-esteem and professional standing (high gains, high demands)

Figure 3. Dimensions of Influential Staff Development (*continued*)

DIMENSIONS	CONTRIBUTIONS	DILEMMAS
	Opportunity for observing and assisting actual practice (e.g., "coaching") Builds faculty morale and sense of individual and group efficacy over time	Coaching is a potentially powerful practice that violates equally powerful and entrenched norms—it is viewed as useful when it happens but happens only when actually structured by someone with influence Hard for newcomers to join—the language and practice are too sophisticated; "closed" collegiality and creeping exclusivity
SETTING: THE WORKPLACE Consistency with expressed values and priorities of building and district	Relevance —professional development is an obligation of the job; participation is rewarded —participation in specific programs is credited and protected Tolerance for struggle Access to resources Rewards for demonstrable success	Multiple and sometimes conflicting priorities Values reflected in teacher contracts Multiple sources of influence over resources and rewards Sheer complexity of groups, interests, and circumstances may place limits on tolerance Success is rarely measured in ways that are programmatically or politically powerful The more complex the practices, the more time it will take and the more difficult it will be to achieve and demonstrate an effect
Norms supporting collegiality among teachers	Extended staff resources—more minds and bodies to concentrate on applying ideas in practice Prospects for "polite coercion" in the face of promising ideas or compelling circumstances Prospects for continuity (life after funding)	Critical practices of collegiality are the exception rather than the rule and may have to be built (rather than simply built upon) by staff development (talk about instruction, observation, shared planning and preparation, reciprocal teaching, or coaching)

Figure 3. Dimensions of Influential Staff Development (*continued*)

DIMENSIONS	CONTRIBUTIONS	DILEMMAS
Norms supporting the routine examination, evaluation, and refinement of practice	Habits of careful scrutiny that separate judgments about practices and consequences from judgments of personal worth	This perspective is in competition with the views that "teaching is a matter of style" and "you don't interfere with another teacher's teaching"
Role of the principal in stimulating, strengthening, sustaining collegiality and continuous improvement	Rights of initiative ("it comes with the territory") Tactics of leadership —announcing expectations for collegial and experimental work —modeling collegial and experimental work —sanctioning teachers' efforts —defending and protecting new efforts against internal and external strain	These are not the practices for which principals are typically selected, prepared or rewarded
FOUR RULES OF THUMB AND A SPECULATION	Four rules of thumb for teachers and staff developers: If you want it, say it If you want it, teach for it If you want it, organize for it If you want it, reward it	And a speculation about what difference it makes: There's no such thing as an "ineffective" or neutral piece of staff development. Every exposure to staff development will either build commitment to professional improvement or will erode that commitment

the study, in a total district budget of more than $200 million), it permitted a single resource coordinator to be assigned full-time to the project. During the same time period, each of the remaining eleven members of the district's staff-development office was charged with organizing minicourses, conducting workshops on a variety of topics, and serving as the assigned resource person for twelve elementary and secondary schools. Their influence was predictably diffuse.

Budget

The successful program was funded with federal dollars as support for desegregation; in this, as in programs described by others,[13] a shift in federal dollars or priorities will jeopardize the project. (That is, although the practices survive in the pilot schools, there is no basis of continued support and expansion.)

Exclusivity

The invitational procedure by which the district's one hundred elementary schools were narrowed first to fifty interested candidates and finally to five selected sites created conditions powerfully conducive to success. On a pilot basis, such a procedure was substantively warranted. Nonetheless, it also permits (even requires) selecting out 95 percent of the district's schools. The district risks a form of "creeping exclusivity" by which the bulk of program resources are devoted to the most sophisticated, most energetic faculties. To maintain an invitational procedure over time would thus require that a district develop a program of preparation that would equip interested schools to compete successfully for participation in the program.

Principals

The successful program was heavily reliant on the direct involvement of building principals, who participated in principals' training sessions, helped to conduct in-service sessions with faculty, joined planning sessions with teachers, observed in classrooms, publicized teachers' accomplishments, organized schedules and other aspects of school work to facilitate teachers' work with one another, and protected teachers against other demands and distractions. In this manner, the program built an enduring system of support that went well beyond the delivery of good skills training.[14] Such a pattern of leadership, however, also calls for practices for which most principals are neither prepared, selected, nor rewarded.[15]

Teachers as Colleagues

The successful program rested on long-term habits of shared work and shared problem solving among teachers. Such patterns of mutual assistance, together with mechanisms by which teachers can emerge as leaders on matters of curriculum and instruction, are also atypical.[16] According to one review, work teams among teachers have proved relatively unstable, particularly in the absence of an explicit "policy of teaming" on the part of building principals.[17] The very success of the pilot project described here calls attention to the character of professional work in schools and the degree to which "reflection-in-action"[18] might be made an integral part of teaching.

The "Fit" or Integration of Staff Development

A fit of staff development with major lines of program development and authority is argued to be both critical and problematic. In tracing the human and material resources devoted to staff development in three districts, Moore and Hyde found staff development was politically weak and programmatically marginal, in spite of higher-than-predicted allocations of money and time.[19] Responsibility for staff development is often widely diffused, low in the bureaucratic hierarchy, and isolated from major initiatives in curriculum and instruction.[20] In many urban districts, the main contribution of staff development in recent years may have been "to keep things from getting worse"[21] by introducing a measure of stability in times of rapid change. There is no evidence that the projects described here were any more centrally connected to the structures of power and policy, nor any less vulnerable to shifts in budget priorities, than the projects described in other studies.

In effect, we are confronted with a tremendous problem, or challenge, of organization, leadership, and scale. It is simply implausible that a small cadre of staff developers in any district will add measurably to the general fund of teachers' knowledge, skill, and enthusiasm, or that programs of the sort just described could be mounted by a district on a scale large enough to exert widespread influence. The lessons are of a different order of magnitude; the guidelines generated by these program examples are properly seen as guidelines for the organization and leadership of professional work in the day-to-day work of teaching.

Notes

1 J. W. Little, *School Success and Staff Development: The Role of Staff Development in Urban Desegregated Schools* (Boulder, Colo.: Center for Action Research, 1981).

2 P. Berman and M. W. McLaughlin, *Federal Programs Supporting Educational Change, Vol. VIII: Implementing and Sustaining Innovations* (Santa Monica, Calif.: The Rand Corporation, 1978); W. J. Tikunoff, J. B. A. Ward, and G. A. Griffin, *Interactive Research and Development on Teaching,* Executive Summary (San Francisco: Far West Laboratory, 1979); Little, *School Success and Staff Development;* G. A. Griffin, A. Lieberman, and J. Jacullo-Noto, *Interactive Research and Development on Schooling, Final Report of the Implementation of the Strategy* (New York: Teachers College, Columbia University, 1982); and T. Bird, "Mutual Adaptation and Mutual Accomplishment: Images of Change in a Field Experiment," *Teachers College Record* 86, no. 1, (Fall 1984): 68–83.

3 J. Lanier, "Tensions in Teaching Teachers the Skills of Pedagogy," in *Staff Development: Eighty-Second Yearbook of the National Society for the Study of Education,* ed. G. Griffin (Chicago: University of Chicago Press, 1983).

4 A negotiation sequence aimed at clarity of understanding does not ensure "receptivity" to a program of staff development. The experience of the mastery learning project is evidence that making an idea clear may serve to *discourage* persons from participating in a collaborative venture. The negotiation does have the virtue of revealing the limits and possibilities of shared work in advance of an agreement to proceed, thus making subsequent steps less tenuous.

5 W. Doyle and G. A. Ponder, "The Practicality Ethic in Teacher Decision Making," *Interchange* 8, no. 3 (1977–1978): 1–12.

6   M. Fullan and A. Pomfret, "Research on Curriculum and Instruction Implementation," *Review of Educational Research* 47, no. 1 (Winter 1977): 335-97; and G. Mohlman, T. Coladarci, and N. L. Gage, "Comprehension and Attitude as Predictors of Implementation of Teacher Training," *Journal of Teacher Education* 33, no. 1 (1982): 31-36.

7   E. Cohen, "Sociology Looks at Team Teaching," *Research in Sociology of Education and Socialization* 2 (1981): 163-93.

8   B. Showers, *The Transfer of Training: The Contribution of Coaching* (Eugene, Oregon: R&D Center Education Policy and Management, 1982); B. Joyce and B. Showers, "Teacher Training Research: Working Hypotheses for Program Design and Directions for Further Study" (Paper presented to the annual meeting of the American Educational Research Association, Los Angeles, 1981); and T. Bird and J. W. Little, "Finding and Founding Peer Coaching" (Paper presented at the annual meeting of the American Educational Research Association, New York City, 1982).

9   T. Coladarci and N. L. Gage, "Minimal Teacher Training Based on Correlational Findings: Effects on Teaching and Achievement" (Paper presented at the annual meeting of the American Educational Research Association, Los Angeles, 1981).

10   Berman and McLaughlin, *Federal Programs Supporting Educational Change, Vol. VIII.*

11   Joan Lipsitz, *Successful Schools for Young Adolescence* (New Brunswick, N.J.: Transaction Press, 1983); and Bird and Little, "Finding and Founding Peer Coaching."

12   Little, *School Success and Staff Development;* and idem, "Norms of Collegiality and Experimentation: Workplace Conditions of School Success," *American Educational Research Journal* 19, no. 3 (Fall 1982): 325-40.

13   D. Moore and A. Hyde, *Making Sense of Staff Development: An Analysis of Staff Development Programs and Their Costs in Three Urban Districts* (Chicago: Designs for Change, 1981).

14   Berman and McLaughlin, *Federal Programs Supporting Educational Change, Vol. VIII.*

15   C. Baltzell and R. A. Dentler, "Local Variations in the Selection of School Principals" (Paper presented at the annual meeting of the American Educational Research Association, New York City, 1982).

16   D. Lortie, *Schoolteacher* (Chicago: University of Chicago Press, 1975).

17   Cohen, "Sociology Looks at Team Teaching."

18   G. Sykes, "Public Policy and the Problem of Teacher Quality: The Need for Screens and Magnets," in *Handbook of Teaching and Policy*, ed. L. S. Shulman and G. Sykes (New York: Longman, 1983).

19   Moore and Hyde, *Making Sense of Staff Development.*

20   P. Schlechty and B. Whitford, "The Organizational Context of School Systems and the Functions of Staff Development," in Griffin, ed., *Staff Development*, pp. 62-91.

21   P. Schlechty and D. Crowell, *Understanding and Managing Staff Development in an Urban School System* (Chapel Hill: University of North Carolina Press, 1983).

Mutual Adaptation and Mutual Accomplishment: Images of Change in a Field Experiment

TOM BIRD

Center for Action Research, Inc., Boulder, Colorado

THE PROBLEM OF IMPLEMENTATION (A RECENT INVENTION)

In schools and communities, there are problems with young people; they do not learn as they should; they steal cars; even if they can get work they do not do a good job. In universities, centers, institutes, central offices, and agencies, there are persons whose jobs are to offer solutions for the problems of and with the young. Thus is born the problem of implementation. Thus was born in 1979 an initiative known to its sponsor[1] as the Delinquency Prevention Research and Development Program (DPRD) and to its participating schools as a school-improvement program.

The problem of implementation has various faces. Sometimes proposed solutions are ignored. Or, when they are adopted, they are found later not to resemble what their authors had in mind. Or they are adopted and documented just well enough to induce others to try them but not documented well enough to show what was done or whether it worked; purported solutions tend to spread even as nothing is learned about them. Or they disappear the moment their backers turn their backs.

From the point of view of a solution's proponents, these failures are made plausible by a raft of confounding factors. There is in the environment of the solution turbulence, which potentially includes a large set of conditions. There is systemic inertia, a general sluggishness having to do with the fact that everything and everybody have to be someplace and tend to resist being moved. There is politics, which tends to include much decision making unfavorable to the solution. There is resistance to change, a selective malady afflicting only those persons whose behavior must change to realize the solution. There are opportunism, indifference, incompetence, and mismanagement, behavior that is regarded with prejudice as hindering the solution and that, given the conditions already mentioned, is not uncommon.

There are personal matters. At any time, about half of the persons needed to pursue a solution are getting married or divorced; tending a sick or well relative; going bankrupt or coming into money; just starting, getting ready to leave, or near retirement; taking care of babies or putting children through college; making up or breaking up; getting sick, getting well, getting chronic, or dying. Living can distract prospective adopters of a solution and thus frustrate its proponents. Fortunately, about half of the proponents of the solution are spared the full frustration because they, too, are getting married or divorced and so forth.

Categories like turbulence, inertia, politics, resistance to change, personal matters, and malfeasance refer to realities. They also are conveniences. After the fact, they allow problems of implementation to be labeled and put aside, placed outside the domain of the solution where they can be termed unfortunate. In the course of implementation, however, they are not so easily dealt with. Having begun with elegance on paper, the proponents of a solution sometimes end in despair, worn out from battling a raft of deviations and confounding influences. Schools and their staffs appear to be stingy.

IMPLEMENTATION AS MUTUAL ADAPTATION (OF A PROPOSED PRACTICE AND AN ACTUAL ORGANIZATION)

The Rand Corporation's study of federal programs to promote change in the structures or practices of schools concluded that those programs often failed to implement those changes and often failed to institutionalize them, largely because the sponsors ignored or failed to deal adequately with local political and organizational circumstances. At best, implementation was "mutual adaptation," in which the intended innovation was modified to fit the local circumstances, and the local circumstances were modified to fit the innovation, so that the solution could survive and work. Even then, the researchers suggested, the effects of programs diminished over the space of a few years, and were hard to replicate in other settings.[2]

The Delinquency Prevention Research and Development program was a case of mutual adaptation. Its five program elements included creation of subschools within schools to reduce anonymity, altered teaching practices intended to increase school success, education about work, and student involvement and parent involvement in the operation of the school. All were significant changes in the structure and practices of the schools involved. As they eventually emerged, the operating projects in the participating schools were less than the program's proponents intended and more than the school staffs bargained for. After one year of planning and one year of implementation in the participating schools, the general magnitude and character of each test was established; subsequent shifts were marginal. Mutual adaptation describes much that happened.

Mutual adaptation has an agreeable political and social flavor; it grants a measure of deserved respect both to the proponents and to the adopters of an innovation and therefore lets them meet on equal terms. It allows them to relax a bit; if there is no alternative to significant diminution of the innovation (if not of the host school), then the participants can keep trying but can regard modifications with equanimity. In the DPRD program, the apparent inevitability of adaptation was a constant rationale for stretching the design a bit further.

But there are flies in the balm. As its coiners recognized, mutual adaptation inevitably implies a reduction in the integrity of the innovation and perhaps in the integrity of the host school as well. When, as in the DPRD program, a school reduces tracking in order to produce more heterogeneous classes to test whether student team learning can produce both academic success and greater social integration, both student team learning and the school are at risk from different points of view.

Presumably, program designs require some minimum of integrity to produce their intended effects. They rely on assumptions. Their propositions are related. They combine parts. If their characteristics are not sufficiently realized, there is no reason to expect a program design to produce the intended result. Little can be expected from an eroded version of a weak design. In current school-improvement programs, an eroded version of an initially weak program design is the most likely condition. There is limited knowledge of teaching and learning, of school characteristics and their effects, and of the processes of school improvement. The adoption of a new practice or policy is a nontrivial accomplishment that often exceeds the resources and energy typically devoted to it.

There is a limit to adaptation beyond which little good, particularly little replicable good, can be expected. What is required is a solution, an organization of the innovation and the school, in which the essential requirements of both are met. This is not likely to be a simple graft or attrition of the two. It is likely to be a third, new creation. Mutual adaptation, at first glance a comfortable reconciliation of diverse forces in implementation, at a second look becomes a highly demanding undertaking that is unlikely to be comfortable for its participants.

IMPLEMENTATION AS MUTUAL ACCOMPLISHMENT (OF AN ACTUAL PROPONENT AND A PROSPECTIVE ADOPTER)

To recognize that adaptation can compromise the integrity of the innovation, or of the host school, or of both is to increase greatly the demands on both the proponents and the adopters of solutions. To come through implementation with enough left to admire will require starting with a lot and doing well along the way. While what happens to the innovation and to the school can be called mutual adaptation, what is required of the proponents and the adopters is a mutual accomplishment. If the participants succeed, the product of their work is not just the remainder of a product of mutual attrition of innovation and school (in which the innovation is likely to lose), but is a new construction.

A basic shift in perspectives is suggested. As Michael Fullan put it:

We found out during the 1970's that there were many different ways to fail, and being able to explain failure was not of direct help in being able to understand, let alone influence success. In 1982 I believe we can honestly say that we can understand success, and even help bring it about under certain conditions.[3]

The shift in views is analogous to the parallel developments in delinquency research and education research on which the DPRD program was founded. Research both in delinquency and in education often has focused on the ways and reasons children fail in school or commit delinquent acts. In both fields, arguments that failure stemmed from specific pathology produced an emphasis on clinical and remedial interventions. Recently, researchers and to a lesser extent practitioners have started to stand that formulation on its head. In delinquency research, the social-control theorists have proposed that the crucial matter is not to explain deviance, but to explain conformity. They urge that that explanation may be found in socialization and social structure: how children and youth are dealt with in the primary socializing institutions of family, school, and work.[4]

In education, researchers are concentrating less on how children fail to learn and are paying more attention to how some schools succeed in teaching them. From analysis of the sources of failure, the enterprise has turned to the requisites and processes of success. And the social aspect of schooling, the "ethos" of the school, has taken a place in these studies.[5]

These similarities led the DPRD program's planners to attempt a program design in which the allied aspects of the respective bodies of research could be applied in schools by means of arrangements and practices gaining prominence in educational research. Thus, for example, it was hypothesized that student team learning methods, which had been shown to increase mutual concern among students and increase students' friendship choices across racial lines,[6] might be capable of pulling apart delinquency-supporting peer groups by drawing their members into successful peer interactions bound to academic success. The central issue was not why students deviate and fail, but how they come to conform and succeed. The central goal was not to correct any supposed pathology producing deviance and failure, but to meet the requisites of success and conventionality. The central strategy was to alter, by adoption of selected practices, the social organization of teaching and learning.

Implementation invites a similar shift in orientation. The problem of implementation is not to protect a paper design from erosion; it is to create the conditions in which the design can be realized. The delinquency theory applied in the DPRD program was reduced to a relatively simple Social Development Model,[7] which proposed that young people will achieve the social bonds that sustain a productive conformity to the degree that they enjoy the opportunity to perform, are supported to attain the skill needed to perform, and are rewarded for appropriate performance, in relevant social settings. That formulation was germane also to implementation by teachers: Until a new practice is being used effectively and routinely, one must assume that the opportunity to use it, the skill to use it, and the rewards for using it are absent and must be created. Experience of the DPRD program suggests that that will be a mutual accomplishment of considerable magnitude.

However, if one's attention shifts from the risk of adaptation to the prospect of accomplishment, it becomes possible that the school is not stingy but generous, and that progress can be made by adequate attention to the obvious. In this view, the problem of implementation is not to squeeze the most out of scarce possibilities but to organize an overabundance of them.

A WEALTH OF WORDS

Mutual adaptation occurs between a proposed solution (a collection of words) and an actual organization in its setting. The proponents of a solution might assume that their written plan will be relevant only to their own behavior. This is not to say that others cannot read, or will not read, or on reading will not attribute significance and behave in a manner predictable to writers. It is to say that no one pays as much attention to a piece of writing as its author, that language is slippery, that persons with different training and experience will read in different ways, and that persons with other jobs and pressures will not assign the same priority to the writing as did the writer. The prospect is not that the words of the innovation will mean too little, but that they will mean too much.

In the DPRD program, the written designs came to have specific and shared meaning for behavior primarily through extensive interaction between the national proponents and the local adopters. Both adopters and proponents were often surprised and dismayed at the concrete requirements of rigor in field experiments and of life in schools. One would say, "Oh, no." The other would say, "Oh, yes." One would say, "It can't be done that way." The other would say, "It must be done in that or in an equivalent fashion." At stake were grants of upward of $50,000 per year. Constitutional principles of the field experiment such as random assignment of students to experimental and control programs were set directly against constitutional principles of the participating schools, such as ability grouping and tracking. Proponents and adopters would quarrel. But they also would argue, probe, and discuss. Proponents and adopters worked together to find out what, if anything, the program and research designs meant. Throughout, there was the constant choice between reducing the rigor of the program and finding the conditions under which its requirements could be attained. There was stubborn pursuit of the latter.

Sometimes, the result was nominal implementation or the agreement not even to attempt one of the program elements. Often enough, however, proponents and adopters discovered or invented a way to do what was needed, both from the point of view of the innovation and from the point of view of the school. In seven secondary schools, randomized field experiments were established involving 160 teachers and more than 3,000 students, multiple and repeated measures of results, and (with one exception) structured observation of experimental and control classes. The research component, by itself a substantial intrusion, was implemented. It appeared that enough of the program was implemented to warrant evaluation on that scale.[8]

As implementation was more a matter of realizing than of protecting an initial design, it was more a matter of making contracts than of enforcing them. The grant documents signed in 1980 contained many specifications, principles, and conditions. Implementation plans were reviewed with the prospect that projects could be terminated; one was. The procedures of contract enforcement were apparent. In light of subsequent experience, however, it is doubtful that the initial contract between the agency and the schools was much longer than one line: "We will try hard, in good faith, to implement a rigorous delinquency prevention/school improvement experiment."

A contract cannot exist without a meeting of the minds. A researcher for whom "random assignment" has to do with systematic determination of probabilities and a principal for whom "random assignment" refers to any procedure that he does not knowingly bias or does not recognize as being biased cannot be making a contract when they agree to a document containing that expression. A program consultant for whom "student team learning" means that he wants to use a specific variant produced at Johns Hopkins and a teacher for whom "student team learning" means nearly any use of groups cannot be making a contract when they agree to try the procedure. The discovered terms of the written agreement were constantly surprising to both parties. Most of the agreements needed to implement the program elements were made after the grants were made. If the proponents and adopters had known in advance all that the project would mean, they might not have started; ignorance has its uses.

The words of the grant awards did not mean too little. They meant too much, from too many perspectives, to too many people. The mutual accomplishment was to make those words mean less and mean the same to proponents and adopters. The important thing about authors of solutions is not so much their brillance as their presence and participation.

GOALS GALORE

If one is seeking explanations for failure in implementation, one possibility is that the prospective adopters lack specific goals, or specifically lack the goals of the proponents. If one is looking for the requirements of success, the problem is that the prospective adopters have so many goals, and that they are so clear.

Persons who agree that young persons should obey the law also believe that they should be educated, reasonably clothed and housed, protected from unacceptable risk, gainfully employed as appropriate, and home in time for supper. Persons who share the goal of reducing juvenile delinquency also want to make a living, retain the good regard of their peers, satisfy those who can help or harm them, retain their pride in what they did or do, and get home in time for supper. At best, one might give these goals a rough order of priority in given cases; they all must be attained to some reasonable degree. Gains in implementation might be made by identifying many of the salient goals of an initiative and of the persons who must participate, and by providing systematically for those goals to be attained wherever possible.

The DPRD program's proponents recognized that schools face a complex array of demands and pursue numerous goals; delinquency prevention is not often in the list. One premise of implementation, therefore, was that schools could attend to delinquency prevention if the experimental elements served both delinquency prevention and the more central aims of schools. There was adequate reason to believe that achievement, attendance, good deportment, and law-abiding behavior are products of favorable socialization. Program elements were chosen primarily from the educational literature on the basis of their protential for preventing delinquent behavior, but usually were presented in terms of their potential contribution to the schools' primary purposes. The central element of the program, mandatory in all schools, was a set of classroom practices including active class management, interactive teaching techniques such as checking for understanding, and cooperative learning by students. Thus, the DPRD program would not call for additional activities in the participating schools, but would call for an appreciable transformation of the schools' methods. And it would affect other goals or values bound up in those methods.

That preparation led the program's proponents to attempt to deal affirmatively with other relevant goals. Proponents would suggest that the classroom-management techniques should reduce disruption in the classroom, contribute to learning, and help to provide a more pleasant and less tiring day for the teacher. Proponents offered that, while student team learning mixed students of varying abilities in order to promote student groups supportive of classroom achievement and thus ran the risk of failing to challenge quick students, team learning also freed the teacher to give individual attention both to students with particular problems and to students who needed extra challenges.

Other goals were not anticipated, or if anticipated, were not adequately negotiated. They were encountered as objections to or flaws in the program. Short of time, in one school the proponents lavished considerable attention on recruiting, informing, and training experimenting teachers, only to find that the method of composing the control classes and neglect of the control teachers led them to deny access to observe their classes—a blow to the research design. The control teachers' goal of preserving their professional stature was not attained; their contribution gained public recognition too late. The task was not unknown; it simply was larger than the proponents wanted to think it was. More systematic attention to the obvious investments of persons in their present practices and arrangements would have advanced implementation.

ABUNDANT RATIONALITY

In implementation as in daily life, persons often find each other unpredictable. Each, mindful of his own or her own aspirations and necessities, encounters the other as an obstacle from his or her point of view, and is inclined to conclude that the other is irrational or even immoral. Such conclusions occasionally are correct, but seldom are useful.

A more likely and quite sufficient explanation for mutual unpredictability is that there is not only a wealth of words and goals galore, but also an abundance of rationality. An action could be said to be rational, scientifically, when the action manipulates a set of independent variables that affect a dependent variable of interest in an objectively verifiable fashion; politically, when sufficient support can be mustered for the action; bureaucratically, when the action conforms to established policy and is routinely resorted to in the same situation; economically, when the action distributes resources to activities so as to maximize benefit from some point of view; ideologically, when the action conforms to important principle regardless of support, custom, or cost; practically, when the action is physically possible; and socially, when the action reconciles diverse goals and techniques in accepted norms of behavior. Established norms tend to express the resolution to date of all these rational considerations. When an innovation changes some of the norms, the whole complex can be called into question to a greater or lesser degree.

With so many possible ways to be rational, persons do not need to be irrational or immoral to find each other unpredictable. The DPRD program's national proponents and their local contacts (school principals and project coordinators) found each other unpredictable and therefore potentially irrational on many occasions. Some reactions to these situations were more useful than others. One of the useful reactions was to pretend that the other person was being rational in a way that was not immediately apparent but might be discerned. In general, asking how an action was rational was more useful than telling how it was not. Proponents and adopters then could educate each other and attempt to satisfy their different points of view.

From the point of view of research, it made sense to support part of a school's teachers to introduce an experimental distinction from the practice in the remainder of the school. Politically, that deprived control teachers of scarce resources and made them scapegoats as well, by creating the sense that one group would improve, or win, or at least have a good time on project money. One possible solution was to minimize the innovation, limit its scale, keep it low key—adapt it—so as to keep the political problem within bounds. Too often, the difference in rationalities was construed as a task of damage control.

Another solution was not to limit the project but to expand it. In one school, control teachers were asked to go without project resources for one year for the sake of introducing an experimental difference in practice. In the second year, the control teachers were supported in the same way as the first group of experimental teachers. The assignment of students was preserved, so that in the second year the experimental difference was in length of exposure to the experimental practices. In the school where the control teachers became angry and refused access to their classrooms, the proponents and their local contacts noticed—after the bridge was burned—that the control teachers might have been provided support that would not have interfered with the program and research designs, and that might have been argued to equalize any effects of the experimentation as such. A more ambitious research design might have made more political sense than a restricted one.

In some cases, it appeared that a principal or project coordinator was personally agreeable to a proposition, but was anticipating problems or resistance elsewhere. Not wishing to appear helpless or to seem to be a mere messenger, the local partner would present the opposition as though it were his own. In such cases, the national proponent could attempt to make the proposition rational from the inferred point of view of the inferred source of resistance, and thus easier for the local partner to propose. The national proponent could attempt to assemble words that would be faithful to the intended innovation and persuasive with the inferred source of resistance, and then model the delivery in the course of conversation with the local partner. The aim was to allow the local partner both to support the proposition and to avoid appearing to be helpless or a mere messenger in the eyes of the inferred source of resistance. That work required a tolerance of ambiguity and a degree of discipline that came more easily when it was assumed that the go-between was not an incompetent.

If national proponents openly granted merit to forms of rationality and points of view other than their own, local partners could feel that their exposing the forces under which they operated would not make them appear to be helpless or mere messengers in the national proponents' eyes. They could agree that all persons operate under various demands and constraints, and together could try to make the proposed innovation rational from the various relevant points of view. By such an accomplishment, they might avoid adapting the innovation.

The proponents of a scientifically rational innovation have additional work to do; sheer thoroughness might produce gains in implementation. In negotiating the DPRD program with its participating schools, the national proponents constantly felt the need to persuade and inform. Many questions had to be answered. Why should this be done? What makes it a good idea? Why should I do what you say instead of what I am doing? Why should it be done that way and not some other way that comes more naturally or conveniently? What makes you think this will all work out?

Oriented to theory and research findings as tools and to research as a method, the proponents were inclined to draw on them to persuade, but that was not easy. Both the perceived and the objective characteristics of science limited its potency as language for implementation. Some persons grow impatient with discussions of "theory" and "evidence." Such reactions may reflect ignorance about science, cynicism about its past uses, or unfruitful encounters with social scientists in the past. In the DPRD program, it helped to point out that theory as such is not rejectable; everyone has assumptions about how the world works or could work. The only choice to be made is whether one will recognize, state, scrutinize, and test those assumptions or not. When persons do take care to recognize, state, examine, and test their assumptions, the product tends to be called "just theory," as in the statement, "That's just theory; let's get down to practical matters." When assumptions are carried out in practice, they tend to be called "just common sense," as in the statement, "Of course it will work, it's just common sense." One of the accomplishments of the proponents and adopters was to turn "just common sense" into "just theory," and vice-versa.

Edward A. Suchman has suggested that there are two main ways in which attempted innovations can fail.[9] An innovation can fail because it was not implemented; this he called a "program failure." Even if adequately implemented, an innovation can fail because its assumptions were invalid; the specified action does not produce the expected result. This Suchman called "theory failure." In practice, the two forms of failure are related; a program failure can be produced by a theory that, however valid, is unpersuasive and unhelpful.

From the national proponents' point of view, student team learning methods might influence juvenile delinquency because systematic heterogeneous grouping would distribute the members of deviance-supporting groups among conventional groups in which they would be minorities; because the task interdependence created by student team learning would create opportunities to succeed both academically and socially; because both social and academic skills would be learned; and because the reward interdependence imposed by a team-points procedure would produce peer pressure and support for good performance in the team and classroom. However, each of these features of student teams required unfamiliar and additional work by the teacher. Further, by its own logic, student team learning could not be expected to show results immediately. Several rounds of team competition would be necessary before the dynamics of team learning could start to exert their intended effects.

So for some time, teachers would have to engage in unfamiliar and demanding activities, the virtue of which would not be seen immediately and which to some extent could only be inferred. One possibility for implementation was to try to create conditions in which a teacher would try the method enough times and obtain sufficiently dramatic results to warrant persistence in all the method's parts, regardless of the theory involved. Even so, a sensible principle of economy would lead the teacher to try to trim anything that can be trimmed from the procedure, just to save energy. The other possibility was to make the underlying theory sufficiently useful as an interpretation of what the teacher could see in the classroom to justify persistence in the vital elements of the method. The task was to turn "just theory" into "just common sense."

In so doing, the proponent runs into the difference between "logical closure" and "empirical closure" in a theory.[10] To attain a degree of specificity and coherence that would permit testing and such proof as science provides, theories necessarily ignore many aspects of the phenomena they treat. Even when the theory is advanced toward a logical closure in which all its assumptions are stated and all the implications of one of its propositions are stated in some other proposition, the theory remains a pale reflection of a part of the phenomenon to which it refers. From the practical perspective, much is seen and goes on that simply is not dealt with in theory. Taken as an argument to a principal or teacher, even the most finished and elegant theories leave much to be desired.

Those who hold that science provides one sound alternative to ignorance can be tempted, by repeated failure to persuade teachers, to doubt its practical powers. They can, from their point of view, lower their standards for discourse. In this view, "the field" cannot meet the demands of science or, as it is more often put, the high standards of science are difficult to meet in the field. That is one possibility. The other possibility is that science finds it hard to meet the exacting requirements of the field. From the latter point of view, the researcher should not lower standards, but should raise them.

Field work tends to escalate some standards that many researchers already hold. A definition of a variable must be precise enough and concrete enough not only to derive a measure, but also to raise that variable from the complex background of the classroom into the foreground for a teacher's attention. A specific and plausible hypothetical mechanism of the sort called for in a causal argument[11] is needed to reveal a process at work, so the teacher can participate in it. A plain and operational explication that avoids potentially misleading and overrich metaphor has virtue in research and yet more virtue in practice. A multivariable theory complex enough to resemble the real thing may be required by practical persons before they bother with theory at all. If the theory is embedded in and expressed in the terms of some larger or more general theoretical tradition, there is a better chance of thinking what to do when the procedures manual runs out of answers.

The DPRD program employed a multivariable theory of social control and social learning bearing on juvenile delinquency. The program design combined a battery of methods to apply that theory. Initially, the connections between the theory and the program elements were only generally drawn. One constant task was to build an analysis in which the theory and the methods were more and more specifically and concretely connected, and to put that analysis in terms that could make the innovation rational from various points of view. Turning "just theory" into "just common sense" will be an important part of the mutual accomplishment of implementation.

A similar argument can be made in regard to research methods. Asked to change their practices to accord with some research findings, or told that their practices have been found in research to be ineffective, most persons immediately become subtle critics of research. They know or soon learn that if you doubt the findings, you should go after the design. "I could get results like that, too, if I worked with the kind of kids they had." "Well you know, those classes also have quite a few kids who take band." "That's Kansas; this is New York."

While its requirements sometimes are surprising or arduous, random assignment of students to programs has explanatory and political virtues. Taken step by step through the random-assignment procedures, persons can examine concretely how hypotheses alternate to program effects are being dealt with. Statistics that provide analogous assurances to researchers tend not to assure others. The visibility and transparency of research methods are likely to be as important as their rigor.

In implementation, it will be useful to assume that rationality is not scarce, but rather is overabundant, and that the task is to organize the innovation so that it is or becomes rational from many points of view. In this undertaking, it appears, the innovations that are most rational or rigorous from a scientific point of view stand the best chance of becoming rational from other viewpoints. The central tasks are concrete explanation and translation. In proceeding from their offices and labs to the field, researchers might sensibly raise their standards.

LOADS OF LATITUDE

By prior experience, the DPRD program's proponents were inclined to think that they were up against the massive inertia of "traditional teaching," typical procedures of long standing that would thwart or limit use of the intended innovations. Much experience in the course of implementation could be construed to confirm that inclination. But the program also provided its proponents a glimpse of an alternate possibility: the prospect that teachers feel little latitude to experiment with their practice because they have little support for experimenting with their practice and that, if effective support can be organized, there is plenty of latitude to experiment in classrooms.

With exceptions, the participating schools lacked interaction that could be construed as significant support for experimentation by teachers. In many cases, the program's initial five-day training for teachers was more training than teachers had received since they started teaching. There seldom were meetings, seminars, or continuing discussions among teachers that could have served as substitutes for training. In most cases, supervision and evaluation could not be construed as support for implementation. Experimentation with teaching sometimes was a visible expectation, but was not often supported in a substantial way.

Under such conditions, persons assigned a complex and demanding task such as teaching rationally may avoid the risks of experimentation. Failure is all too possible. Beyond the cost for the students, to try something new is to risk sending a noisy, boisterous class into another teacher's room the following period, and to hear about that later. Only by individual effort will a teacher be exposed to potential innovations. The difficult work of turning a paper proposal into a behavioral reality will have to be done alone. Tried-and-true techniques will be mastered painfully and individually. One's habits in the classroom are likely to seem like manifestations of one's style, personality, or philosophy. Those habits will be hard to see as objectifiable or examinable practices. In such conditions, a well-founded conservatism would not lead a teacher either to experiment or to act readily on advice from others.

As the time approached to design training for teachers, the magnitude of the program's request of teachers became more and more apparent. Either the program would have to be scaled down, or the support would have to be increased. The latter was the first choice.

One decision was that the trainers should design and conduct the training so that, to the maximum feasible extent, they would train teachers by the methods that the teachers would be asked to use. The training would itself be an extended demonstration of the experimental methods. A teaching technique thus could be taught either by explicit attention or by demonstration and experience, or by both methods. As a result, both the content and the procedure of the training were applied to the objectives of the training. At any moment, either the nominal content of the session or the trainer's procedure could be a topic for discussion.

These features made the training complex, and some interesting problems arose. Literal modeling of teaching techniques sometimes required the trainer to treat the adult trainees as though they were junior high school students.

Some trainers and some trainees were hesitant to enter such a relation, but it appeared that many adopted the stance that much of the training was an extended role-playing exercise. That convention was helpful; for example, a desire to discuss the training procedure could be treated as the sort of "time out" taken by role-players in order to discuss their exercise.

The utility for implementation of including student team learning among the experimental techniques was anticipated but underrated. Teachers often studied experimental methods in student team format. From the first day of training, a recurring remark on evaluation forms completed at day's end was that teachers were being provided considerably more interaction with each other than they had enjoyed previously. Use of the student team learning as a training device laid a foundation for other work on professional relations in the school.

The intensification of the training was judged not to be sufficient for implementation. Ongoing support would have to be provided in the school. A strategy was devised from the proponents' combined experience. That strategy was informed particularly by a study then being conducted by one of the proponents.[12] The strategy had several parts. First was to cultivate the expectation that teaching practices not only are matters of personal style, preference, or philosophy, but also are tools of a public profession, to be examined publicly and professionally. In training, trainers invited feedback on their methods from the trainees and tried to model how such feedback could be received and used. Teachers were hesitant to describe and assess the work of their trainers at first, but they soon warmed to that chore. They would be asked to give and receive such feedback in their own work.

Second was to promote the norm that teaching practices should be improved continuously by deliberate experimentation and careful evaluation. In training and implementation, the proponents adopted the stance that improvement is something that all teachers do and want to do. One strand of this position was that new practices cannot be adopted smoothly, that "everybody knows" that things will not always go smoothly at first, and that they should give each other the latitude to blow it now and then, even if that meant putting up with the agitation of failure.

Third, teachers would talk—concretely, specifically, and often—about teaching practices. The training was intended to provide them a well-developed, concrete, and precise language for these exchanges. The proponents encouraged regular meetings or seminars of experimenting faculty to continue the conversation.

To obtain shared experience to which the shared terms could be applied, teachers would be observed at work in the classroom, and would talk about lessons with observers. At the time, the first choice for providing in-school support would have been a program of expert clinical supervision provided by specialists. Lacking these technical capacities, the proponents resorted to the less expert but possibly more available and tenacious form of peer coaching among teachers, which project and school administrators could complement. By the end of the year of planning in the participating schools, the attempt to build a system of coaching became a central feature of the projects.[13]

The immediate results of these efforts varied. The attempt to provide shared language was seen as an imposition by some teachers and as a service by others. Coaching apparently was experienced as support by some teachers, but as an additional demand by others; that demand may have led some teachers to withdraw from participation. Other measures taken to help teachers, project coordinators, and school administrators to participate in supporting each other to alter their behavior also produced mixed results. Neither the proponents nor the adopters had had much experience in organizing, providing, or receiving such support.

Nevertheless, there grew groups of teachers, project administrators, and school administrators who entered into mutually supportive relations, took satisfaction in coaching and in being coached, grew more energetic, spent more time with each other, and devoted considerable energy to adopting the experimental practices. It appeared that their latitude to experiment in the classroom increased in proportion to the support they enjoyed.

Under conditions common in many schools, it appears, staff receive so little support for experimentation with their practices that they are likely to adapt, sometimes severely, any innovation suggested to them. Provided little support, they are likely to be stingy with the proponents of any innovation. But in the presence of persistent efforts to make shared sense, to pursue the variety of relevant goals of a faculty, and to provide adequate support, they can be generous. Organizing that support will be no small accomplishment; it will be a mutual accomplishment of the proponent and the adopter. The prospect of that accomplishment, rather than the risk of adaptation, will be the more fruitful focus of proponents' efforts.

Notes

1   The Deliquency Prevention Research and Development Program was sponsored by the Office of Juvenile Justice and Delinquency Prevention, U.S. Department of Justice. The national proponents were staff of the Westinghouse National Issues Center and the Center for Action Research, who provided technical assistance to the schools, and of the Center for Law and Justice, University of Washington, Seattle, who conducted the research.

2   Paul Berman and Milbrey Wallin McLaughlin, *Federal Programs Supporting Educational Change, Vol. VIII: Implementing and Sustaining Innovations* (Santa Monica, Calif.: The Rand Corporation, 1978).

3   Michael Fullan, "Implementing Educational Change: Progress at Last" (Ontario, Canada: Ontario Institute for Studies in Education, 1982), p. 1.

4   Travis Hirsch, *Causes of Delinquency* (Berkeley: University of California Press, 1969).

5   Michael Rutter et al., *Fifteen Thousand Hours: Secondary Schools and Their Effects on Children* (Cambridge: Harvard University Press, 1979).

6   Robert E. Slavin, "Cooperative Learning," *Review of Educational Research* 50, no. 2 (1980): 315-42.

7   Joseph G. Weis and J. David Hawkins, *The Social Development Model: An Integrated Approach to Delinquency Prevention* (Seattle, Wash.: Center for Law and Justice, University of Washington, 1980).

8   Research reports are now being prepared by Joseph G. Weis and J. David Hawkins.

9   Edward A. Suchman, "Evaluating Educational Programs: A Symposium," *Urban Review* 3, no. 4 (1969): 15-17.

10   Talcott Parsons, *The Structure of Social Action* (New York: McGraw-Hill, 1937).

11   David R. Heise, *Causal Analysis* (New York: John Wiley, 1975).

12   Judith Warren Little, "Norms of Collegiality and Experimentation: Workplace Conditions of School Success," *American Education Research Journal* 19, no. 3 (1982): 32-40.

13   Tom Bird and Judith Warren Little, "Finding and Founding Peer Coaching" (Paper presented at the American Educational Research Association Annual Meeting at Montreal, Canada, 1983).

Rethinking the Quest for School Improvement: Some Findings from the DESSI Study

A. MICHAEL HUBERMAN
University of Geneva

MATTHEW B. MILES
Center for Policy Research, New York City

Definitive formulas—seen in craft *and* science terms—for achieving school improvement have often proved elusive. Elusive because the normative nature of the term makes it slippery; one persons's version of improvement is another's version of wastefulness, or even of worsening. Elusive also because researchers have ridden off in all directions, armed with different conceptual and methodological trappings, and have returned with formulas that often appeared incompatible or incommensurate. Elusive, finally, because of implementation problems: even though we may know what successful school-based innovation looks like, *delivering* it is another question. Too many of the key variables seem unmanipulable, and too many success stories look more providential than intentional.

It is dangerously easy for school people and researchers to conclude that the quest is hopeless, and turn to other matters. The risk, of course, is that of abandoning "school improvement" to the opportunists and zealots, making it into little more than an ideological banner, thus paving the way for rhetoric-laden "programs" with little real benefit for schools.

Yet we believe the quest is not at all hopeless, on two counts. First, it is increasingly clear that we know a good deal more about implementing changes that improve school-based practice than we let on. If one compares recent studies, whether they define improvement as increased achievement scores, as classroom mastery, as use of new instructional modules, or as improved academic self-concept, the findings across studies[1] are far from inconsistent. The same macro-variables crop up, from "adaptation" to "assistance" to "involvement," "problem solving" and "institutionalization." Often, the *configurations* of these variables are constant across studies and settings, and one begins to get a glimpse of which families of predictors will influence which families of mediators and of outcomes, in which families of settings. In short, we are getting a progressively better fix on school-improvement processes and outcomes, though it is a far more differentiated and multilayered fix than we expected and might have preferred. We may not have a technology, but we do have a series of very promising cottage industries.

Our second reason for optimism about the quest is grounded in the belief that we can reorganize the way we have been going about it. Many researchers in the "dissemination and utilization of knowledge" tradition, of which the study of school improvement is a subset, have been guilty of a certain hubris. We have been imbued, often unconsciously, with the rationalist paradigm of change, and this has oriented us toward the quest for an uncontingent technology of "innovations" that make for "improvement" that may not exist empirically. We have tried to derive context-stripped "factors" or "variables" that somehow lay behind the welter of phenomena in idiosyncratic school settings. And we have inferred as well that the process within individual settings was orderly and intentional—or at least could be made so if educational affairs were managed properly. In short, we leapt too quickly and perhaps illegitimately from the descriptive to the prescriptive, and nurtured the Promethean illusion that by following our *conceptual* tracks, policy planners and administrators could get there *operationally* as well.

Correcting these biases requires us to reorganize the quest, but not to abandon it. The first, most obvious need is to abandon the master plan and accept a more modest scenario of generating smaller parts, multiple formulas, and clearer specifications of the contextual conditions under which the formulas may be expected to produce desired results. The second need is for improvement researchers to move deliberately into another paradigm, the "conflict" paradigm, in which the explanation of social change is rife with power, uncertainty, continuous negotiation, loose-endedness, and local history. We need only to survey the drift in the literature on organizations to get a sense of the exodus from the rational paradigm to the conflict paradigm in the past decade.[2] Clearly, there is a fund of explanatory power here, and, obviously, a good deal of school improvement has to do with careerism, interpersonal conflict, politics, posturing, bungling, arbitrary power plays, temporary and opportunistic coalitions, and the like. But how much? And does this necessarily rule out a more planful or consensual approach? For example, conspiratorial behavior can be both technocratic and consensual in a sense very close to that of the rational model of change; the assumptions are different, but it is not obvious that they are incompatible. Adherents of both paradigms like the term "strategy," for instance, and although one paradigm may be naive and the other overly conspiratorial, it is not clear that the meanings they impute to strategy are incompatible.

The point is that the rational, meliorist approach to educational innovation can and should be enlarged—made more conceptually street-wise—by the more conflictual, open-ended perspective in order to yield more powerful and useful studies. The search for "usefulness" may be harder than that for conceptual powerfulness—for example, we may find out that a lot of the critical variables can only be "managed" under exceptional conditions, and that those conditions fluctuate over time—but we need to know these things, too. Knowing what not to try is as serviceable as knowing what to try. And enlarging the meliorist approach does not oblige us to fully integrate the two perspectives. Rather, it saves us from having to choose between competing conceptual paradigms that are incompatible only at the extremes, and to concentrate on the middle ground—where the bulk of the data and the meaningful concepts are.

BACKGROUND OF THE DESSI STUDY

For the better part of the past five years we and our colleagues have been trying to take a serious crack at that conceptual and methodological enlargement, with some promising results. The chief product of that work has been the ten-volume *Study of Dissemination Efforts Supporting School Improvement*,[3] whose findings have been distilled at successive American Educational Research Association (AERA) sessions and in practitioner journals.[4] The DESSI study itself was of gargantuan proportions: 45 innovative programs, analysis at the federal and state levels, studies of 146 schools and school districts in 10 states with 5,000 interviews and questionnaires and a parallel, multiple-site field study keyed to the sampling frame and research questions being addressed in the survey component. While the size of the study created many logistical complications and problems in data interpretation, it did allow for a comprehensive analysis of federal and state dissemination activities throughout the country, and it brought together the contributions of five research centers active in the field of school improvement research.[5]

We were involved in most facets of the DESSI project, but most intensively in the field study, and the "learnings" we shall be reporting on come primarily from there. We did, however, work closely enough with the survey data base to see the substantial degree of overlap in findings, so the generalizations we offer can go beyond the twelve-site sample comprising the field-study component.

In many ways, the survey component of the DESSI study embodied the "rational" paradigm of school improvement, and the field study the more "conflict-theoretic" paradigm. To some extent, this was a methodological artifact. Surveys are inappropriate vehicles for picking up on subterranean career agendas or internecine rivalries or people's incoherent behaviors, and when they do get such data, the statistical analyses often yield interpretations that border on the surreal. Field studies, on the other hand, can handle only a few settings and can get so mired in local-setting variables that they lose the programmatic thrust of the study initially undertaken. Surveys and field studies combined not only extend and deepen the data set; they also keep one another analytically honest and on target.

The field study mobilized four people for eighteen months, with about twelve months of spaced visits to schools. One of its purposes was to compensate for a survey's typical weaknesses (predesigned instrumentation, one "snapshot" pass at a site, difficulties in unraveling over-time processes, clumsiness in the face of unanticipated or unequivocal findings). Another objective was historical and descriptive: that of "telling the story," and of identifying and documenting typical patterns and local determinants. There was the additional hope of validating, or at least of lending more plausibility to, survey-analytical findings. More fundamentally, the field study was designed to capture the everyday properties of local sites and to follow how they change and are changed by the process of implementing new practices— what school improvement is an improvement *of* or *from*, what the "baseline" or "receiving context" is. Capturing these properties invariably entails getting underneath the official, noncontroversial, and socially desirable renditions often given by survey respondents, and dredging up more latent issues, agendas, conflicts, and contextual features.

The field study sample itself comprised twelve sites drawn from the survey sample and varying along the dimensions shown in Chart 1. For program sponsorship, only two programs were studied (National Diffusion Network, or NDN, and Title IV-C), so as to compare locally generated (IV-C) and externally introduced (NDN) innovations.

The conceptual model underlying the field research roughly paralleled that of the survey, although it took more deliberate aim at motives, conflicts, and organizational issues characterizing the everyday life of the school. It hypothesized a series of reciprocal "transformations" among users, the properties of the innovation, and the organizational unit affected—much along the lines of the mutual-adaptation phenomenon described by Berman and McLaughlin.[6] As a set, however, the thirty-four research questions forming the basis for field-study data collection overlapped and mapped well onto the main foci of the survey.

We visited sites between 3 and 7 times each for a total of 5 to 11 days, depending on the site. Researchers worked with a general interview guide, keyed to the research questions, and supplemented this with observations and document collection. In all, there were some 440 interviews, 75 observations, and 259 document analyses. The interview and observation data, along with researchers' comments, were dictated and transcribed (field notes for one site ran about 250 pages), then coded. Raw survey data were also fed into later fieldwork. The coded field notes went through a series of interim analyses, and were written up in identically formatted case reports and fed into the cross-site analysis. We used a variety of conventional and experimental methods for formatting, reducing, displaying, and analyzing qualitative data, including qualitative analogues of cluster and causal analyses, and have since extended them into a methodological sourcebook.[7] The field study itself was published

Chart 1: Characteristics of Field Study Sample

	Site Context				Aspects of the Innovation			
Site	Program sponsorship[a]	U.S. Region	Setting	Year began project	Status (as initially assessed)	Program type	Program name or initials[b]	Program content
ASTORIA	NDN	Southeast	Small city	1978	Expanding	Add-on	EPSF	Early Childhood
BANESTOWN	NDN	Southeast	Rural	1979	Expanding	Pull-out	Catch-Up	Reading/Math
BURTON	NDN	Midwest	Suburban	1979	Expanding	Add-on	IPLE	Law and government
CALSTON	NDN	Midwest	Center city	1978	Ongoing	Drop-in	Mateson 4D	Reading
CARSON	IV-C	Plains	Rural	1977	Expanding	Add-on	IPA	Individualized educational planning[c]
DUN HOLLOW	IV-C	Northeast	Urban sprawl	1977	Dwindling	Add-on	Eskimo Studies	Social studies[c]
LIDO	NDN	Northeast	Rural	1976	Dwindling	Add-on	KARE	Environment
MASEPA	NDN	Plains	Rural	1978	Ongoing	Drop-in	ECRI	Language Arts[c]
PERRY-PARKDALE	NDN	Midwest	Suburban	1977	Ongoing	Sub-system	EBCE	Career education
PLUMMET	IV-C	Southwest	Center city	1976	Ongoing	Sub-system	Bentley Center	Alternative school
PROVILLE	IV-C	Southwest	Urban sprawl	1977	Dwindling	Pull-out	CEP	Vocational education
TINDALE	IV-C	Midwest	Urban sprawl	1976	Ongoing	Drop-in	Tindale Reading Model	Reading

[a] NDN = National Diffusion Network; IV-C = Title IV-C

[b] IV-C program names are pseudonyms, to avoid identifying specific sites.

[c] Program is used in this site with a comprehensive sample of learners, rather than with low-achieving or marginal populations.

both as a technical volume (vol. IV) in the DESSI report series and in an abridged form for a wider public.[8]

Finally, we should note that though we used many familiar ethnographic methods, the nature of this field study—short, interrupted time on site, presence of multiple sites; integration with a survey data base—moved it toward another species, one closer to the investigative reporting and investigative social research tradition.[9] A distinctive quality of that tradition is its "recycling" or "forensic focusing" property. Field researchers use successive waves of interviewing and observing to establish and flesh out what appears to be the most plausible version of local events. Through a series of progressive revisions and cross-checks, that version undergoes a fairly merciless verification before field researchers and their critical readers settle on it. These procedures are also described in detail in Huberman and Miles.[10]

SOME FINDINGS

There is no fruitful way of summarizing the corpus of findings briefly; it would read like an incoherent shopping list. Let us try to be discriminatingly selective. In particular, we want to follow through on the arguments and the agenda laid out in the initial section by presenting carefully three main findings that are consonant with either a conflict paradigm or a rational paradigm, then try to show how they can be consonant with both paradigms at a conceptually superordinate level. These are also findings that may not have been brought home sharply enough in prior studies; in addition, they indulge our—probably decadent—bent for highlighting controversiality.

Let us begin at the "front end," with the question of why innovations are initially implemented. Here is the finding:

1. *The merits of the innovation itself, including its potential for solving local problems, are one reason for adoption, but not necessarily the main one.*

This is a finding that a more conflict-theoretic analyst might take in one direction and a rationalist-meliorist in another. For instance, Yin et al. found that the main motives for adopting public service innovations were not primarily service- or client-oriented but involved facilitating working conditions on the part of the adopters.[11] But there was a *mix* of motives, and the configuration was different for different groups of adopters and users. There was, in many cases, a problem to be solved and the innovations tended to constitute solutions. So motives are multiple (for a given adopter), different (for different users), and even contradictory (wanting better working conditions *and* higher service payoff when both may not in fact be possible).

We found a similar pattern, with a few surprises. For example (see Chart 2) nearly two-thirds of the "users" in the sample (usually teachers) adopted primarily because of *administrative pressure*.

Chart 2. Reasons Given for Adoption by Administrators and Users.

Reasons	Administrators (N = 41)	Users (N = 56)
	No. %	No. %*
Improves classroom instruction	21 (51)	16 (29)
Improves school capacity	10 (24)	—
Solves problems	7 (17)	2 (4)
Access to funds	6 (15)	1 (2)
Improves teacher capacity	4 (10)	5 (9)
Administrative pressure	4 (10)	35 (62)
Helps meet goals, follow philosophy	3 (7)	—
Enhances own professional image	3 (7)	—
Meets external demands	2 (5)	—
Increases own power/authority	2 (5)	—
Novelty value, challenge	1 (2)	10 (19)
Improves achievement scores	1 (2)	—
Social influence (teachers spoke well of it)	1 (2)	9 (16)
Good politics	1 (2)	—
Opportunity to shape projects	—	5 (9)
Gets better working conditions	—	3 (5)

*Percentages add to more than 100% because of multiple responses.

There were degrees of pressure. In some projects just under way, teachers said that they had been "strongly encouraged" to volunteer. One respondent put it concisely: "The principal wanted it in; we got the message." There was sometimes an element of seduction at this phase, but underneath it was the clear understanding that demands for compliance could not be countermanded.

Still, being pressured is not inconsistent with wanting to adopt. If the innovation looked good, and the supporting conditions (preparation for implementation) were satisfactory, there was no strong reason *not* to adopt. There were relatively few users who felt "violated" by the pressure, and some who saw such an exertion of pressure as a legitimate leadership role for the administrator.

The findings beg immediately for some contextualizing. What kind of innovations imply that teachers are essentially targets? Obviously, these are not classroom-generated changes, but rather changes initiated from without and affecting several classrooms at once. As such, these are exceptional efforts. They are also, as we have noted, efforts involving outside assistance, for example, federal or state seed money, provision of outside consultants or materials. So this is only one species of school-improvement project, albeit one whose potential impact is likely to be greater (more funding, more political clout, more local units affected) than that of isolated efforts.

Less than a third of the users said that their reasons for adoption had to do with instructional improvement. Of these, very few mentioned any chronic or severe instructional problem to be solved. Rather, they liked the added resources, the enrichment value for the curriculum they taught, the overall appeal of the unit or technique or project.

Another fascinating finding: Users' motives often centered around professional growth. Many respondents thought these innovations could counter professional stagnation through their novelty value, could stretch existing instructional repertoires, could add to professional qualifications. When these individual items are grouped, they exceed the frequency of "practice improvement" motives. This underscores the need to broaden perspectives when we look at incentives and rewards. Although innovations are supposedly introduced for instrumental reasons—for example, to increase achievement scores—they are not necessarily construed this way at the classroom level, at least not in this sample. For example, no teacher mentioned "achievement gains" as a motive for adoption, although one administrator did. On the other hand, professional growth was a strong motive in many cases, and acted as a catalyst for the introduction of new practices, many of which did, in fact, improve academic performance. This pattern intersects nicely with the results of previous studies.[12]

Administrators gave more diverse reasons for adoption and configured them differently from users'. Pressure was far less frequently reported, but was still there, notably among principals, and sometimes had a sharp bite:

Just another dumb program being shoved down our throats.

For a principal to cross the district openly [and refuse to adopt] is almost like suicide.

Instructional and schoolwide improvement was a salient motive for administrators: The new practice "had merits"; it was "a good alternative"; it "could be used elsewhere" in the system and would improve working conditions in the classroom. Here again, however, local problem solving was not a dominant theme—nor was it more prevalent in the locally initiated change (IV-C) sites than in the externally introduced (NDN) change sites. Nor was there—with one exception in forty-one cases—an explicit expectation that achievement scores (or any specific student outcome) would improve as a result of program adoption. The emphasis was on school capacity - enhancing characteristics of the innovation (for example, enriching curricula, providing remedial materials) that administrators believed could mean achievement gains further down the line.

As with the teachers, administrators had multiple motives. Obviously, the greater the number of incentives and their relative importance to a key administrative actor, the more assertive and consequential the decision to adopt. And the closer we got to the full agendas of principals and central office personnel, the more numerous and various the incentives. Here is an illustration from the field notes:

> Summary of inferred and explicit motives for her: [the innovation] resolved the local problem of low achievement, [helps her] compete with elementary-level rival in central office; increases relative clout of elementary education sector; meets [her] emotional needs [attention to disadvantaged]; enhances professional image, responds to pressures external to the district. All of roughly equal importance to her. (Supervisor, Banestown site)

Career Pursuit as Motive The "conflict" paradigm makes us attentive to the fact that, in making available new resources, an innovation often alters career opportunities.[13] First, it often creates new roles facilitating upward mobility. Teachers can become local trainers. Administrators are appointed program directors. Second, innovations also attract attention: Teachers involved with their execution frequently get higher visibility than in their conventional work, and higher visibility can enhance professional advancement. Finally, central office administrators, often active advocates of new practices, come into more direct contact with principals and teachers, thereby multiplying the opportunities for school-level personnel to forge useful interpersonal links. In short, innovations can accelerate promotions or other career shifts for both teachers and administrators.

We found many career-related incentives for adopting innovations at the twelve field sites. But we should be careful. At only one site was career advancement the paramount motive for adoption; it was usually one of several reasons. Also, career incentives were not always obvious at the time of adoption, but materialized later, when local actors saw more clearly what the institutional implications of the new practice were. So local personnel were neither overly cynical nor Machiavellian; they simply looked out for themselves and capitalized on opportunities crossing their paths. The important thing to remember is that paths exist.

What kinds of career shifts did site informants mention? We chose to sort out these motives as derived from what we called "trajectories." School people may have been going nowhere or going someplace in their career progression, so the innovation was an asylum, a way station, a vehicle, or a final destination. Logically enough, there were four gross trajectories: The innovation provided as opportunity to *move in* (for example, from a prolonged leave or from a distasteful job elsewhere), to *stay in* (securing, solidifying a new role; avoiding demotion), to *move up* (e.g., from aide to teacher, teacher to principal, principal to central office administrator), or to *move away* (to a lateral job, to another line of work).

Roughly half of the administrators and teachers for whom there were data had no discernible career motive. Either they were not interested in changing roles, did not see the innovation as a good vehicle for career shifts, or simply focused fully on the contribution of the new practice to their immediate settings without regard to their own career progression.

The remaining half had plans. For both teachers and administrators, these plans frequently involved promotions, but teachers' career motives were quite varied, whereas administrators were more often setting up a promotion or solidifying one. Informants usually spoke to us openly about these plans, but were often discreet in their formulations, speaking of the innovation as "an intermediate step" or "a way to get more responsibility."[14] Sometimes, there were two-step trajectories;

> I figured it was a good way to get back in after my leave. The program had a good reputation and I liked the one-on-one work in it. . . . It was an interesting job while I was waiting to get my own class. (Teacher at Banestown)

"Moving someone else in" was a dominant motive in only one site, but a sub rosa one at two others. In two cases (Proville, Banestown) this led to intense jockeying that took its toll on program execution. The innovations did not create these perturbations, but amplified interpersonal tensions already present, adding noise and friction to the system.

In contrast, at three of the five sites where administrative careerism was low (Carson, Masepa, Tindale) implementation was smoother: more task-focused, more collaborative between central office administrators and building-level personnel, and less perturbed when staff turned over. (In passing, the two other sites—Dun Hollow and Lido—seemed to suffer from a lack of central office investment, which might have been stronger if a career motive had been present.)

In the five remaining sites, administrative careerism was strong, without being manic or exploitative; it appeared to inject energy into the adoption process by accelerating the time line, mobilizing resources, and, in some cases, generating enthusiasm at the school-building level.

So we can see that the configuration of motives is both less disinterested and less problem-focused than the rationalist paradigm would have it—but it also has meliorative, task-centered components. Moreover, even some of the more apparently opportunistic phenomena (e.g., career pursuit among administrators) have positive results and can probably even be incorporated into an innovation "strategy" from a rationalist's perspective. A larger, more ecumenical conceptual framework is helpful.

Let's move on to the next proposition:

2. *Administrative decisiveness bordering on coercion, but intelligently and supportively exercised, may be the surest path to significant school improvement.*

This may be an objectionable proposition, but it is also a logical one. It nests well in the rationalist paradigm in assuming that school improvement can be managed and achieved as the product of a social technology. But the rationalist paradigm also assumes, with disarming naiveté, that people will achieve and be managed because they are convinced of the merits of the project, along with its problem-solving potential. One needs the conflict-theoretic paradigm here to get much closer to the ways in which organizational changes are actually played out. Put crudely, organizational change occurs in a complex, continuously negotiated power field, in which some parties wield more influence than others, but the others are never powerless.[15] Senior administrators in a school system generally have the power to adopt innovations, to mandate them, to finance and backstop them, even to institutionalize them. This goes a long way toward actually *delivering* an innovation. But managers don't *execute* innovations, teachers do; and if teachers decide not to execute the innovation, managers will find themselves institutionalizing placebos, perhaps unwittingly. So administrators have to leaven an enforcement strategy with something that teachers are interested in and that, at the same time, will facilitate execution. This turns out, logically enough, to be sustained *assistance*. Administrative bullying—the superintendent or principal as thug—is an ineffective strategy, but assistance-rich enforcement—tough-minded help—appears to pay off.

All of this needs empirical substantiation. First, however, let us spell out the first part of the proposition. We are saying that a more power-coercive strategy, when blended with a normative-reeducative strategy in the classic sense of Chin and Benne,[16] is potentially a surer path to school improvement because powerful people tend to be able to exert directional control over the environment—to shape the surround, to reduce the uncertainties, to reduce the degree of freedom of actors having countervailing plans—and to offer assistance resources.

In assessing the nature and the degree of school improvement, we came to focus on five normative outcomes—normative in the sense that having achieved more of them at higher levels was perceived as more desirable than having achieved fewer at lower levels. They are:

Stabilization of use of the innovation at high levels of technical mastery
Percentage of use: proportion of actual users relative to the total pool of eligible users of the innovation
User capacity change: increments in teachers' professional competence as a by-product of the innovation
Student impact: the effects of the innovation on pupils
Institutionalization: the "built-in-ness" of the innovation in local regulations, procedures, budget and procurement, cycles, training programs, and the like

The final outcome variable is an especially important one. New educational practices that do not hang on beyond one or two years are clearly not worth the investment, and the gist of relevant research is that hangers-on are fewer in number than one had thought.[17] The notion that a technically mastered, well-administered, impactful innovation will lock automatically into the local setting is, once again, a Panglossian and potentially self-delusive view of the world. We found that technically mastering a new program, even one that demonstrated better pupil performance than had its predecessor, did not ensure and sometimes had no bearing on the likelihood of its continuation. But we also found that continuation *can* be ensured when administrators attend to the requisite parameters.

The Supported-Enforcement Scenario Let us focus on the "institutionalization" outcome, with attention to some of the others as well. In the DESSI field study, we drew a "causal network" for each of the twelve sites describing the course of local events in terms of a core list of empirically derived variables.[18] We were analytically able to sort the twelve sites into four different "families" according to the configural clustering of the key variables. The first family performed well on all the main outcome variables. We came to call it the "supported-enforcement" scenario, in that it achieved stable, institutionalized use through administrative mandating *and* sustained assistance that led through teachers' energies to stable use. Figure 1 shows one of the cases in that family:

Here, a powerful central office administrator (2), the director of curriculum and special projects, working from a centralized power base (3), put considerable pressure on users (5) to implement the new, locally developed reading program. Initially, this lowered users' commitment (8); they resented and feared the pressure. But substantial assistance (1) was supplied, which increased users' practice mastery (4) a good deal and subsequently their commitment (8). In addition, organizational rearrangements (9), including scheduling, pupil rotation, and teacher teaming, were made, increasing student impact (11). User mastery and commitment, along with stability of program staff (6), led to stabilized use (10), which both increased percentage of use (12) and led to institutionalization (13). Stability of program leadership (7) also aided institutionalization. The general picture is one of administrative decisiveness, accompanied by enough assistance to increase user skill, ownership, and stable use in the context of a stable system. The cases in this supported-enforcement family share some characteristics that are worth underlining:

1. Sustained administrative commitment. Senior administrators, often central office staff in a coordinator or curriculum slot, wanted to see the project implemented. They therefore exerted pressure, made the necessary procedural and structural changes, and provided sustained backstopping: materials, training, authorizations, consultancies, planning sessions on

Figure 1

Mandated, Stable Use as a Route to Institutionalization: Tindale (IV-C)

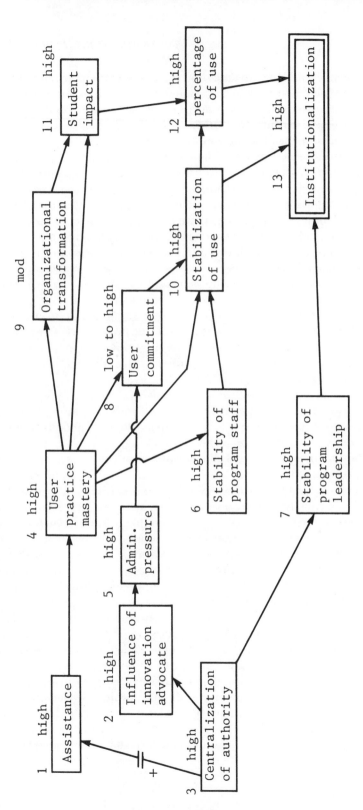

+Influence of other variables not discussed

school time. They did *not* get the project going and then turn their attention elsewhere, which is the modal pattern in this and in most empirical studies. Nor did they assume that assistance at the front end (prior to program execution) would suffice, but rather redistributed these resources to make proportionately more of them available later on.

2. Technical mastery as a stimulant. Some teachers initially did not like the innovations in this family and did not appreciate the pressure. They did, however, make a serious attempt to get on top of the new practice instructionally—in part owing to the pressure, in part to the assistance, in part to the challenge of mastering a demanding technical task. As that level of mastery rose, two things happened. First, as the figure shows, user commitment (8) increased. When one follows this process in the field, it is more the mastery that drives the commitment than the reverse; commitment is not a precondition, but rather an *achievement*, the result of effortful and technical application. Teachers talked of "being on top of it," of "getting it to go *my* way." Second, heightened practice mastery (4) led to stronger student impact (11), in terms of achievement or attitude increments. The innovation had started to deliver, and the users, increasingly effective in manipulating it at the classroom or school level, could increase, differentiate, and more consistently produce those impacts.

3. Deliberate focus on institutionalization. Innovations are highly perishable goods. New practices that get built into the training, regulatory, staffing, and budgetary cycle survive; others do not, notably when their original champions move on. The administrators in this family attended specifically to these issues and did not move on until the innovation was satisfactorily locked in.[19]

The Overreaching Scenario We said that administrative enforcement was *a* family in our data; there were others, at least one of which could also lead to positive outcomes. It was, however, a less certain path, and it entailed slightly lower levels of outcome. We called these projects "overreachers." They also entered the district through central office advocacy. Administrators provided initial and some follow-up support, and authorized users to make execution more manageable by changing the innovation—something the administrators in the first family of projects did not allow in the early stages. Most of the support, however, was peer support rather than administrative support, and it brought users through to fairly strong levels of commitment and mastery. Project outcomes were fairly high, but users tended toward exhaustion, and responded by reducing the gradient of practice change (which lowered the outcome levels) or by reviving career pursuits that led out of the district. Personnel turnover, both among staff and project leadership, reduced commitment to the project and thereby made for an uncertain longevity of use at the site.

This family of projects illustrates the fact that new practices *can* be introduced and consolidated without administrative strong-arming. The problem, however, is that as users reach masterful ownership of the practice, some burn out, others revive career ambitions, and most are working with a somewhat watered-down project relative to its initial scale and impact. Nor do administrators appear to build lasting commitments to the projects they sponsor or lead, so that success or environmental turbulence are prompts to move on. We shall return to this point in a moment.

So this family, while more democratic and lateral than the first one, is also less "managed." It achieves somewhat weaker results than the first set—but in a more adventurous way. These projects are not "implemented" as much as they are collectively "crusaded." They have a lot more uncertainty, in part because the senior administrators run them with a lighter hand. They run the innovations even less, however, in the later stages, when institutionalization issues are paramount. The scenario here is more appealing to those of us nurtured on nondirective leadership, but it is also less reliable than the first one, which tends more to *deliver* the improvements it pursues. In other words, implementation can be a social technology—school improvement can be enacted—but one pays a price for it in the degrees of freedom allotted most of the main actors.

The Dark Side of Adaptation: Blunting and Downsizing We are now ready to spell out the second part of proposition two, in which we endorsed intelligent, supportive coercion as a surer path to significant school improvement. The claim we are making here is that innovations that are managerially handed over to teachers often become "blunted" or "downsized" in such a way as to trivialize their outcomes.

We found a third family of projects with a basic theme: Innovations that might have been major ventures, either at the district or classroom level, had been progressively reduced in scale and scope to the point where outcomes could be, at best, only modest. Typically, the reductions took place at the instructional level. Given wide latitude by administrators to make changes, teachers redid the innovations, stabilizing them as minor add-ons or drop-ins. To redo them, teachers unbundled external (NDN) projects, using only those components that were congenial to personal teaching styles and that called for few changes in ongoing instructional routines.

An additional thread tied this group together and connected it thematically to the second family of cases for three of the four sites: Continuing administrative leadership was low. Key advocates at the building and district level backed off, left, or were reassigned.

As an example of the scenarios, in the Astoria site the districtwide mandate for using an early childhood screening and skill-development program created new and stiff demands on the kindergartens. This made for a poor fit between program and building characteristics, already potentially poor because of the heavy requirements of the program design. The central office administrator then gave wide latitude to building administrators to "adapt" the project, thereby restoring the teacher-administrator harmony that had been compromised by the innovation and its requirements. As a result, there was substantial program change, resulting in less impact on pupils than its developers expected.

The scenario at other sites was similar. At the Burton site, the central office advocate considered the program to be in a "pilot" year, when teachers could "pick and choose" promising aspects, then, supposedly, build them into the curriculum. But teachers quite naturally shied away from the more demanding or adventurous components (for example, emphasis on activist community experience and more student-directed learning activities). Because these aspects of the program were central to its success, the impact on pupils was minimal.

The point here is not that local adaptation is a poor policy, but that fiddling with a project to improve the fit between the school and the innovation can often trivialize results. The whole point about innovating is that it creates a discrepancy between local practices and the demands of the new practice—and in that discrepancy lie the changes that can produce significant results. Reduce that discrepancy and you throw away important outcomes. The logical—and understandable—response of teachers is to improve the fit, to begin gently, and to avoid situations of high uncertainty, all of which create pressures on administrators to give teachers their heads. Such latitude usually leads to down-sizing—which is rarely followed by up-sizing later on. In particular, administrators who give a lot of leeway (often in order to get the innovation accepted) and then turn their attention elsewhere are asking for placebos. More often than not, that is precisely what they get.

There are, of course, many caveats here. Supported enforcement is, as we have said, not the only way to get significant practice change, although it might be the most literally manageable way. Also, we are talking about innovations intended for several schools and therefore engaging the central office directly. There is also the assumption that the innovation's quality is high—or at least that it can be made so. Enforcing lemons, with or without assistance, is a flawed enterprise, and the projects comprising our fourth family (i.e., cases of failure) are of that kind, with a strong dash of administrative indifference thrown in.

A final caveat: Our discussion of the second proposition has drifted into the realm of the Promethean; we have depicted muscular administrators sagely manipulating resources to enact impactful, well-rooted changes. The assumptions are that muscular administrators will not abuse their muscles and that the resources are there; both assumptions are questionable in many instances. There are also two other problematic assumptions: (1) that the achievement of some outcomes does not undo the achievement of others, and (2) that the external environment is benign. In other words, human affairs may be manageable—but only up to a point. Uncertainty and perversity have a way of confounding our best-orchestrated efforts. That brings us to our third proposition.

3. *Well executed, high-quality innovations do bring about measurable improvements, but some of them may destabilize the very conditions that have produced the improvements.*

Let us address this proposition, which might be captioned "the failure of success," with the two remaining outcome variables we have not yet illustrated: the normative outcome, "user capacity change," and a more descriptive outcome that we called "job mobility." The former has already been defined; the other warrants some added discussion.

As we saw in the analysis of informants' motives, about 40 percent of users and 50 percent of administrators had career plans tied in with the adoption of the innovation. One is naturally curious as to whether and when people got where they wanted to go. How much job mobility occurred? And how much of it was related to the innovation, or was adventitious? Finally, what were its local effects?

This is the kind of variable that surveys either ignore or are ill-designed to capture, but that field studies can identify and document when it looms large empirically, as was the case in our study. When we arrayed the projects by program type, numbers of key actors involved, job shifts at different moments in the life of the project and the degree of program-relatedness of those shifts, there was a good deal of moving around related to the innovation (63 moves among 123 key actors—people closely involved with the innovation—for our 12 sites, of which 83 percent were clearly innovation-related). Activity was high at the outset, when the project created new, often upwardly mobile roles. But activity was also high much later on, when administrators moved out and up or simply within the district, and teachers associated with the project took over their places. About 35 percent of the innovation-related job mobility was upward.

Some job mobility (14 moves, or 17 percent of the total) was *not* related to the innovation. It was of two types: (1) project staff had planned to leave or retire, or were moved elsewhere independently of the project; (2) environmental turbulence, usually in the form of sudden budget cuts, ejected people from the project, usually into unwanted jobs. More on this latter type in a moment.

At four of the twelve sites, there was little evidence of innovation-related job mobility. At the eight others, career moves were clearly tangled up with the fate of the innovation. Within these eight, we identified four somewhat distinct families. Let us illustrate one case that straddles two families and, thereby, accounts for five of the eight high-mobility cases. Figure 2 presents the causal network:

The first stream leading to job mobility is an ominous one; it goes from low

Figure 2
Job Mobility as Win-Lose Scenario: Perry-Parkdale (NDN)

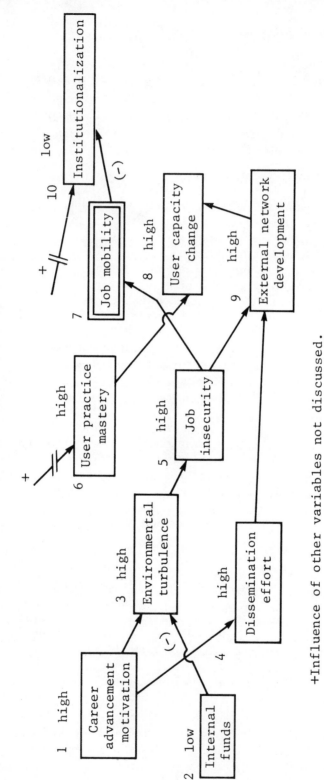

+Influence of other variables not discussed.

internal funds (2) to environmental turbulence (3) in the form of unexpected budget cuts to job insecurity (5) and to job mobility (7) for two of three core staff. Job mobility was mostly unwanted; people were essentially casualties of external events over which virtually no one had much control. Three of the eight cases have similar casualty scenarios.

However, there is another, more upbeat stream to job mobility: the one leading from user practice mastery (6) through user capacity change (8) to job mobility. Through progressive mastery of the project, users and administrators developed new skills they were interested in using elsewhere—preferably but not necessarily at a higher level. Paradoxically, it was the success of the project at the individual level that triggered mobility and, in so doing, lowered its institutionalization (10) at the local level. A similar phenomenon is afoot in the stream leading from career advancement motivation (1) through dissemination effort (4) and external network development (9), then up to user capacity change and job mobility. In brief, disseminating a largely successful program brought on opportunities for self-advertisement and new jobs that, when taken, reduced the local stability of the innovation. Some actors won, some lost (the "casualty" cases), but both kinds moved and the project's continuation was made uncertain by their departure.

Lest we be accused, as some qualitative researchers have been, of overusing irony as an analytical device, we should note that nondisruptive cases of job mobility did exist at two of our eight high-mobility sites. Both, interestingly enough, were highly effective supported-enforcement sites. At Tindale, users moved into building-level administrative jobs, a department head went to the central office, and a central office administrator shifted to another district. But the movement was seen as a legitimate payoff for successful program execution, and the key staff remained, continuing to provide leadership for the innovation. At the Masepa site, two users moved into full-time teaching, a principal's "visibility" was aided, and another user became first a turnkey trainer and later a Title I coordinator. No one left the district because of involvement with the innovation. So career advancement needs and innovative success are not incompatible. The question is whether this balance can be planfully managed. In most of our high-mobility sites it was not.

It could be argued that mobility that disrupts local programs contributes to another educational enterprise; those who move will use their new capacities, or as one of the principals we studied did, replicate the innovation in a new position. Nevertheless, it is important to maintain social capital. On balance, we might wish for school-improvement programs that could accommodate individuals' needs for capacity development and career advancement without destabilizing the local gains achieved.

But educational change is manipulable only up to a point. Project success at the individual or even the institutional level can create the kernel of longer-term failure by unsettling the project, and there may not be much that can be done about it. Environmental turbulence can do in a well-executed, impact-bearing innovation in a matter of months; innovations are typically the first victims when budget crises strike. We would do well to be modest, not only in the claims we can make within a rational, social-engineering paradigm, but also concerning the control over events that is possible within a conflict paradigm. Within the bounds of that modesty, as we have seen, there are identifiable and probably replicable ways of bringing about school-based improvement.

CONCLUSION

In conducting this selective tour of the findings of the DESSI field study, we have tried to show that the conceptual paradigms used to account for the school-improvement process need enlargement and articulation if they are to mirror the real world and provide useful explanations of it. The advocates of highly managerial, meliorist perspectives need to wallow around more in the untidy, often disruptive empirical realities we find in the field. Those pushing conflict-theoretic perspectives may be equally simplistic in their endemic emphasis on conspiratorial strategizing, an emphasis that obscures much of the goal-centered activity to which different actors actually commit themselves within schools. Being more ecumenical within and between these paradigms strikes us as both conceptually plausible and empirically robust.

Finally, we have suggested that school improvement is a reachable objective, and that we are beginning to understand the conditions for reaching it. Most of our field-study (and survey) cases achieved moderate to strong positive outcomes. Though administrators and teachers live in different worlds and have different agendas, they can, under the right circumstances, complement each others' efforts productively. Committed administrators can push, protect the innovation from casual adaptation, and supply supportive assistance. Users can follow their own professional growth motivation to master the innovation, help each other, extend their own classroom practice, and deepen their commitment.

Getting all the pieces of that formula in place, however, is difficult and only partly manageable. The conditions for attaining school improvement are stringent—and sometimes undesirable for one or more of the parties involved. Perhaps that is why there is less school improvement going on than we would like. If it were easy, we could simply follow the craft and mold our concepts around it. As it is, the craft of school improvement is unevenly successful, and we need newer, tougher concepts to reorient the quest.

Notes

1 Paul Berman and Milbrey Wallin McLaughlin, *Federal Programs Supporting Educational Change*, Vols. I-VIII (Santa Monica, Calif.: Rand Corporation, 1974-1978); Karen S. Louis et al., *Strategies for Knowledge Use and School Improvement* (Washington, D.C.: National Institute of Education, 1981); and John Emrick and S. Peterson, *A Synthesis of Findings*

across Five Recent Studies in Educational Dissemination and Change (San Francisco: Far West Laboratory for Educational Research and Development, 1978).

2 David Clark, Sue McKibbin, and M. Malkas, eds., *Alternative Perspectives for Viewing Educational Organizations* (San Francisco: Far West Laboratory for Educational Research and Development, 1981); Michael Crozier et E. Friedberg, *L'Acteur et le Systeme* (Paris: Editions du Seuil, 1977); and Karl Weick, *The Social Psychology of Organizing*, 2nd ed. (Reading, Mass.: Addison-Wesley, 1979).

3 David Crandall et al., *A Study of Dissemination Efforts Supporting School Improvement*, Vols. I-X (Andover, Mass.: The Network, 1982).

4 "Transplanting Success: Good News from a Study of School Improvement," 8 articles devoted to the DESSI study in *Educational Leadership* 41, no. 3 (November 1983): 3-37.

5 The Network Inc., Andover, Mass.; Center for Policy Research, New York; Knowledge Transfer Institute, American University, R&D Center for Teacher Education, University of Texas; and Center for the Study of Evaluation, UCLA.

6 Berman and McLaughlin, *Federal Programs Supporting Educational Change*, Vols. I-VIII.

7 Matthew B. Miles and A. Michael Huberman, *Qualitative Data Analysis: A Sourcebook of New Methods* (Beverly Hills: Sage, 1984).

8 A. Michael Huberman and Matthew B. Miles, *Innovation Up Close: How School Improvement Works* (New York: Plenum, 1984).

9 Jack Douglas, *Investigative Social Research* (Beverly Hills: Sage, 1976).

10 Huberman and Miles, *Innovation Up Close.*

11 Robert K. Yin et al., *Changing Urban Bureaucracies: How New Practices Become Routinized*, Vols. I-II (Santa Monica: Rand Corporation, 1978).

12 Emrick and Peterson, *A Synthesis of Findings across Five Recent Studies in Educational Dissemination and Change;* and Michael Fullan, *The Meaning of Educational Change* (Toronto: OISE Press, and New York: Teachers College Press, 1982).

13 For a more systematic and detailed treatment of this topic, see A. Michael Huberman, "Educational Change and Career Pursuit: Some Findings from the Field," *Interchange* (forthcoming).

14 In almost all cases, teachers were well aware of the career plans of one another and of their principals, as were principals of central office personnel's career plans.

15 Cf. Richard Elmore, "Organizational Models of Social Program Implementation," *Public Policy* 26 (1978): 185-228.

16 Robert Chin and Kenneth D. Benne, "General Strategies for Effecting Changes in Human Systems," in *The Planning of Change*, 3rd ed., ed. Warren Bennis et al. (New York: Holt, Rinehart & Winston, 1976.

17 Berman and McLaughlin, *Federal Programs Supporting Educational Change*, Vols. I-VIII; and Yin et al., *Changing Urban Bureaucracies.*

18 The techniques for elaborating and validating causal networks are described in Miles and Huberman, *Qualitative Data Analysis.*

19 It might be argued that our supported-enforcement findings are restricted to the specific sort of school improvement we are studying—the adoption and implementation of locally or externally developed innovations. However, we should note that Berman found an almost identical pattern of strong, proactive leadership accompanied by extended assistance in an extensive study of the California School Improvement Program, an approach emphasizing general capacity building of the school, beyond the use of specific innovations (Paul Berman, *Improving School Improvement*, Vol. 1: *Executive Summary and Recommendations*, R-103/1; Vol. 2 (with Thomas Gjelten), *Findings*, R-103/2 [Berkeley: Berman-Weiler Associates, 1984]). The finding is not inconsistent, either, with what is known about the properties of "effective schools" (cf. David Clark, Linda S. Lotto, and Terry A. Astuto, "Effective Schools and School Improvement: A Comparative Analysis of Two Lines of Inquiry," *Educational Administration Quarterly* (forthcoming).

Reconstruing Educational Innovation

LOUIS M. SMITH
Washington University, St. Louis

JOHN J. PRUNTY
Maritz Communication Company, St. Louis

DAVID C. DWYER
*Far West Laboratory for Educational Research and
Development, San Francisco*

PAUL F. KLEINE
University of Oklahoma, Norman

INTRODUCTION

This article, as the title indicates, presents one of the central conclusions from our recent research on the Kensington Elementary School in the Milford School District. Essentially we want to argue that our early view of the Kensington School was severely limited due to several sets of assumptions we did not make problematic at the time.[1] Second, we argue that our original proposal to the National Institute of Education (NIE) for *Kensington Revisited*, which stated our current "problem," had similar limits.[2] Third, we argue that one of the most provocative recent summary statements has similar limitations.[3] Finally, we want to make the case that our revised position is more clearly in the literature, especially in the work of C. Wright Mills[4] and Robert Redfield,[5] than we and others (e.g., Whiteside and Sarason[6]) realized. Most of us who do intensive case-study or qualitative field research recognize a redefinition of a problem, a theoretical reconceptualization, or a reconstrual of a domain as worthy objectives, even though we seldom attain such goals.

This article is based on the project Innovation and Change in American Education—Kensington Revisited: A Fifteen Year Follow-up of an Innovative Elementary School and Its Faculty *supported by NIE grant no. G78-0074. The analysis and interpretation represent official policy of neither the National Institute of Education nor the Milford School District. As we have commented on several occasions, the support by Dr. Ronald George, superintendent of Milford, and by Frederick Mulhauser, our NIE project officer, has been overwhelmingly positive at every turn.*

In a sense, and after we were underway, Ernie House might be said to have set our task with his integrative "ten year perspective on innovation."[7] He argued that three broad perspectives—technological, political, and cultural—have dominated recent thought about educational innovation. In House's view, the technological model was developed in agriculture and industry and formalized in education as the RD&D model—Research, Development, and Diffusion. It provided the basic set of assumptions for much of the curriculum reform and government effort in educational innovation in the 1960s. The political perspective arose as a competing model and cast the problems and difficulties in changing schools as issues of value pluralism involving multiple interest groups and processes of conflict, negotiation, and compromise in making decisions, securing resources, and distributing incentives and rewards. The cultural perspective took a more holistic and contextualist point of view, usually with concern for the meaning of the actors in the setting. It was an anthropological perspective, frequently carried out by nonanthropologists.

In this context, the part of our study dealing with the life histories of educational innovators and accenting the theme of natural history of belief systems is an attempt to redress the scant attention given to and, in some instances, the complete omission of the individual person in the innovative process. Our *Educational Innovators: Then and Now* (Volume V) accents the biography, the life history of the individuals involved. In a sense it reflects a position among the multiple theories of personality currently in debate in social science and, as a point of view about human personality, can be seen as a kind of psychological perspective. As a psychological perspective it is considerably different both methodologically and substantively from most of the psychological theories and efforts applied to educational innovation. From our viewpoint such a difference is important and constitutes one main contribution of our effort. In effect, we are proposing a fourth perspective to the three raised by House.[8]

Further, we were led into a historical perspective in other parts of our study through a series of serendipitous events, and quite commonsense puzzlements. By chance we stumbled on a closet full of the Milford School District board minutes from 1915 to the present day. They seemed an amazing record of human action and events that illuminated the historical and contemporaneous district context of the Kensington Elementary School. Concomitantly, the change in the makeup of the student body at Kensington School—from 100 percent white in 1964/1965 to 40 percent white and 60 percent black in 1979/1980—led us into demography and the history of community change. We believe now that a historical perspective is very important.

In sum, in our view, an overall model must have technological, political, cultural, biographical, and historical dimensions if the phenomenon of educational innovation is to be understood. That is a part of the reconstrual for which we are arguing. Twenty-five year ago Mills set such aspirations succinctly:

> The sociological imagination enables us to grasp *history* and *biography* and the relations between the two within *society*. That is its task and its promise. To recognize this task and this promise is the mark of the classic social analyst.
>
> No social study that does not come back to the problems of biography, of history and of their intersections within a society has completed its intellectual journey.[9]

Though we are neither sociologists nor "classic social analysts," our problems and ideas mirror those concerns and our aspirations are in those directions.

THE KENSINGTON-REVISITED CASE STUDY

OVERVIEW

Our research is about innovation and change in American education. It began as *Kensington Revisited: A Fifteen Year Follow-up of an Innovative Elementary School and Its Faculty,*[10] supported by the National Institute of Education. As in most of our case-study research, the initial problem was buffeted about by the reality of settings, events, and people as captured by our several modes of inquiry—participant observation, intensive open-ended interviews, and the collection and analysis of multiple documents. The setting was Kensington, an elementary school built fifteen years ago as a prototypical innovative building with open space, laboratory suites instead of classrooms, a perception core instead of a library, and a nerve center for the latest in educational technology. The ideology was caught in team teaching, individualized curriculum and instruction, and democratic administration. The people were the series of administrators, teachers, pupils, and parents who worked in, attended, or sent their children to the school. Three principals have come and gone, the fourth is in his first year. None of the original faculty remains at the school. Several cadres of faculty have staffed the building. The events were the activities of those people as they built and transformed the school over the years. This story we found, and constructed, as part of a larger setting, the Milford School District, which had its own story, actors, and events and which provided an important context for Kensington.

"Innovation and change in American education" became the guiding theme around which our developing ideas and data could be integrated. That broad rubric is composed of a half dozen subthemes, each of which makes up a separate book-length volume in the final report. While we believe the totality of the study has its own kind of integrity and that each volume extends the meanings of the others, we have written each as a "stand-alone" piece. That is, we believe each speaks to an important domain of innovation and change in American education, each draws most heavily on a particular subset of our data, and each contains important descriptive narratives and substantive grounded interpretations and generalizations. We present brief summaries of each volume, which are intended, in a few sentences, to keep the totality and each of the pieces in the forefront of the reader's consciousness.

SUBSTANTIVE CONCERNS

Volume I   Chronicling the Milford School District: An Historical Context of the Kensington School

Kensington's fifteen-year existence is but one small segment of the Milford School District's sixty-five years of recorded history and one school in a district with a dozen other schools. Stephen Spanman, the superintendent who built the school, is but one of five individuals who have held the post. As we have told the story, we have raised generalizations regarding innovation and change, and have presaged themes of policy; of local, state, and national influences on the school district; of organizational structure and process; and of curriculum and teaching. More abstractly, we moved toward concerns as broad as the many faces of democracy in education and schooling, policymaking and administration, and a longitudinal nested systems model of innovation and change. These are conceptualizations that have been underemphasized in the theory and practice of innovation. The key documents in developing the perspective were the official school board minutes. Newsletters to patrons, newpaper accounts, other records, and interviews, formal and informal, supplemented the basic documents.

Volume II Milford: The School District as Contemporary Context

In a fundamental sense, Volume II is a continuation, a final chapter as it were, of the historical context of the Milford School District. It is a long chapter, however, for the central actors and events that immediately and directly shaped the Kensington School are in place, just as the school is in place. The ebb and flow of the district, in its recent history, is brought to a particular focus, one that will illuminate the events and themes that appear in the development and change in the Kensington School over its fifteen-year history and in its current status. The board of education, the superintendent, the central office staff, and their interrelationships lead toward a governance and organizational perspective on innovation and change. We move finally and more abstractly to a reconsideration of the Griffiths/Greenfield debate[11] in the light of our findings regarding the Milford School District as context for the Kensington School innovation. Board minutes remain the central core of the data with increasing amounts of information from public documents (e.g., newspapers), interviews with central actors, and observation of meetings.

Volume III   Innovation and Change at Kensington: Annals of a Community and School

This volume begins by tracing the origins and development of a community that became part of the Milford School District in 1949 and a neighborhood that began sending its children to Kensington School in 1964. With the opening of Kensington, the annals of the community are joined by a history of the school. As we develop the stories of Kensington and its neighborhood in tandem, we begin to tell of the interdependency of school and community and to further our understanding of innovation and change in schooling in contemporary American society. Our search for an explanation of the profound changes that have taken place in a once innovative school has pushed us back in time and obliged us to consider such wider topics as demography; ethnic, religious, and racial groups; neighborhoods; and political jurisdiction.

Volume IV   Kensington Today: Sailing Stormy Straits, a View of Educational Policy in Action

An ethnographic account of the school today with particular reference to educational policy in action at the day-to-day school level is presented here. The major metaphor is a ship sailing through stormy straits on a perilous journey during the 1979/1980 school year. Staff and students produce vivid scenes reflecting issues in racial integration, special education, discipline, and instruction in basic subjects. Turbulent environments and organizational identity emerge as key conceptions. Policymaking seems analogous to the fine art of navigation.

Volume V   Educational Innovators: Then and Now

Crucial to any educational enterprise are the people who staff the schools. Smith and Keith characterized the original faculty of Kensington as true believers.[12] In this volume we sketch life histories; careers; serials of the original faculty based on extended open-ended interviews (2-7 hours); comments by spouses, friends, and colleagues; and various writings—books, brochures, reports, and dissertations. Patterns and themes arise in the form of secular religion, you *do* go home again, organizational niches and career opportunities for educationists, maintenance of educational ideology, continuity and change in personality, and doctoral education—a disaster for reform-oriented practitioners. The natural history of belief systems is the major integrating conception.

Volume VI   Case Study Research Methodology: The Intersect of Participant Observation, Historical Method, Life History Research, and Follow-Up Studies

Regularly in our inquiry we have produced methodological appendices to our research reports. We saw our efforts as clarifying the craft of research as we practiced it, ordering its evolving nature, and continuously attempting to integrate it with other ways of knowing. This volume continues in that tradition. Specifically our mode of participant observation now has enlarged itself by a substantial historical thrust and a substantial life-history and biographical thrust. In addition, our research is an instance of a special methodological stance, a follow-up or return to the setting of an earlier major study. In a way it takes on a time-series quality with repeated observations. In doing the descriptive and analytical pieces, Volumes I through V; in reading about how others have done similar work; and in talking with proponents of the various methods we have reached for a broader synthesis of case-study research methods in the intersection of these several approaches. We see all this as an important addition to the methodological literature in educational inquiry in general and to the more specific research tradition in educational innovation.

SUMMARY

In summary, our research is a unique blend of approaches to the problems and issues of innovation and change in American education. It is grounded in the multiple aspects of a single school in a single school district. As in all case studies, the particular events have major meanings for the actors in the setting, but we also believe that these events often capture images and ideas that have relevance for other people in other times and places. These "inner" and "outer" perspectives, which Geertz labeled as "experience-near" and "experience-distant"[13] conceptions, were part of our early concerns. Even here we found our practices outrunning our initial analytical distinctions. Finally, when we looked back over our shoulders at what we had, we were able to see an intersection of problems, methods, and perspectives. These are contained in Figure 1. In effect we have half a dozen key problems and themes tapped by several major research methods and framed by multiple inner and outer or experience-near and experience-distant perspectives. In each form we hope to be providing mirrors for educationists to see themselves better, that is, more clearly, to be conscious of rephrased problems, and to create more viable options and alternatives. The present article argues that this too is part of a reconstrual of educational innovation.

Volume	Problem/Content/Theme	Major Research Method	Dominant Perspective/ Point of View
I	Genesis and Evolution of a School District	Historical	Natural History
II	Innovation and Its Contemporary Context	Historical	Board of Education/ Central Administration
III	Community and Neighborhood Change	Historical	Minority Population
IV	Kensington Today/ Policy Implications	Ethnography	Liberal Reformer
V	Faculty Careers/ Life History of True Believers	Life History	Participants/ Outside Theorists
VI	Theory of Methodology	Analytic/ Reflective	Researchers

Figure 1: An Overview of Kensington Revisited:
Intersection of Problems, Methods, and Perspectives

ARGUMENTS FOR A RECONSTRUAL

HISTORY

In an earlier circulation of one of the historical volumes of the extended report we had reactions and comments regarding the need for such an intensive history of the Milford School District. In a sense we were asked, What is the question to which that long monograph was the answer? We built a perspective that culminated in the phrasing of that question.

Several beliefs coalesced in our view. First, we thought that most educational innovators and researchers of educational innovation had not taken up the issues in the relationship between educational innovation and educational change. Very simply put, we see educational innovation as a specific planned improvement. As such it is just one class of phenomena in the larger category of educational change. When viewed in this larger context, innovation takes on considerably different meaning. Our hunch is that most innovators have been so busy with their own specific problems and programs that they have not pursued the implications of events occurring in the larger category. As we thought about these issues, other related concepts entered our analysis. Educational reform became a major or large-scale innovation often blended with idealism. Utopias seemed to be extreme kinds of reforms. Other concepts of change seemed to imply other assumptions or root metaphors. For instance, the genesis of a school district is a specific kind of innovation with a time referent. The evolution of a district implies gradual change over a period of time. Growth and decline suggest change in size and perhaps an evaluative disclaimer. In American culture, growth is bigger and better and decline is smaller and lesser. Clustered, these concepts also implied a more organismic or naturalistic metaphor. Other concepts used by people involved in educational innovation—for example, expansion, contraction, reorganization, and merger—although not mutually exclusive of our early classes of terms, seem to fit more comfortably a technical perspective and, perhaps, imply a more mechanistic root metaphor, as Pepper argues.[14] Our point is simple: The very language one uses to talk about change in schools and schooling brings major and usually implicit "excess baggage" or meanings into the discussion.

For the moment, we settled on the outline in Figure 2, a beginning analytical context for the concept of educational innovation. As we worked through the data and analysis in volumes I, II, and III, the history of the changing school district and community helped us "see" the nature of Kensington School as an educational innovation, a specific planned change. The magnitude of this insight on change is caught in the restatement of the overall title of our study. What began as *Kensington Revisited: A Fifteen Year Follow-up of an Innovation Elementary School and Its Faculty* has become *Innovation and Change in American Education*, with the original wording now a subtitle.

1. Educational change—the general category
2. Change from a "planned" perspective
   2.1 Innovation
   2.2 Reform
   2.3 Utopia
3. Change from a "naturalistic" perspective
   3.1 Genesis
   3.2 Evolution
   3.3 Growth
   3.4 Decline
4. Change from a "technical" perspective
   4.1 Expansion—add on
   4.2 Contraction—subtract
   4.3 Differentiation
   4.4 Reorganization
   4.5 Merger

Figure 2. A Beginning Analytical Context of the Concept "Innovation"

Our history of the growing, evolving, changing Milford School District helped us see more clearly a related set of issues, the political context of innovation. If educational innovation is only one kind of change and if it is, as colloquially expressed, your or my "baby," that is, attached to someone's political interests—as often is the case, and was in Milford—then a further idea follows. At a minimum, other individuals may have other interests and ideas they see as desirable, special, and, possibly, innovative. If their ideas are not perfectly congruent with yours or mine then we begin to have a problem of priorities, resources, power, and persuasion. In short, your or my innovation may well be just one small part of a political process. Goodness and truth may not lie in your or my project to the degree we had assumed. At this point, our specific planned change is more than a technical or scientific problem. Illuminating that cluster of events, the give-and-take of conflict, compromise, and political maneuvering became very important to us.

Third, it is our belief that many if not most educational innovators do not know much educational history. We believe that this is a tragedy for them and their ideas and a tragedy for many of the individuals in the schools on which they "inflict" their innovations, for example, new open-space buildings, individualized curriculum and instruction, or democratic administration. This belief is one of the major results of our study. As one of our colleagues commented on listening to our enthusiasm and stories, "Lou, you've discovered history." And so we have. This concern for history in general and for history of the Milford District in particular is part of a major shift in our concept of paradigms or root metaphors underlying our approach to educational research, theory, and practice. We feel we are operating from a contextualist metaphor as Pepper[15] and Sarbin[16] use the term. With them, we believe the power of social science and educational inquiry will be enhanced as others move in this direction also.

Fourth, even so, there is still enough of the natural scientist in each of us to feel that an outsider's reasonably detached view of the "natural history" of *a* or, better, *this* school district might be more important than just the pursuit of idle curiosity. We believe that the genesis and evolution of the district from this more naturalistic perspective shades into our more contextualist perspective. As such, we can view "the new elementary education of Kensington" as one superintendent's vision, in a history of five superintendents and seventy-five years of schooling in Milford. Where does that superintendent, Spanman, fit in the evolution of the Milford School District? Where did he come from? Why did he build the innovative Kensington School here?

Fifth, when we accidently fell into the huge body of data, bound volumes of Milford board minutes reaching back to 1915, the practicality and possibility of this historical dimension became a reality. Beyond a Mount Everest being there to be climbed, we have found that vague, general, and often ill-founded ideas take on another kind of vitality when they are moved into the concrete reality of data on human events. As we argue elsewhere,[17] school board minutes are public records of an unusual sort. Finding a closet full of them opened up unimagined vistas. The historical context was there.

Sixth, one of the truisms in our field research is that "the problem" evolves over the course of the project. This is the best of what is sometimes called responsive research design rather than preset research design. Rather than being a producer of anxiety, this becomes part of the excitement and joy of the unexpected in field research.

In short, Volume I, *Chronicling the Milford School District: An Historical Context of the Kensington School,* is just that, a historical context. Volumes II and III extend that context. They answer the question "Where does the Kensington School as an innovation fit into the larger picture?" Because this picture is treated historically as the genesis and evolution of a school district it permits us to deal with the broader reconceptualization or phrasing of our problem as "innovation and change in American education." By introducing "American" into the statement we have gone from the instance of the Milford School District to a larger class or category of events, "American education." And that is a major issue in its own right. We believe that one of the best ways, although not the only way, of understanding that larger set of events is to know intimately one highly detailed but integrated case. With such an image at hand, one can begin to come to terms with any other case and with the larger category. As we commented in jest with the current superintendent of Milford, "We know more about Milford than anyone ever has known and probably more than anyone will want to know." That is, unless one wants to "really" understand innovation and change in American education. Such is the question, and hope, of these historical volumes in the overall report.

LIFE HISTORY

The argument for a life-history component of educational innovation has been with us implicitly since our labeling of the Kensington teachers as "true believers," after Hoffer's use of the term,[18] men and women of fanatical faith willing to die for a cause. In *Anatomy of Educational Innovation* we did not make this issue problematic in the sense either of asking for the reasons these individuals chose to come to the Milford School District or of asking about the genesis of such a personal point of view. Now our speculations run in multiple directions. For instance, if educational innovators differ from educational reformers only in the size of the planned change they contemplate, and if both are linked with being true believers, and if educational reform has a quality of secularized religion, as we have argued in the main report, then the phenomenon of educational innovation has roots well beyond a simple technological, cost-benefit, or surface change in schooling practices. More specifically, our hypothesis of educational reform as secular religion grew out of our surprise at finding religious views and experiences entangled in multiple ways in the backgrounds and beliefs of our group from Kensington. Several had trained for the ministry; many, both men and women, were quite active as Sunday school teachers with adult groups; one had become a born-again Christian. These ideas, with others, have broadened into a theme we call "the natural history of belief systems." Our results suggest that beliefs about innovation are not simple, peripheral, fly-by-night add-ons to the personalities of educational innovators.

To return to our data and interpretations, our study of life histories argues that theories of educational innovation must include other concepts and propositions about the personality of the innovators. "Proactive" is a term that runs through multiple levels of abstraction regarding innovation. At a concrete situational level our people tended to be planning, choosing, self-determining people who looked for, found, and got into situations supportive of their positions. Theoretically it argues for a theory-of-action alternative to more reactive, behavioristic positions. Paradigmatically such terms take a stance on root metaphors—contextualist versus mechanical. In short, the domain of educational innovation requires a place for life history as a special perspective on personality theory.

Major life events—schools, peer networks, jobs, marriages, and deaths in one's family—are the class of variables influencing belief systems and personality styles. Our interests have been rekindled in concepts such as developmental tasks and have been moved toward creating ideas such as "experiential funnel," which captures the long-term channeling of experiences and resultant belief systems.

These issues of biography, life history, and personality, while significant in their own right, seem especially important as one moves along the continuum or across the domains of educational change from educational innovation to educational reform to educational utopian idealism. Critiquing, rewriting, or extending Matson's *Idea of Man*[19] is not on our agenda now, although that is what is called for as we look at life-history implications for educational innovation. As we have detailed elsewhere,[20] our data have pushed us a long way on the road away from mechanistic or biological images of human nature. Matson's "creator image," the person as free agent, as creative actor on the world stage, whose existence is open-ended and characterized "by choice, contingency, and chance,"[21] is the direction in which we find ourselves going. Such a perspective raises questions with many of the assumptions underlying much of academic psychology, and, in our view, represents a part of a basic paradigmatic shift in social science.[22] This, also, is a part of the needed reconstrual of educational innovation.

CONCLUSION: REDISCOVERING ROBERT REDFIELD

We have indicated that C. Wright Mills was "already there," while we were stumbling along.[23] An even more fully differentiated position is that of Robert

Redfield in *The Little Community*.[24] If one approaches Redfield analogically, that is, if one looks at a school or school district as a little community, then one can bring his distinctions to bear on the problems of educational innovation. Briefly, in his low-key phrasing:

> This book is about some of the several ways in which the organized life of man can be viewed and understood. The subject is the forms of thought for understanding humanity; it is a book about "method," if one means by that word not merely the techniques of observation and analysis, but also the conceptions which allow us to characterize and compare.[25]

Later, he seems to finish the thought:

> We shall be required, then, as we proceed, to accustom ourselves to thinking at two levels. First, we look at an Indian or African village or a peasant settlement, and we think about it. We think about it, as far as we are able, as a whole. We find what there is to say about all of it. And then we turn to the form of thought we have used in thinking about it so, and we think about this thought. The kinds of thinking about communities as wholes become the second and derivative subject matter of these chapters. This is an invitation to consider the mental apparatus for characterizing human societies.[26]

In a sentence or two we try to capture Redfield's distinctions and the flavor of his approach. Perhaps most significant is the formatting or the grammar of his book, that is, "the little community as: . . . " with each chapter providing an alternative perspective.

His first chapter accents the holistic/analytic controversy and he puts himself fully in the tradition seeking syntheses. His next holistic perspective, "An Ecological System," accents the community's relationship to its environment, particularly the physical environment. Later, in Chapter 7, "A Community within Communities," he turns to the community's relationship to its multiple social environments. Other holistic social scientists have accented such issues in a concern for the group's survival in its environment.[27] Redfield's "social structure" perspective (Chapter 3) accents the ahistorical, cross-sectional relationships of the parts of communities. It is the structural/functionalist set of concepts and issues that has dominated much of social anthropology over the last seventy-five years. Positions, statuses, roles, make up structures that in turn make up systems.

Redfield then develops three lines of discussion that parallel many of the ideas raised by our life-history concerns. Chapter 4, a "typical biography," presents the human career characteristic of a community, and leads easily into Chapter 5, "a kind of person," and from this view of a modal or prototypical person he moves to the ethos or "an outlook on life." In his view this is the domain of the philosophers. Life histories, modal personalities, and value systems woven together create a powerful lens for looking at the little community and, metaphorically, at innovative schooling. If we had seen all that clearly earlier, we would have moved differently. Chapter 7 raises "a history," and probes the problems and issues in history and ethnography. As we have indicated, we think we did better here than we had any right to expect.

The last two chapters of Redfield's book seem to shift toward another level of discourse: "a combination of opposites" and "whole and parts." Dialectic thought, the "this" on the one hand and the "that" on the other, vies with internal and external dialogue. Finally, he is back to fundamental issues in the mental structures for considering parts and wholes and carrying out specific research projects. In part, these are issues of figure and ground and the productive ways in which a social scientist can shift back and forth. Into this discussion comes again the vantage point taken by the researcher. As illustrated in Figure 2, we found and took multiple positions across the volumes and topics of our report. In Redfield's view readers will bring additional and different perspectives to the accounts as written.

Through these multiple views run a number of polarities, dichotomies, and dilemmas existing in today's literature: structural versus processual conceptions, historical versus contemporaneous context, inner versus outer view, portrayal versus analytical view, understanding versus action purposes, real versus ideal conceptions, and dialectical thought versus part-whole thought versus analytical thought. These, in our view, are the issues at a tertiary or meta level.[28] Most significantly, Redfield is simultaneously anticipating, speaking to, and suggesting practical alternatives regarding the paradigmatic crisis in education and the social sciences. These items are in the domain in which the most abstract reconstrual of educational innovation will occur.

Our thesis in this article is relatively simple. We believe that the phenomenon of educational innovation needs to be reconstrued. We concur with House that most of the theory and practice has been from technological, political, or cultural perspectives. These are important: however, we believe that history and life-history approaches would add significantly to the discussion of educational innovation. Well after we were into our own empirical effort we found the work of Mills and Redfield provocative in their call for multiple interrelated perspectives in social science inquiry. Our strong emphasis on fitting the Kensington innovation into the history of the Milford School District and the Milford community, and our strong emphasis on the life histories of the faculty and administration, have been coupled with a detailed history and ethnography of the school itself. That, we think, is a powerful way of looking at educational innovation. Our hope is that the multiple perspectives, methods, and data from *Kensington Revisited* give a concrete, particularistic case for entertaining the needed reconstrual.

Notes

1   L. M. Smith and P. Keith, *Anatomy of Educational Innovation* (New York: John Wiley, 1971).

2   L. Smith, *Kensington Revisited: A Fifteen Year Follow-up of an Innovative Elementary School and Its Faculty, Original Proposal* (Washington, D.C.: NIE, 1977).

3   E. House, "Technology as Craft: A Ten-Year Perspective on Innovation," *Journal of Curriculum Studies* 11 (1979): 1-15.

4   C. W. Mills, *The Sociological Imagination* (London: Oxford University Press, 1959).

5   R. Redfield, *The Little Community* (Chicago: University of Chicago Press, 1955).

6   T. Whiteside, *The Sociology of Educational Innovation* (London: Methuen, 1978); S. Sarason, *The Creation of Settings and the Future Societies* (San Francisco: Jossey-Bass, 1971); and idem, *The Culture of the School and the Problem of Change*, 2nd ed. (Boston: Allyn and Bacon, 1982).

7   House, "Technology as Craft," p. 1.

8   Ibid.

9   Mills, *The Sociological Imagination*, p. 6.

10   L. M. Smith, J. J. Prunty, D. C. Dwyer, and P. F. Kleine. *Kensington Revisited: A Fifteen Year Follow-up of an Innovative Elementary School and Its Faculty*, vol. 1-6 (Washington, D. C.: NIE, 1984).

11   Daniel Griffiths, "Intellectual Turmoil in Educational Administration," *Educational Administration Quarterly* 15 (1979): 43-65; and Thomas B. Greenfield, "Reflections on Organizational Theory and the Truth of Irreconcilable Realities," *Educational Administration Quarterly* 14 (1978): 43-65.

12   Smith and Keith, *Anatomy of Educational Innovation*.

13   C. Geertz, *The Interpretation of Cultures* (New York: Basic Books, 1973).

14   S. Pepper, *World Hypotheses: A Study in Evidence* (Berkeley: University of California Press, 1942).

15   Ibid.

16   T. R. Sarbin, "Contextualism: A World View for Modern Psychology," in *Personal Construct Psychology, Nebraska Symposium on Motivation 1976*, ed. J. Cole (Lincoln: University of Nebraska Press, 1977).

17   Smith et al., *Kensington Revisited*, vol. 6.

18   E. Hoffer, *The True Believer* (New York: Mentor, 1951).

19   F. W. Matson, *The Idea of Man* (New York: Delacorte Press, 1976).

20   Smith et al., *Kensington Revisited*, vol. 6.

21   Matson, *The Idea of Man*, pp. xiii-xxii.

22   R. Bernstein, *The Restructuring of Social and Political Theory* (Philadelphia: University of Pennsylvania Press, 1978); B. Fay, *Social Theory and Political Practice* (London: George Allen and Unwin, 1975); and E. Bredo and W. Feinberg, ed., *Knowledge and Values in Social and Educational Research* (Philadelphia: Temple University Press, 1982).

23   Mills does not cite Redfield's *The Little Community*. Our search indicates that he is not in the cognitive map of most educational innovators, nor even most educational anthropologists—if one looks at citations.

24   Much of Redfield's thinking *seems* stirred by the catastrophic impact of Oscar Lewis's restudy of Tepoztlán (Oscar Lewis, *Tepoztlán* [Champaign: University of Illinois Press, 1951]).

25   Redfield, *The Little Community*, p. 1.

26   Ibid., p. 16

27   G. C. Homans, *The Human Group* (New York: Harcourt, Brace and World, 1950); and F. Emery and E. Trist, *Towards a Social Ecology* (London: Plenum, 1975).

28   L. M. Smith, "An Evolving Logic of Participant Observation, Educational Ethnography and Other Case Studies," in *Review of Research in Education 6*, ed. L. Shulman (Itasca, Ill.: Peacock, 1979).

School Improvement:
Themes and Variations

ANN LIEBERMAN
Teachers College, Columbia University

LYNNE MILLER
South Bend Schools, Indiana

In 1978 we published an article entitled "The Social Realities of Teaching" in a special issue of the *Teachers College Record* devoted to staff development.[1] In that article, we tried to establish a basis for viewing staff-development activities. We developed a perspective that focused on the lived experiences of teachers in schools as the basis for establishing programs and strategies for school improvement and staff development.

In that earlier work, we began with a set of understandings about the nature and dailiness of teaching. Included as understandings were the following:

Style is personalized.
Rewards are derived from students.
Teaching and learning links are uncertain.
The knowledge base is weak.
Teaching is an art.
Goals are vague.
Controls norms are necessary.
Professional support is lacking.

When we examined the dailiness of teaching, we found that rhythms, rules, interactions, and feelings all played powerful roles in the lives of teachers and of schools. We struggled to link our emerging understanding about teachers and schools with the movement toward staff development that was gaining strength in 1978. We found, to our disappointment, that we were long on analysis and woefully short on application. Now, some six years later, we return to our original purpose—enriched by new knowledge and understanding through the work of others as well as through our own continued engagement in the field.

But times have changed. The catchword of the day is "excellence." The emphasis is not on process and development, but on product and mandate. A plethora of reports has captivated the attention of the nation and educators are implored to lengthen school days and school years, to raise graduation requirements, to institute competency tests for teachers and for students, to develop merit pay incentives, and to redefine the very nature of the teaching profession. New research has focused on what makes "effective schools";[2] characteristics such as a sense of order, high expectations, strong leadership, schoolwide control of instructional decisions, and clear and agreed-upon goals are identified as leading to improved instruction and raised student achievement.

All of the commissions, reports, and studies provide their own, often contradictory, destinations for schools, but they do not provide much in the way of practical suggestions about how to get there. While we do not believe that we need detailed itineraries, we do believe that we need maps to guide our efforts toward improved schools. And we still believe that it is through teachers and through working with teachers that we have our best hope of succeeding.

Our tone is meant to be optimistic. We have good examples of how to build schools that work for both students and adults. In the past decade, we have learned a great deal about the process and products of school improvement. It is the new information that we want to bring to bear on our understanding of staff development. We want to link what we know about schools and teachers and how they change and improve to the dialogue about school improvement. We begin with a discussion of guidelines for school improvement that have emerged over the past few years and then continue to build our knowledge base with a description of learnings from experience about the strategies and substance of school improvement. We close by connecting issues of school improvement to issues of staff development and by delineating some of the dimensions of the map we will need to guide our staff-development practices, as part of our school-improvement efforts.[3]

TOWARD A SET OF WORKING GUIDELINES
FOR SCHOOL IMPROVEMENT

Much of the literature on school change is dominated by a policy or managerial perspective. One gets the view that teachers and school principals can be manipulated by mere exhortation. One can also make a strong case from the literature for reformers to start where the teachers are, understanding the dilemmas that shape their reality. For the elementary teacher, these are issues of more subjects to teach than time to teach them, coverage versus mastery, large group versus small group versus individualized instruction, when to stay with a subject and when to shift, and how to keep discipline without destroying the momentum in the class.[4] For the secondary teacher there are dilemmas rooted in the complexity of the formal and informal system, such as personal versus organizational constraints, dealing with the classroom and the school, packaging and pacing instruction to fit into allocated time periods, proportioning subject-matter expertise and affective needs in some way, and figuring out how to deal with mixed loyalties to the faculty and to the student culture.[5] For both elementary and secondary teachers, there are also dilemmas endemic to our understanding about teaching that were discussed previously.[6]

In this section we examine the nonmanagerial literature on school change and develop guidelines that may be useful for school improvement.

THE SCHOOL CULTURE

Several studies have alerted us to the special nature of the school culture, from the routinization and regularities of school life to the strong informal norms that grow up among teachers governing their work life.[7] Even when attempts are made to radically change the organization with enlightened leadership, plenty of outside help, and highly motivated teachers, one must contend with the gap between the ideals of building a school with all the advanced knowledge we have and the social realities of what is possible in practice.[8]

Given the isolation of most teachers from one another, the variability in the quality of leadership, and the differences in social context of schools from state to state and from community to community, it is not difficult to see that people on the inside develop all kinds of adaptations to their work. Would-be reformers tend to oversimplify and underestimate the complexity of these relationships and the difficulties of making change. But it is just these kinds of problems that need to be considered in school-improvement efforts: how to get teachers involved and get them to work collectively; how to get the principal and his or her team to understand their role in facilitation of such efforts; how to get superintendents to understand that expectations must be matched with help in resources, time, perhaps realignment of personnel; supporting projects that help people learn to work with one another.

The Nonlinear Path to School Improvement

Although we now have some good descriptors of what makes effective schools, they cannot be sold as recipes. We cannot overlook or underplay the significance of individual variations among schools and the real messiness and idiosyncratic nature of the real stories of school improvement.[9] Linear expectations of policymakers give unrealistic messages to local school implementors. The real process has many stories and only a few have been printed for public understanding.[10] We are just beginning to get a good idea of the necessary conditions that appear to make school improvement work.[11] For Huberman and Miles, the paths to school improvement include four different patterns among schools implementing major innovations from science units to alternative schools. In reasonably stable environments, they find (in two sites) that *forced stablized use* resulted in the best overall outcomes. In these sites administrators kept the pressure on, required faithful implementation, and gave collaborative assistance to teachers "struggling to achieve mastery." In yet another pattern, *overreaching projects* (four sites), the administrators pressured less and teachers who were committed learned to do the practices well, but "burnout, job mobility and weak institutionalization reduced the overall impact."[12] *Blunting/downsizing* where the projects were weakened by adapting the ideas (four sites) and *indifference/discouragement* where there was much pressure without assistance (two sites) were additional patterns. The authors conclude that where administrators and teachers aim high and work together to mediate and link their separate worlds, where administrators stay committed, where there is pressure and assistance, where teachers use the innovation, are mutually supportive, gain professional development and develop commitment, there is a likelihood of success.[13] Those are all big "wheres." Popkewitz et al. described three patterns of educational reform as they studied the implementation of the Individually Guided Education (IGE) program. Their study schools fall into three patterns based on teachers' understanding of their concepts of knowledge. They found schools to be *technical* where techniques become the ends of school activities rather than the means. In this case the teachers implemented programs built on a structured curriculum of goals, activities, monitoring, and testing. The *constructivist* pattern focused on curriculum in which problem solving and integration were the cornerstones of the teachers' concept of knowledge. Last, there was the *illusory* pattern, in which teachers and principal had learned the words but activities and purposes seemed unrelated.[14] We begin to see the tangled web of introducing new ideas and the conditions that work to both constrain and promote school improvement that changes and enhances the teacher's repertoire and eventually gets into the classroom. The appearance of simplicity covers the complicated paths of the movement from idea to implementation to institutionalization.

These studies show the marked difference in what researchers are studying: Early researchers were concerned with how and under what conditions implementation and institutionalization took place, while later researchers looked at the quality and ideology of the teacher's concept of knowledge.

Collaboration, Voluntarism, and Practicality

In two landmark studies of the early 1970s[15] and some others several years later,[16] we begin to get important descriptions of the critical importance of collaboration, teacher participation, and the practical nature of school improvement. But more than that, the descriptions include how the collaborations were made and what people actually did to make them happen.

In the Rand studies, descriptions included the importance of early participation of teachers in the thinking and planning of school-improvement efforts. Teachers volunteered to participate. Some managers who are in a hurry for other people to change and grow underestimate the need for people to be committed and involved in the beginnings of projects. The building of norms of collegiality comes over time. It cannot be mandated.

For example, in the League study,[17] a core of teachers were initially involved in coming to meetings, listening to new ideas, and working in their own classrooms. But over time teachers who were negative and resistant also became less threatened as they saw their colleagues trying new ideas, working on a new curriculum, and trying new pedagogical techniques.

In a study of schools implementing mastery learning, Little[18] describes the actual behaviors manifested by both principals and teachers who learned to be colleagues by planning together, creating curriculum, teaching and critiquing each other, publicly announcing the expectations for sharing, and then doing it together. In this way principal and teachers became learning colleagues. The focus for the provision of a mastery approach to the students was created by *both* teachers and principals, neither of whom knew anything about this approach. Teachers came to staff-development meetings with the idea that they were participants in building a learning community where all were involved, rather than that they were remediating some failure on their part. This subtle yet important distinction makes the difference between professional development programs or activities that enhance teachers' sense of professionalism and mandates that make assumptions that negate teachers' past experience and knowledge. Collaboration between principal and teacher and between teacher and teacher is critical in school-improvement efforts. Where the ideas come from is not nearly as important as how staff development is organized, how people are supported, and how teachers' sense of efficacy can be enhanced.[19]

Top-down/Bottom-up

To improve schools by expanding the repertoire of both principal and teacher requires both announced expectations from top-level leadership and organization for improvement from the local level. Posing the problem as strictly managerial puts the focus only on the leadership. But looking to teachers to create and sustain improvement efforts puts the focus only on teachers. It is the sustained support from the leadership by facilitating time, a focus, resources, and protection from additional responsibilities coupled with the organization of continuous, practical, hands-on, classroom support that builds commitment, sustains improvement, and makes real improvement work in the classroom.[20]

Massive amounts of federal dollars have been spent telling school people what to do and sometimes how to do it. We have only recently had descriptions of the supportive processes that need to be practiced connecting what the teachers actually do in their classrooms with the organizational structures that need to be built. Mandating new policy from the top without attending to organizing, supporting, and providing teachers and principals with the necessary learnings they need to carry out any school improvement efforts will be ineffective. We know more now than we did several decades ago.

Universalistic solutions to idiosyncratic situations will not be effective. The tough work of creating and sustaining school improvement building by building is what needs to be done. Harsh, punitive measures from the top, encouraged by the language of a crisis mentality coupled with linear schemes, paperwork, and lots of monitoring, will not penetrate the differences among schools, nor will it create places where both adults and students want to fully participate. Past reform efforts have often been blunted at the classroom door, but few strategies call for spending the time working with teachers in their schools as they teach.

Teacher Ownership and Collegiality

What actually happens in the classroom as a result of a new mandate, new reading program, new thrust by the district, or pressure for raising expectations brought about by a large number of studies and commission reports and state plans? As has been suggested, little will happen unless attention is paid to the necessity for building an ethos, a climate for collective effort on the part of teachers and principals.

Discussion of new instructional strategies or new texts or new curricular efforts must be mated with discussions of how best to engage teachers in dialogue about their own teaching, how to find ways for teachers to have a greater sense of their own professionalism, their own sense of excitement as teachers. This can come about only through strategies that involve teachers in experiences where they can work together as colleagues, where they can be involved in the plans, and where their concerns can be made primary. Although it will upset some who are looking for the universal solution for how to improve schools, we must realize that there is no one strategy. There are many ways to make provisions for teacher ownership of an improvement idea and many ways for people to work together. But it does not just happen. We must all learn how to work in a way that nourishes people and helps them grow rather than exhort people to make changes without the necessary conditions to make this happen. But how can this come about? Where does one look for such ideas? It is here that we have more experience than research, more practical knowledge than neat packages, and more inference than prescription. We must continue to do research to find out under what conditions different strategies work best, but until then we must use what we have learned over the last few decades.

LEARNINGS FROM EXPERIENCE

STRATEGIES AND SUBSTANCE OF SCHOOL IMPROVEMENT

There have been scores of projects in the last three decades ranging from large-scale federally funded projects to local school efforts. Some have books written about them,[21] but many more of the stories of what people have learned have not been written; they nevertheless provide important knowledge for school reformers. Perhaps the single most important learning has been that there are a variety of ways to work with people—no single mode works for everybody. How efforts are organized and what people will engage in has much to do with the differences in context, the history of school efforts, and the makeup of the personnel in a school. Scant attention has been paid to the high school except to say that it is more complex than and clearly different from the elementary school. But what we have learned is worth public discussion.

Because most teachers have learned to teach by doing it, much of their repertoire is home grown, experiential, and idiosyncratic. Attempts to make changes in style and substance must involve teachers in doing things that help expand their repertoire. There are many ways for this to happen.

Local Problem Solving

Building collective effort and improving school climate are often at the root of the problem of schools' not working for the teachers and the students. Local problem-solving efforts are one way to get at what is going on. Consider this effort:

Mid-city High School A new assistant principal decided that she was not going to be cast in the mode of the typical disciplinarian. She began to listen to teachers in the lunchroom and teachers' room. Teachers complained about the discipline in the school and the fact that attendance was a problem (a large problem in urban high schools). Teachers said that the administrators were not tough enough, were not consistent, let the students roam around in the halls and blamed the teachers for the problem. Many of the students were already alienated from school. Teachers were told to stop "whining" and to improve instruction and the problem would go away.

The assistant principal decided that the issue was pervasive enough to call together a teacher committee to discuss the problem. She had just read about action research and decided to use the method to get at "the problem." She worked through a mode of problem solving that helped her with a structure and moved the process along with the teachers. She followed these steps: (1) define the problem; (2) gather some evidence; (3) come up with some alternatives; (4) decide on one agreeable to the teachers; (5) explain the plans to other teachers; (6) implement a new policy.

In defining the problem, the committee members decided that the issue was letting the young people know that they wanted them to be in class and to be there on time. They wanted them to know that they were concerned about their learning and that they had some expectations that could not be ignored without some consequences. Teachers were asked to submit names of students who had unexcused absences. After discovering who these students were and when they cut class, the committee found that some students cut all day, while others cut only specific classes. Tardiness was as much a problem as cutting and teachers had made accommodations by starting class late. Students came later, teachers started class later, and everyone accepted the situation. The committee came up with two simple rules:

1. All students are expected to go to class.
2. All students are expected to be on time.

After three unexcused absences the teacher would make a home contact. After five unexcused absences the teacher would refer the student to the administration to follow up with pupil personnel services. Students were expected to make up work before readmittance to class. Committee members met with small groups of teachers to explain the new policy and to highlight problems that the committee might have overlooked. In addition, teachers were asked to volunteer to be in the halls to escort students to class. Results were phenomenal. Students joked, but enjoyed being escorted to class. Teachers enjoyed seeing the students in informal situations outside of class. But more importantly teachers felt that they had won back their authority in ways that were positive.

Any problem can be used to get teachers and administration working together. In this example:

1. Teachers feel a sense of collegueship with each other; they have united to do something rather than making do on their own in isolation.
2. Teachers feel supported by the administration rather than being blamed for the problems in the school.
3. There is a sense in the school that adults have authority that they can use in constructive ways.
4. Students like the concern shown and support the policy, writing about it in the school newspaper and giving verbal feedback to the teachers.
5. Teachers are involved in the creation of the policy and in implementing it.
6. The attendance issue and how it was dealt with provide a frame for working on development issues of curriculum and instruction.

This may seem like a small problem and an obvious way to work on it. But underlying this description is an example of the nuances of a school culture. Teachers as a group are sometimes scapegoated by a principal. Teachers and principal do not work through a problem with each other and therefore the breach between their worlds becomes larger and larger. Organizational members make adaptations to bad situations, often unconsciously (teachers began to start class late and students came later). Through collective effort with such small and varied problems, organizations do change and the people gain renewed commitment.

Research Transformed into Usable Improved Practices

Sometimes the content and the strategies for improvement come directly from research findings or studies. But those findings are made real for teachers only when the referent is their own classroom.

Several people have taken the research on teacher effectiveness and found ways to organize it in such a way that teachers can use it in their classrooms. One such effort has been carried on in secondary schools by Jane Stallings.[22] She has done research on reading where several variables have been found to be related to high reading scores. The variables reported were:

Discussing or reviewing seatwork or homework
Instructing new work
Drill and practice
Students reading aloud
Focusing instruction on a small group or total group
Praise and support of success
Positive corrective feedback
Short quizzes

These findings would not move most teachers, because they would find them so commonplace. The problem is to provide for the engagement of teachers that helps them look at their own practices. Stallings took the findings and created an observational checklist for teachers. This list serves as the beginning of a series of workshops in which teachers receive a profile based on observation of how they are doing on a number of classroom variables such as praise and feedback. Through role playing, specific incidents (provided by teachers) and discussion of students who are having difficulties, teachers work together in small groups but work on their own profiles. In this way both collective effort in looking at practice and individual needs and problems of teachers receive attention. Research findings are made real by checking them with one's own practices in a supportive group setting.

In another example, in a school district in a large urban area, it was decided to introduce mastery learning as a technique for the improvement of reading in both elementary and junior high schools in the district. The district was concerned with problems of integration as well as low reading scores. This instructional strategy was tried in several schools with the help of a small districtwide staff-development team. Again, what is demonstrated here is the importance of introducing technical knowledge with accompanying social arrangements that provide the supportive conditions to learn new knowledge.[23] One without the other does not provide the important interplay between the learning of new knowledge and skills and the daily supportive social conditions that help support teacher learning. Little's painstaking analysis of what happened in the schools that successfully implemented mastery learning begins to unlock some of the catchwords thrown around—

"climate," "support," "trust," and "ethos," for example. In schools where new norms of collegiality and experimentation were practiced, four patterns were observed:

> *Teachers talk about practice.* Teachers begin to build a shared language about what they are doing. The focus is off children and on to the substance, the process, the interaction, and the materials they are creating. The focus is on *practice*, not *teachers.*
>
> *Teachers and administrators plan, design, research, evaluate, and prepare materials together.* It is in the interaction of ideas and plans and in execution of these plans that people become committed.[24]
>
> *Teachers and administrators observe each other working.* Colleagueship in a collective struggle to learn is more apt to build commitment and involvement than control and evaluation.
>
> *Teachers and administrators teach each other the practice of teaching.* The resources of the school are recognized. People see each other as colleagues. People share resources with each other. Past and current learnings are discussed.

Little draws attention to the subtleties of "relevant interaction" as opposed to "demanding" interaction. The day-to-day descriptions of what people do when they develop new practices describes both the content and the processes that go on in school-improvement efforts that really make a difference. Teachers design and prepare materials, review and discuss plans, persuade others to try things out, credit new ideas, invite others to observe, observe other teachers, teach each other both formally and informally, talk publicly about what is being learned, evaluate both their own and the principal's performance. *This is what building high expectations is all about.* The principal models collegiality not by talking about it, but by doing it. Staff development becomes a process for both teacher and principal.

In the past year, the Research in Teacher Education group (RITE) of the Research and Development Center at the University of Texas designed and implemented a staff-development program based on selected teaching behaviors and selected staff-development strategies.[25] In this case they took particular teaching behaviors found in the research: (1) learning environment (warm and supportive); (2) classroom management (well organized); (3) classroom instruction (work orientation); (4) productive use of time (brisk pacing).

In addition, specific behaviors such as gaining student attention, making presentation clear, practicing new skills, monitoring, providing feedback, and evaluating student responses provided the content. From the school-improvement literature the team took the following strategies: (1) teacher interaction on professional issues; (2) technical assistance to teachers; (3) adaptation of ideas to fit school and classroom regularities; (4) opportunities for reflection; (5) focused and concrete substance. Principals and staff developers used workshops to learn both teacher behaviors and the strategies. The workshops took place before school opened in the fall. The results of this study were so strongly in favor of teaching staff developers these strategies that the district, a large urban city, has adopted these procedures for the 175 schools in the district. Again, both substance and process, or content and structure for work, are necessary to engage faculty in their own professional development.

The American Federation of Teachers (AFT) has developed still another way of transforming research for teacher use. In this case, three different sites were selected in different parts of the country. Teacher Research Linkers (TRLS) were selected at building sites. These teachers are viewed by other teachers as innovative, task-oriented risk takers and generally people who combine both personal strengths in working with people and professional strengths as teachers. During a two-year project the union prepared a resource manual that describes the teacher's transformation of research in areas such as classroom management, praise, and so forth. The materials describe activities for teachers that were tried out that make the research understandable in teacher terms. The use of this research is led by a teacher who has been specially trained to understand the research and furthermore to teach it to peers.[26] An expanded role for some teachers is explored here as well as activities that relate selected research to teacher's own classrooms.

Action Research Revisited

Over thirty years ago at Teachers College, Columbia University, a group of university professors worked with several school districts to create a collaborative research effort. The research differed from traditional research in that the problem was one identified by the school people themselves.[27] Several new versions of action research have been created that hold promise for still another way to reduce the gap between research and practice to involve school people with university people in work that allows for a mutuality and sharing of two worlds of experience.

In the mid 1970s action research was rediscovered and renamed Interactive Research and Development on Teaching (IR&DT).[28] Again, the major idea was to organize a team of teachers, a researcher, and a staff developer. In this project, two teams were organized—one within a school district and one with a university and school linkage. In one instance, the teachers on the team were concerned about a district mandate to increase student time on task. The problem that concerned the team was: What are the distractions that keep us from spending more time on task and what coping techniques do we use? This question formed the basis for their team effort.

Teachers found out that most of the distractions that worried them were inside the classroom rather than outside and that their coping techniques varied from verbal reprimands to body language. Interventions included teachers' trying to expand their coping techniques and getting rid of those that were ineffective. The team then taught other teachers in the district the process they had gone through.

In still another version of interactive research, Griffin, Lieberman, and Noto participated to form three teams in the New York area.[29] One team was from a suburban school district, one from an intermediate agency, and one from an urban teacher center consortium. In this instance we were interested in the degree to which this strategy contributed to the improvement of practice regardless of such issues as problem differences, context differences, organizational missions, and the like. Three different problems were researched by the teams. The school district studied the qualities of good writing in children, the Teacher Center team studied the factors that enable teachers to maintain positive attitudes toward their work, and the intermediate agency studied several interventions designed to deal with reducing disruptive behavior in the classroom. Again, what we learned was the powerful impact of involving school people in a way that stretched both the university people *and* the teachers, where engagement in understanding their own problems brought not only significant learning but a heightened sense of self-esteem based on their newfound abilities as they participated in doing research.[30]

Networks for School Improvement

We now have some good experience in the formation of networks for school improvement and a better understanding of their purposes. We rarely think of forming coalitions or networks outside existing formal channels. And it is even rarer that we think of these loose, informal coalitions of people as catalysts for change. Most of us working in formal organizations do not think of providing informal settings as legitimate places where we can share resources, gain new knowledge, be supportive of one another, and participate voluntarily.[31] Two networks have been written about extensively—the League of Cooperating Schools[32] and, more recently, the study of dissemination efforts supporting school improvement.[33] Both document the power of people working together to learn, to support, to practice new skills and attitudes to improve schools and the relationships among the people in them.

One of the writers runs a network that connects Teachers College with thirty-four school districts. We have learned that teachers, principals, and superintendents enjoy and profit from interaction with people from the university and from other school districts. We all gain a heightened sensitivity to the complex problems that schools struggle with and we collectively organize to better understand them and work on them. We create new structures to share knowledge, to increase our skills, to learn from one another.[34]

There are many other forms of school-improvement efforts that consider the realities of classroom and school life and provide different organizational structures to help school people participate.

SCHOOL IMPROVEMENT: THEMES AND VARIATIONS

We have come full circle in our thinking and discussion. We began in 1978 with a description of the social realities of teaching as we looked inside schools to see how teachers think about and carry out their work. We argued then that any effort to improve schools must be grounded in the social realities of the classroom and the school. In 1984, we took as our point of departure the work of a decade of school-improvement efforts and examined just how the most successful of these efforts have evolved and taken form. And, as we would have predicted six years ago, we found that the most promising strategies placed their emphasis on the teacher, the classroom, and the interactions within the school. Whether we looked at local problem solving, research transformed into practice, action research, or networking, we were drawn to the teachers, their world, and their work as the starting points for improving schools.

What, then, are our new understandings about staff development and school improvement? As Seymour Sarason is wont to tell us, there is not much new under the sun.[35] Rather, what we have rediscovered are some tried and true notions that have become enriched and expanded over time. Among them:

Working *with* people rather than working *on* people.

Recognizing the complexity and craft nature of the teacher's work.

Understanding that there are unique cultural differences in each school and how these affect development efforts.

Providing time to learn.

Building collaboration and cooperation, involving the provisions for people to do things together, talking together, sharing concerns.

Starting where people are, not where you are.

Making private knowledge public, by being sensitive to the effects of teacher isolation and the power of trial and error.

Resisting simplistic solutions to complex problems; getting comfortable with reworking issues and finding enhanced understanding and enlightenment.

Appreciating that there are many variations of development efforts; there is no one best way.

Using knowledge as a way of helping people grow rather than pointing up their deficits.

Supporting development efforts by protecting ideas, announcing expectations, making provisions for necessary resources.

Sharing leadership functions as a team, so that people can provide complementary skills and get experience in role taking.

Organizing development efforts around a particular focus.

Understanding that content and process are both essential, that you cannot have one without the other.

Being aware of and sensitive to the differences in the worlds of teachers and other actors within or outside of the school setting.

We know that this list is not all-inclusive, that our knowledge about staff development and school improvement is still incomplete. We know that it is not easy to "reconcile the legitimate requirements the organization imposes and the authentic needs of teachers as persons."[36] But we also know that we are on the right track, that by attending to how teachers approach their work and how the "real world" of school is, we are gathering the craft knowledge and professional insights we need to develop and maintain effective staff-development and school-improvement practices.

Notes

1 Ann Lieberman and Lynne Miller, "The Social Realities of Teaching," *Teachers College Record* 80, no. 1 (September 1978): 54–68.

2 See, for example, Wilber B. Brookover and Lawrence Lezotte, *Changes in School Characteristics Coincident with Changes in Student Achievement*, Occasional Paper 17 (Washington, D.C.: Institute for Research on Teaching, 1979); and Dale Mann, "The Politics and Administration of the Instructionally Effective School" (Paper delivered at the American Educational Research Association, Boston, April 1980).

3 Portions of this paper have been adapted from Ann Lieberman, "Is School Improvement Possible?" Preconference papers of *Excellence in Our Schools: Making It Happen: A National Forum on Educational Reform* (San Francisco: Far West Laboratory, 1984), pp. 63–90.

4 Karen B. Kepler, "B.T.E.S.: Implications of Pre-Service Education of Teachers," in *Time to Learn*, ed. C. Denham and Ann Lieberman (Washington, D.C.: National Institute of Education, 1980), pp. 139–57.

5 Ann Lieberman and Lynne Miller, *Teachers, Their World and Their Work: Implications for School Improvement* (Alexandria, Va.: Association for Supervision and Curriculum Development, 1984).

6 Lieberman and Miller, "The Social Realities of Teaching."

7 See for example: Seymour Sarason, *The Culture of the School and the Problem of Change* (Boston: Allyn and Bacon, 1971); Gertrude McPherson, *Small Town Teacher* (Cambridge: Harvard University Press, 1971); Gerald Grace, *Teachers, Ideology and Control* (London: Routledge & Kegan Paul, 1978); and Dan Lortie, *Schoolteacher* (Chicago: University of Chicago Press, 1975).

8 Louis Smith and P. Keith, *Anatomy of Educational Innovation* (New York: John Wiley, 1971).

9 Stewart C. Purkey and Marshall S. Smith, "Too Soon to Cheer? Synthesis of Research on Effective Schools in Educational Leadership," *Educational Leadership* 40, no. 3 (1982): 64–69.

10 See for example: Judith Warren Little, *School Success and Staff Development: The Role of Staff Development in Urban Desegregated Schools* (Boulder, Colo.: Center for Action Research, January 1981); and A. Michael Huberman and Matthew Miles, *People, Policies and Practices: Examining the Claim of School Improvement, Vol. IV: Innovation Up Close: A Field Study in Twelve School Settings* (Andover, Mass.: The Network, 1982).

11   See for example: T. B. Popkewitz, B. Tabachnick, and G. Ovehlage, *The Myth of School Reform* (Madison: University of Wisconsin Press, 1982); and Susan Loucks, "At Last: Some Good News from a Study of School Improvement," *Educational Leadership,* November 1983, p.4.

12   Huberman and Miles, *Innovation Up Close.*

13   Ibid., pp. viii and xi.

14   Popkewitz, Tabachnick, and Ovehlage, *The Myth of School Reform.*

15   See for example, Paul Berman and Milbrey Wallin McLaughlin, *Federal Programs Supporting Educational Change, Vol. VII: Factors Affecting Implementation and Continuity* (Santa Monica, Calif.: Rand Corporation, 1977); and John I. Goodlad, *The Dynamics of Educational Change* (New York: McGraw-Hill, 1975).

16   See for example: Tony Gibson, *Teachers Talkings, Aimes, Methods, Attitudes to Change* (London: Allen Lane, 1973); Little, *School Success and Staff Development;* and Leila Sussman, *Tales Out of School* (Philadelphia: Temple University Press, 1977).

17   Goodlad, *The Dynamics of Educational Change.*

18   Little, *School Success and Staff Development.*

19   Richard Daft and Selwyn Becker, *The Innovative Organization* (New York: Elsevier, 1978).

20   Patricia Cox, "Complementary Roles in Successful Change," *Educational Leadership,* November 1983, pp. 10-13.

21   See for example: Neal J. Gross, J. Giacquinta, and M. Bernstein, *Implementing Organizational Innovations* (New York: Basic Books, 1971); and Smith and Keith, *Anatomy of Educational Innovation.*

22   Jane Stallings, "Changing Teacher Behavior: A Challenge for the Eighties" (Paper delivered at the American Educational Research Association, Los Angeles, 1981).

23   Little, *School Success and Staff Development.*

24   Such a process was described earlier by M. Bentzen as D(ialog), D(ecision) Making, A(ction), and E(valuation): in M. Bentzen, "School Characteristics and DDAE," in her *The Magic Feather Principle* (New York: McGraw-Hill, 1974), pp. 75–108.

25   Gary Griffin et al., *Changing Teacher Practice: Final Report of an Experimental Study* (Austin, Tex.: Research and Development Center for Teachers Education, October 1984).

26   Brenda Biles, L. Billups, and S. Veitch, *Educational Research Dissemination: Program Training and Resource Manual* (Washington, D.C.: American Federation of Teachers, Education Issues Dept., 1983).

27   Stephen Corey, *Action Research to Improve School Practices* (New York: Bureau of Publications, Teachers College, Columbia University, 1953).

28   William Tikunoff, B. Ward, and G. Griffin, *Interactive Research and Development on Teaching Study* (San Francisco: Far West Laboratory, 1975).

29   Gary Griffin, Ann Lieberman, and Joann Jacullo-Noto, *Executive Summary Final Report, Interactive Research and Development on Schooling* (Washington, D.C.: National Institute of Education, April 1983).

30   Ibid.

31   Seymour Sarason et al., *Resources, Community Exchange Network* (San Francisco: Jossey-Bass, 1977).

32   Goodlad, *The Dynamics of Educational Change.*

33   Susan Loucks et al., *People, Policies and Practices, Examining the Chain of School Improvement, Vol: II: Portraits of the Changes, the Players, and the Contexts* (Andover, Mass.: The Network, 1982).

34   Workgroups are organized on subjects varying from Cooperative Learning to using the computer in writing. Special sessions and groups concern themselves with particular problems such as a principals' group or a supervisors' group. Special interest groups form on the basis of sub-groups sharing information and teaching each other. (i.e., a writing group and a computer

group). The power in the network comes from being with people in a supporting environment where both ideas and support flow freely. The network is called the Metropolitan School Study Council (M.S.S.C.).

35   Sarason, *The Culture of the School and the Problem of Change.*

36   Philip Schlechty et al., *Staff Development and School Improvement: A School District Examines its Potential for Excellence.* Executive summary of a study sponsored by the National Institute of Education (Washington, D.C.: National Institute of Education, n.d.).

Part II
New Images and Metaphors

Educational Change: Revival Tent, Tinkertoys, Jungle, or Carnival?

TERRENCE E. DEAL

Peabody College of Vanderbilt University

I recently visited a high school near Minneapolis. Per normal protocol, the principal assigned a student as my tour guide. My tour took me through the school's various departments and classrooms. As we entered a U.S. history class, vivid memories flooded my mind. The classroom was a replica of the 1950s' version I remembered as a high school student. It was almost identical to my classroom in the 1960s when I was a high school teacher. The students looked somewhat different—younger than I remembered. The teacher looked younger too—not the mature educator that I remember being. But the smells, the sounds, the desks arranged in rows, the teacher talking while some students listened, the rich repertoire of unengaged behavior that only adolescent energy can produce—they were all the same. It was to me the classroom I had left twice before. I could have moved effortlessly into a lesson on the Civil War or the American Constitution. In many ways, I really wanted to—the old ritual still in fashion despite all those years.

As my tour continued, I observed a group of students engaged earnestly at computer terminals. "A revolution in the way we teach," noted the math chairman. Then my eyes moved to an overhead projector atop a cabinet at the rear of the room. I noticed a television set sitting unused on a nearby table. I vaguely remembered forecasts of similar revolutions in teaching. Many of the prophesies were mine; most materialized about as much as those regarding classroom television and overhead projectors. As my tour continued, I looked for other familiar innovations: the language lab, team teaching, open-space classrooms, or a school-within-a-school. All of these have been replaced with new forms strange to me. In some ways, the school periphery was different. But the differences seemed superficial. The school was almost the same. What was happening inside the classroom was almost exactly the same.

On the plane ride back to Nashville, I began to reminisce about planned efforts to make schools different—to improve the quality of education. In my own professional lifetime: the Trump Plan of the 1950s, innovation and alternative schools of the 1960s, the reform initiatives of the 1970s, school improvement, effective schools, and educational excellence of the 1980s. Any historian could identify other general movements launched during the three decades my career encompasses. Any teacher or principal could easily create a long list of specific new programs created during the same time span. And I am sure that there were many more efforts to change, reform, or improve schools long before that. With all this activity to make education different, why does the fundamental reality of the classroom or the school remain so constant across time? Some point to the recalcitrance of educators. Others argue that we need to develop a technology of change through university-based research and development (R&D). Others advocate the use of temporary change agents imported from the outside. Still others look to a stronger role for the state in providing incentives to improve. The explanations are as numerous as the proposed changes themselves. But none seems to capture the essence of why schools and classrooms remain stable in spite of repeated and sizable efforts to change education.

Maybe it is time to reexamine how we think about changing schools: to begin with, our theories and philosophy of change—how we approach the task, our basic assumptions, how we justify or explain our successes, difficulties, or failures. Our theories form what we see and determine how we interpret experience. Theories are behind strategies, policies, and programs. Theories guide evaluation and other efforts to examine the impact of change.[1] Schools are complex organizations. If our images of schools are distorted or limited, or if our philosophy of how to change them is off the mark, then we cannot expect either to succeed or to explain why we cannot do better.

POPULAR THEORIES OF CHANGE

In the literature of organizational change, two perspectives have enjoyed a prominent position. The first has origins in psychology and social psychology.[2] These disciplines focus attention on individuals and small groups in organizations. To make schools different we need to focus on the attitudes and beliefs of people and the norms that develop in small social collectives. Attitudes, beliefs, skills, and norms are the catalysts for new directions. The concepts also form powerful barriers, or offer resistance in support of the status quo. In action, the individual perspective emphasizes T-groups, sensitivity sessions, group problem solving, and training to pro-vide new skills, understanding, attitudes, and norms. A quick look at the approaches of the last three decades would demonstrate how pervasive the influence of the individual prospective has been—and continues to be.

The second perspective directs attention to the formal side of schools as organizational settings.[3] Sociology and systems theory emphasize the properties of larger social systems. The role of goals, roles, and linkages is change. Organizational characteristics—patterns of the social setting— become the primary targets of change as a direct strategy for improvement. Formal patterns also provide indirect support for changes in other areas. Efforts to establish and clarify goals, pinpoint accountability, increase specialization, promote collaboration, alter roles and relationships, increase problem-solving capacity, or provide formal incentives are guided by a structural logic of change. The perspective emphasizes formal patterns and processes, both as levers for change and as reasons why initiatives succeed or fail. The canons of the approach are visible in the literature, in policy, and in the way consultants or practitioners try to change or to improve schools as organizations.

Individual and structural theories have been—and will continue to be—very helpful in understanding and guiding school change and improvement. But underneath both is a collection of rational assumptions about how people and organizations work. The assumptions of purpose, purposeful action, reasonableness, and certainty are the primary virtues of the individual and structural approaches. The assumptions are also restricting blinders that leave powerful, less rational forces unidentified and unexamined. For that reason, other views must be entertained.

POLITICAL THEORIES OF CHANGE

In Timber River, Oregon, the school district had been involved in a major improvement effort for five years prior to the announcement of the Experimental Schools (ES) competition by the U.S. Office of Education. The superintendent saw the additional federal resources as a way of moving beyond mere improvement to a lighthouse school district. He and two of his district administrators drafted the initial letter of interest. That letter and subsequent negotiations secured award of $1.2 million for the district. When the administration announced the award to the faculty at an orientation meeting opening the 1973 school year, expecting that it would be met with approval and enthusiasm, one faculty member stood up, pointed his finger at the superintendent, and shouted. "You dared to make such a decision without consulting the faculty?"

In Clayville, Montana, a consultant assumed that a workshop designed to attract teachers to diagnostic-prescriptive instruction would be well received by teachers. To teachers, however, the event represented a potential encroachment by the administration on their turf. (The consultant had been retained by the superintendent.) The consultant's optimism was based on an assumption that agreements that had been reached during the planning stage of the project would carry over as the plans were implemented. During the workshop, teachers began to complain about the ES project and then virtually ignored the consultant until he finally remarked, "I came here assuming that everyone was complying with the agreement we made last August. One thing I learned tonight is to make sure that I know what is going on before I made a damned fool of myself."

These vignettes are drawn from a large-scale, federally sponsored initiative to change schools in rural areas.[4] But examples like these are common in the experience of changing schools. Despite this, the politics of change have not received the attention shown the other two perspectives. House[5] and Baldridge,[6] for example, have studied the political side of change and innovation. Baldridge has relied heavily on political ideas to formulate his rules for practitioners who wish to emulate Machiavelli.

But the volume of political ideas has not matched the role that politics plays in changing or neutralizing changes in schools. People enjoy their stature and power in organizations. Even those who have neither relish the time that they will. People also have self-interests they wish to protect. When their interests are threatened, they form coalitions with others. Struggles among coalitions decide whose interests will prevail in an arena of combative conflict. In the struggle the champions of the status quo usually emerge victorious while the agents of change lick their wounds and wonder why they lost. In the ten rural school districts that tried to implement comprehensive changes under the Experimental Schools Program, for example, only one superintendent remained at the end of the five-year grant. The administrators become victims of powerful coalitions of teachers and local residents who for different reasons rallied together in protest against change.

High rates of administrative turnover are only part of the legacy of the politics of changing schools. Scars and unresolved tensions remain for years in schools and communities after changes have temporarily come and quickly gone. From a political perspective, the reasons seem obvious. Change always will have its winners and losers, its contests and conflicts, its exchange of power. Scholars who embrace political concepts will be able to explain variance that others will see as error or confusion. Practitioners who understand the law of the jungle and exercise their power wisely will probably enjoy more success than those who cling to a world they believe should behave more sensibly. But even the political approach has its own attachment to rational assumptions. It assumes that interests can be identified, that power can directly influence outcomes, and that conflicts will decide winners and losers. While the political view adds to the individual and structural perspectives, it also leaves something important untouched.

SYMBOLIC THEORIES OF CHANGE

Several years ago, we developed and tested a model relying heavily on structural theory and reporting information to small discussion groups as a vehicle for improving schools. In a large urban high school, we attempted to change a situation that had deteriorated to the point of either all-out warfare or total collapse. The principal and faculty agreed to engage in the process as it appeared their only hope. Over a one-year period, we interviewed people and tried to report information in a form that would allow problems to be identified and ultimately resolved. Instead of small group problem solving discussions, however, our sessions became large scale arenas of conflict and carnival. We would arrive to a faculty of seventy, start reporting our information, and end up in a large-scale shouting match. In any early session, the following exchange occurred: "We had a lot of terrible consultants here," an older teacher screamed. "You are the worst." "The best thing you can give this faculty is a book of jokes." We replied, "The best thing we can do for you is to give you a bottle of wine and loan you a straw." "What the hell do you want us to do?" yelled another. "Nothing," we replied. "At this point we don't even know why we are here."

In a session toward the end of the year, another vitriolic exchange erupted between the faculty and us. During the heated free-for-all, an elderly faculty member rose to his feet and yelled, "I've been on this faculty for twenty-five years and all you people do is bitch and spear outsiders and each other. I still don't even know what these people want us to do. But I'm behind whatever it is 100%." The session ended with some positive exchanges and we said a benediction and left. A year later the principal called us and asked us to fly across the country to visit the school. "Something's different," he said, "and I can't quite put my finger on it." He was right. Nothing had really changed, and yet everything had. The school was a vibrant, alive, positive place to be. We spent two days trying to find an unhappy teacher. There was none to be found. At the end of our visit, the faculty held a party in our honor, and everyone ignored us. We left totally perplexed.

The school never really used the survey-feedback model, yet the nonevent had an overwhelming impact.[7] Explaining this situation would tax individual, structural, and political theories to their limit. Less rational concepts and ideas are needed to press below the surface of the events for a symbolic interpretation.

In the 1930s Willard Waller characterized schools as museums of virtue or theaters of social drama and ceremony.[8] This strand was picked up by Seymour Sarason's concept of behavioral regularities, identifying the culture of a school as a powerful barrier to change or improvement.[9] From a symbolic view, assumptions of rationality are relaxed or discarded to reveal the expressive side of change in organizations.

There are several versions of the symbolic aspects of change. The first comes from Meyer and Rowen's[10] institutional theory of organizations. In their view, change is often sought by those outside the organization rather than those within. To maintain the support and faith of the external environment—clients, consumers, governmental agencies, ideas in good currency, experts, or benefactors—organizations engage in the ceremony of changing, an expressive activity of pomp and circumstance. Deep down, actors have neither intention nor hope that core features or process will emerge differently. The ceremony is a dance of legitimacy, not a strategy of change. It can be important to insiders, but the ceremony is usually played to an audience outside. For the last three decades, schools have been dancing, some with considerable verve and style. People enjoy the dance, while schools and classrooms retain their character. Only scholars who mistake dancing for purposeful activity seem puzzled and confused. Only practitioners who take the dance too seriously become disillusioned and demoralized. Schools, like any business or nonprofit organization, engage in a continual dance with constituencies. Their core identity and social support are preserved—sometimes transformed—through the dance.

In the high school case cited above, the changes in the high school may have been influenced by changes in expectations on the part of outsiders. For a long time, the school had been seen as the worst in the district. The fact that the school's professional staff was using a survey-feedback model developed by "those people at Stanford" was a high ceremony. The principal often told us that he passed copies of our manuscript to every parent, administrator, or other district employee who inquired about the activity under way at the high school. "I told them they would have trouble understanding the ideas," the principal noted, "they're pretty complex, but awfully powerful." People thereby came to expect that something positive might happen. As people looked for improvements, they appeared; Pygmalion in a school. A similar effect has been described by Sopolsky in the development of the Polaris missile.[11]

The second, symbolic interpretation of change comes from ideas about the role of culture in organizations.[12] Culture is an evolving human invention that shapes behavior and gives meaning to any social collective. Core values define the essential character. Heroes and heroines embody and represent values, providing role models and symbols of virtue. Rituals enact the values, binding people together, providing reassurance, and reinforcing core understandings and beliefs. Ceremonies offer episodic occasions for the culture to be displayed dramatically, to be revitalized and reinforced. Stories personify and carry values and spread the exploits of heroes and heroines. An informal network of priests and priestesses, storytellers, gossips, spies, and whisperers conspires to keep the culture strong and stable. Where the elements of culture are consistent and mutually reinforcing, productivity, continuity, morale, and confidence are assured—as long as the culture fits the requirements posed by the external environment.

Cultural change becomes necessary because of external influences or the influx of newcomers—usually a new leader. But the change is a loss for most people.[13] Individuals become attached to values, heroes and heroines, rituals and ceremonies, stories, and key cultural players. When change breaks the attachment,[14] individuals experience loss akin to that if a close friend or relative dies. Their meaning is shattered. This loss triggers two impulses: one to cling to the past, the other to rush pell mell to embrace the present or future. Either impulse creates problems for an organization and threatens productivity and morale. Only through mourning rites, transformation rituals, the anointing of new heroes or heroines, or the telling of new stories can cultural cohesion be reinstated and meaning be restored.

In the large urban high school, survey feedback discussions served as a ritual of mourning and transformation. The school had once been the flagship of the district. But a long-time principal's retirement, the departure of several core faculty, and the influx of different students undermined the culture. Enter a new administration with ideas for even more extensive change.

In the survey-feedback exchange, faculty were able to vent their anger and grief, and finally to celebrate their emerging phoenix. One teacher later told us that "in the sessions, we found a piece of flotsam floating in the ocean where we had been drowning before. We clung to it, found other pieces drifting around and built a raft. It's flying the same colors now as the new version of the old ship we once lost." In this interpretation, our treatment by the faculty on the occasion of our return visit had the following meaning: "Something special happened here, and we don't really understand it. You were here when it happened and we wanted you to see it too. You may have even played a role in it. But it's ours. Thanks for coming. Goodbye."—a closing ritual to a major symbolic event through which a school's culture was revitalized and transformed in the wake of change and loss.

Such dramatic events occur also in businesses when cultural changes occur. Consider two additional examples:

A large division of AT&T. Several hundred people attending an occasion to mark the transition from comfortable tradition to an uncertain future. The final night was an elaborate ceremony of food and frolic. At the height of the festivities, a group entered with a small coffin with the words "Ma Bell" written on the outside. The reaction was electric, but unspoken. Some laughed, some cried. That night I had a death dream. Hearses carrying loved ones I'd known passed in review, each person waving goodbye. Then a dark form leaped at me. I awoke in a cold sweat. I had somehow internalized the collective sentiments.[15]

During a three-day retreat for a group of executives from a large manufac-turing firm, an issue arose. They were all happy; we were very depressed. At lunch on the third day, we discovered why. The group was engaged in animated lunchtime chatter. The chairman of the board turned to us and said, "Companies are strange. When we dedicated the new plant several weeks ago, people came from all over the world and cried." We responded: "John, maybe they needed a funeral." The group suddenly became hushed. When we reconvened in the seminar, we said, "We think your corporate landscape is littered with dead bodies—people lost in the merger. Before you can move on, you must bury the old and celebrate the new." From the back of the room, a brother of one of the old heroes yelled, "You sonofabitch, my brother is alive and well." "Not to me, he's not," responded a vice-president, "Your brother to me is dead." For the next two hours, the group engaged in a spirited debate filled with anger, tears, and nostalgia. At the end, the chairman rose to his feet and mumbled something. People rose in standing ovation.[16]

These are powerful examples that none of the other theories of change can explain adequately. Both institutional and cultural theory explain the missing dynamics of change and support creative ways that schools can be improved symbolically.

CONCEPTUAL PLURALISM OR CONCEPTUAL WAR?

Each theoretical approach—individual, structural, political, and symbolic— has its own ideas, language, assumptions, prophecies, and prescriptions for changing organizations.[17] Each has rules for how information can be collected to test the validity of major tenets and minor hypotheses. Rational theorists favor large-scale, empirical studies with quantitative data. Political and symbolic theorists tend to favor case studies, anecdotes, and metaphors.[18]

Each approach also has a cadre of gurus, scholars, advocates, and disciples who righteously defend one view against criticism from other camps. The end result is a cacophony of voices: a dialogue of the deaf among academics, usually a source of confusion among those struggling with how to improve schools.

"Staff development is the key to school improvement."

"Effective schools are more well coordinated than their less successful counterparts."

"Successful changes result from confrontation, conflict, and negotiation among major constituencies."

"Change is the result of blending old and new within rituals of transformation."

Depending on whom one calls for advice, it is possible to get a variety of opinions. It is probable that none of the advice-givers would recognize the validity of the knowledge or wisdom shared by others.

Some would take a different position in the face of diverse perspectives. Each of the conceptual approaches highlights an important aspect of change in organization. Change affects and is affected by individual skills and attitudes. Change alters and requires formal patterns of roles and relationships. Change attracts and stimulates issues of power and conflict. Change alters and is influenced by culture. It serves both instrumental and symbolic purposes.

To a conceptual pluralist, change is not one thing; it is many. Change is like a revival tent or training ground where individuals are saved or new skills are learned to meet new challenges. Change is like a set of tinkertoys where roles and relationships are rearranged into a stronger, more workable design. Change is like a jungle where beasts, herds, and flora compete for scarce resources and struggle for survival. Change is like carnival or theater, an activity in which deep-seated values are dramatized and transformed. If we can embrace the variety of roles change can play in organizations, we are much better equipped to understand it.[19] If we understand the process, we are in a better position to improve organizations—especially public schools. Conceptual pluralism, rather than conceptual warfare or myopia, is a prerequisite to making schools better—or recognizing that maybe they are already better than most would think.

CHANGE AS INTERPLAY AMONG ELEMENTS

By employing all four conceptual lenses, different aspects of change in organizations focus into clear images.[20] The images help to capture the dynamic interplay among the various elements of any organization in flux. The complex process of change becomes more understandable and more predictable. Consider some hypothetical examples from education.

Management training seminars for principals find origins in the individual approach to change. Since the principal is the key to school effectiveness, improving the principal's ability to lead should result in schoolwide improvement. Suppose the training works and the principal alters his or her role. The principal role is set in a constellation of other roles—teachers, superintendents, students, and parents. The principal's behavioral change may require structural changes. Structural changes have political implications and may engender power struggles among various groups. And the entire episode will take place in an ongoing culture. The changes in the principal may be supported by values and symbols. Or the changes may topple a hero, alter a ritual, or otherwise threaten the pattern of existential stability and meaning.

Take another example. Contemporary efforts advocate additional career opportunities for teachers through teacher incentive or merit pay plans. The rationale for these changes comes through a combination of individual and structural frames: needs and formal incentives. But the details of most plans also threaten the interests of teacher unions and can threaten the power of the principal or local school board. They may also foster competition between teachers and district, between teachers and administrators. Teacher incentive plans potentially undermine the cultural norms of teacher autonomy and equality and demand that evaluation become a basis for decisions rather than an important cultural ritual. The drama of teacher incentive systems may signal to outside constituencies that teachers will improve. Or the squabbles around how master teachers will be selected may again reinforce the image of schools as a battleground for interest groups rather than a place where children learn.

School closings provide still another example. The need to close schools arises from a complicated relationship among declining enrollments, dwindling resources, and reduced political support for schools. As decisions are approached, the logic is initially structural. What criteria do we employ in making the decision and who will be involved? The decision usually becomes politicized. Various interest groups exercise their power and build coalitions to influence the decision. Conflict quickly escalates and the school closing becomes an arena of power politics. Underneath school closings is the reality that schools provide a symbol for neighborhoods. Schools become places of memories and meaning. People become attached to values schools embody, heroes and heroines that serve inside, rituals and ceremonies that they remember or anticipate. Closing creates potential loss, and loss always threatens meaning. School closings thus become cultural dramas of mourning, transformation, and realignment.

A final example: Alternative schools were efforts to create new educational cultures. But as these schools were launched in the 1960s and 1970s, their founders forgot the strength of the existing myths of education. As the schools began, individuals began to search for meaning that the old culture provided—rebels who railed against existing symbols. The new culture, however, had not yet crystallized. Internal politics or struggles between various factions were commonplace because a shared sense of community did not exist and because people hurt, but did not know why. Communities became involved politically when people saw learning facilitators, couches, and active experience rather than teachers, desks, blackboards, and books. Alternative schools that succeeded developed cohesive cultures based on positive values, developed through trial and error, reinforced in ritual, and extolled in legend and stories.

In each of these examples, the link between needs, roles, power, and symbols in change is obvious. Studies of change guided by one—even two—conceptual lenses have not been able to capture the central issues of changing, thus limiting understanding and prediction. Strategies of change that have overlooked any aspect of organizations—especially power and symbols—have typically ended in disaster or have unintentionally reinforced the status quo. As a result, our legacy of change is not as dramatic as it might be. Classrooms and schools have emerged from innovation, reform, improvement, and school-effectiveness initiatives very much the same as they always were. While each of the frames would interpret this legacy differently, only the symbolic frame would question the outcome—either in fact or desirability. Maybe schools are better than we think they are. Maybe efforts to improve schools are directed at the wrong audience. Maybe deeper changes have been made that rational lenses cannot capture. Maybe our constant efforts to change, reform, and improve schools are making them worse instead of better. Maybe our approaches are not only conceptually limited, but philosophically mis-directed.

SEARCHING FOR THE WIZARD:
THE QUEST FOR CHANGE IN EDUCATION

The search for better schools has many goals: innovation, reform, improvement, or effectiveness. And now the excellence movement has captured our imagination, stimulating almost a stampede among educators in pursuit of an elusive quality. The quest has a familiar ring:

"I am going to the Great Oz to ask him to give me some brains," remarked the Scarecrow, "for my head is stuffed with straw."

"And I'm going to ask him to give me a heart," said the Tin Woodman.

"And I'm going to ask him to send Toto and me back to Kansas," added Dorothy.

"Do you think the Wizard could give me courage?" asked the cowardly Lion.

"Just as easily as he could give me brains," said the Scarecrow.

"Or send me back to Kansas," said Dorothy.

"Then if you don't mind, I'll go with you," said the cowardly Lion."[21]

We're off to see the Wizard" was the rallying cry that propelled Dorothy and her colleagues along the yellow brick road in search of their dreams. But the dreams were always to be realized through the Wizard, never through the inner resources that each character already possessed. As we search for improved schools, for excellence in education, we too come to place most of our confidence in external knowledge resources, people, or policies.[22]

Philosophically, we have little confidence that schools will change if left to their own devices—or rightfully choose to retain their existing virtues. They either do not know how to change, or will not even though they need to. External guidance, wisdom, or force are required. There is a literature that outlines the characteristics of effective schools, a book that lists the characteristics of high-performing companies, and countless commission reports filled with recommendations for how excellence can be achieved. These—along with other research findings or popular wisdom—will undoubtedly form the new foundation for state and local policies to improve schools. Educators in local schools typically may welcome the clear directions that guidelines or policies provide. In addition, policies will provide incentives for schools that "adopt" or "implement" these changes and penalties for those that do not. And there we will be—back in the old predicament of changing organizations with little hope that schools will emerge any more excellent, or even any different from what they already are.

There are two main problems with this top-down, externally driven philosophy. The first is that the research and policies may not be as adequate or as powerful as we would like to believe.

"You are all wrong," said the little man meekly. "I have been making believe."

"Making believe!" cried Dorothy. "Are you not a great Wizard?"

"Hush my dear," he said. "Don't speak so loud or you will be overheard, and I should be ruined. I'm supposed to be a great Wizard."

"And aren't you?" she asked.

"Not a bit of it, my dear; I'm just a common man."[23]

Our need to believe that there is some specific rational answer to social crises may help maintain our confidence and spirit. But as policies, guidelines, and recommendations enter the complex reality of social institutions, they often become less powerful than they once appeared. Knowledge of experts, opinions of influential persons, and values of diverse groups meld into guidelines that apply across the boards—and slip between the cracks.

The second problem with our philosophy of change is related to the first. Practitioners at all levels, across sectors, have been trained and encouraged to look outside rather than within for solutions to problems, criteria for improvements, or directions for change. This is especially true in public schools, where wave after wave of reform has weakened cultural values and beliefs, where constant criticism and ridicule have eroded professional confidence, where experience has been devalued in favor of youth, where main avenues for survival have been to hunker down, burn out, or leave. All this fosters an attitude of looking outward and upward for direction and solutions:

"You are a very bad man," said Dorothy.

"Oh no, my dear, I'm a very good man; it's just that I'm a very bad Wizard."

"Can't you give me brains?" asked the Scarecrow.

"You don't need them. You are learning something everyday. A baby has brains, but it doesn't know much. Experience is the only thing that brings knowledge, and the longer you are on this earth, the more experience you are sure to get."

"That may all be true," said the Scarecrow, "but I shall be very unhappy unless you give me brains."

The false Wizard looked at him carefully. "Well," he said with a sigh, "I'm not much of a magician, but if you come to me tomorrow morning, I will stuff your head with brains. I cannot tell you how to use them, however; you must find that out for yourself."

"But what about my courage?", asked the Lion anxiously.

"You have plenty of courage, I'm sure," answered the Wizard. "All you need is confidence in yourself. There is no living thing that is not afraid when it faces danger. True courage is facing danger when you are afraid, and that kind of courage you have in plenty."

"Perhaps I have, but I'm scared just the same," said the Lion. "I shall really be unhappy unless you give me the sort of courage that makes one forget he is afraid."

"Very well, I will give you that kind of courage tomorrow," said the Wizard.[24]

Experience—the very characteristic we now devalue. Confidence—the feeling the public schools often lack. And heart—if we include the Tin Woodman—which in many schools pumps faintly. All essential to revitalize public schools. Excellence or improvement cannot be installed or mandated from outside; it must be developed from within. It must arise from collective conversations, behaviors, and spirit among teachers, administrators, students, and parents within a local school community.

There is a revolution underway in the way we think about human organizations. The movement does not require that we throw away everything we have learned in the last ten or twenty years. It does require that we reach back to revive and refurbish some time-worn ideas about the role of power and conflict, or symbols and meaning in human experience.

The changes in our thinking about organizations is influencing dramatically the way in which modern businesses are being managed or changed.[25] The new approach to management is built on a realization that the most successful businesses in America have evolved and have continued to cultivate and reinforce a strong symbolic sense, a culture that gives meaning to the work place. This insight has encouraged many businesses to look within, to identify and nourish values and symbols that experience has proven over time. For others, the look inside has revealed the need to change. A strong, cohesive culture designed for one set of stable circumstances cannot continue to be productive in a highly competitive environment. Banks, insurance companies, airlines, and especially the telephone company are struggling to adapt internal values and mores to new demands. But many of these companies, as they change, are paying attention to the symbolic side of the process. They know that it is impossible to break completely with the past. They also know that the roots that are severed must be mourned if people are to seek nourishment and derive meaning from new sources.

In improving schools, we need to follow a similar pathway. We need to change our thinking about change. We need to conceptualize and embrace the political and symbolic side of schools. We need to think about the complex interplay among different aspects of an organization before, during, and after implementation of new policies and programs. Even more important, we need to recognize the value of a strong cohesive identity to a school's productivity and image. School improvement ought to emphasize building from within. Those of us who claim to be wizards ought to make sure that our primary role is to help people see the power that they themselves have to make things better.

Notes

1 Lee G. Bolman and Terrence E. Deal, *Modern Approaches to Understanding and Managing Organizations* (San Francisco: Jossey-Bass, 1984).

2 A full review of literature in the individual perspective, as well as the other three, can be found in ibid., chaps. 11 and 13.

3 J. Victor Baldridge and Terrence E. Deal, *Managing Change in Educational Organizations: Sociological Theories, Strategies and Case Studies* (Berkeley: McCutchan, 1975).

4 Terrence E. Deal and Samuel C. Nutt, *Promoting, Guiding, and Surviving Change in School Districts* (Cambridge, Mass.: Abt Associates, n.d.).

5   Ernest House, *Three Perspectives on Innovations—The Technological, the Political, and the Cultural* (Beverly Hills: Sage Publications, 1981).

6   J. Victor Baldridge, *Power and Conflict in the University* (New York: John Wiley, 1971).

7   Gail P. Houghton, *Using Survey Feedback as a Problem Solving Strategy in a Suburban High School* (Dissertation Abstracts International, 1979), 40/05A, p. 2385, 79-24564.

8   Willard Waller, *The Sociology of Teaching* (New York: John Wiley, 1932).

9   Seymour S. Sarason, *The Culture of the School and the Problem of Change* (Boston: Allyn and Bacon, 1971).

10   John W. Meyer and Brian Rowan, "Institutional Organizations—Formal Structure as Myth and Ceremony," *American Journal of Sociology* 27, no. 3 (1977): 16-26.

11   Harvey M. Sopolsky, "PERT and the Myth of Managerial Effectiveness," in *The Polaris Systems Development,* (Cambridge: Harvard University Press, 1972).

12   Terrence E. Deal and Allan Kennedy, *Corporate Cultures: The Rites and Rituals of Corporate Life* (Reading, Mass.: Addison-Wesley, 1982).

13   Peter Marris, *Loss and Change* (London: Routledge & Kegan Paul, 1974).

14   Lee G. Bolman, Class lecture, Harvard University, 1982.

15   Terrence E. Deal and Allan Kennedy, "Tales from the Trails," *Hospital Forum: The Journal of the Association of Western Hospitals,* May/June 1984, p. 16.

16   Ibid., p. 24.

17   Bolman and Deal, *Modern Approaches to Understanding and Managing Organizations.*

18   Terrence E. Deal and Allan Kennedy, "Culture: A New Look Through Old Lenses," *The Journal of Applied Behavioral Science* 19, no. 4 (1983): 498-505.

19   J. Victor Baldridge and Terrence E. Deal, *The Dynamics of Organizational Change in Education* (Berkeley, Calif.: McCutchan, 1983).

20   Bolman and Deal, *Modern Approach to Understanding and Managing Organizations.*

21   Frank L. Baum, *The Wizard of Oz* (New York: Grosset and Dunlop, 1944), p. 51. These references to the *Wizard of Oz* also appear in my paper "Searching for the Wizard: The Quest for Excellence in Education," appearing in *Issues in Education* 1 (Summer 1984).

22   Deal, "Searching for the Wizard."

23   Baum, *The Wizard of Oz,* p. 147.

24   Ibid., p. 152, 153.

25   Thomas J. Peters and Robert H. Waterman, Jr., *In Search of Excellence* (New York: Harper & Row, 1982); and Deal and Kennedy, *Corporate Cultures.*

Teachers and Mothers:
Facing New Beginnings

KAREN KEPLER ZUMWALT

Teachers College, Columbia University

Beginning . . . is a great moment in a person's life. It is a time of high expectations, special joys and, often, punishing difficulties.[1]

Memories of [one's] own experiences—both good and bad—help to create a sense of familiarity and idealized visions.[2]

You're happy and excited . . . but you wonder whether you are going to know how to do a good job.[3]

It is easy to spend most of [one's] time and energy taking care of others' needs all day. . . . What is left is not much of you—not one who can really enrich the lives of the people you love.[4]

Experiences of new teachers and new mothers evoke many similar feelings—so similar that some descriptions of the experience seem almost interchangeable. The above quotations—the first two on teaching, the last two on mothering—could be describing either experience.

Because I am a teacher educator recently inducted into motherhood, the striking similarities as well as the differences between these two beginnings have reinforced my sense that we could do a better job of inducting teachers into our profession. Doing a better job of this seems critical at this point when teaching is having difficulty attracting the most able college graduates; reports of burned-out, demoralized teachers flood the public press; and experienced teachers are leaving (or say they wish they could leave) the profession for easier, more lucrative, higher-status careers. Although there are definitely compelling external factors contributing to the situation, as a profession generally committed to a "trial by fire" induction for neophytes, we have not really paid enough attention to these crucial early years, which leave a mark on one's teaching and on one's commitment to the profession. As a recent request for proposals from the National Institute of Education asserts:

> The conditions under which a person carries out the first year of teaching have a strong influence on the level of effectiveness which that teacher is able to achieve and sustain over the years; on the attitudes which govern teacher behavior over even a forty year career; and, indeed, on the decision whether or not to continue in the teaching profession.[5]

The first section of this article focuses on the similarities faced by beginning mothers and teachers as they cope with new experiences and feelings. Highlighting the commonalities provides a vivid picture for new teachers and for colleagues long past their own induction. We then turn to the differences in the "induction process" highlighted by comparing new teachers and new mothers. In the last section, these similarities and differences are explored for the implications they suggest for the induction of teachers. In some cases, the differences suggest changes to make beginning teaching more like beginning motherhood, and, in some cases, the differences suggest unique features of beginning teaching that deserve special attention.

NEW TEACHERS, NEW MOTHERS: SIMILARITIES

Watching and helping the next generation grow and develop provides involved adults with a natural high—and an incredible learning opportunity. It is a time of learning about yourself, testing your competencies and values, and deepening your understanding of the human experience.

But such learning is not always exciting or easy. Child-care books speak about "postpartum blues" and teacher educators refer to the "curve of disenchantment."[6] New beginnings generate new joys and "constant, unremitting self-confrontation."[7] Between swings of self-assuredness and overconfidence and self-doubts and fear of failure, the newly initiated has to come to grips with her identity as a teacher or as a mother. Adjusting to a new role involves reshaping present roles and guarding against the new demands overshadowing other aspects of personal identity. Given the demands on their time and energy, it is easy for the new mother or new teacher to gravitate toward meeting personal needs through the new baby or the students. In both cases, there is a danger of "needless self-sacrifice and excessive preoccupation."[8] Restructuring one's identity in a healthy manner is one of the personal challenges of the first years.

Labor Day heralds the beginning of the separation of romance from reality. The new teacher and new mother begin actively redefining the ideal in light of the real. The trick is to grow more realistic without losing your enjoyment and positive orientation. A more pragmatic form of idealism rather than a mere survival attitude will develop, it is hoped, as the new teacher and new mother discover that "it's not as easy as it looks."

Having many years of experience as children and as students, new mothers and new teachers think they have a pretty good idea of what the new job entails. But being on the other side of the desk or highchair, the familiar unexpectedly becomes foreign. Slowly your body adjusts to the physical and emotional exhaustion that at first seems overwhelming. Sleeping when the baby naps and the "afterschool/before dinner" collapse complement a new adherence to Ben Franklin's "Early to bed, early to rise." You learn that the excitement of teaching and mothering brings with it an acceptance of much that is sheer drudgery—mounds of paperwork and procedural details, dirty clothes and diapers, which seem to be perpetually regenerated. Being responsible for the development of others, you learn to accept the fact that the job is never done—you could always have prepared more for class or done more with your child. You learn to structure life around bells and grading periods, feedings and naps. Many of your responses are on other people's schedules rather than self-determined. There is no time for mothers and teachers to get sick, even though they tend to get sick more often during their first year with children. Unexpected events—an infant's first sudden 104° fever or an unplanned observation from the principal at the "worst time"—demand a good dose of flexibility and calmness in a world that is not as controllable or predictable as the one experienced in pre-mother or pre-teacher days. You have to learn to accept the good days and bad days, the ups and downs that seem inevitable during the induction process. You learn to take pride in small accomplishments—a smashing lesson, one more hour of sleep at night—and continue onward despite never being really sure of your impact. You learn that a teacher is not a friend, nor a parent a pal, as you struggle with being an authority figure and being liked by your charges.

Perhaps the biggest shock in coping with reality comes with the realization that perfection is an impossibility—that your images of what teachers/mothers should and should not do and what babies/students should and should not do need to be tempered by the realities, the complexities and constraints, of everyday life. Mistakes are inevitable, and something to learn from rather than indicators of failure. It is hard to maintain "consistency" and everything seems to take much longer than you ever expected. And despite your prior convictions, you learn that there are few "nevers" in teaching and in mothering. The once-derided pacifier or playpen, behavior-modification technique or multiplication drill, is quickly placed in a more acceptable context. While you learn to accept the fact that "less than ideal" practices of mothers and teachers from your own past will become part of your present practices, you also develop your own characteristic ways of dealing with the new role, ways that do reflect some of your earlier images of teachers and mothers that are "more ideal" than the ones you experienced.

In juggling dreams with reality, you inevitably make some compromises; you revise some commitments and fight for others. Regardless of preparation, struggling and coping is the norm—something that is a desirable stance of a growing adult rather than a sign of personal failure or an indication of inadequate preparation. The new teacher and the new mother are constantly experimenting—with different management techniques and instructional strategies, with different approaches to feeding and sleeping. One hopes that most of the experimentation is more rational than frantic, yet sometimes out of desperation comes something that "works."

Deciding on and balancing priorities is a major task facing the new mother and the new teacher. There are so many choices available as you decide how to approach each week. You just cannot do everything you want or think others want. Swamped with papers to grade, you learn to assign fewer or give detailed comments only on selected ones. Swamped with child-care choices, you learn that the daily bath or walk is not sacred. For both the new mother and the new teacher, planning, organizing, and managing time become critical skills to prevent the job from becoming overwhelming, to prevent survival from becoming the only goal.

In coping with new demands, the new mother and the new teacher are faced with much advice but "little of it offers her support for her own individual reactions and intuitions."[9] Such counsel tells her how to be perfect, it is often contradictory, and it leaves her confused and guilty when she cannot follow it. In the extreme, knowing too much can lead to "analysis paralysis"[10] or a sense of failure as the neophyte tries to duplicate the master instantaneously. A noted pediatrician comments that "in spite of this avalanche of advice, of 'sure ways' to mother a child, a new mother must realize that no one of them is the only answer. She must find her own way as a mother with her own special baby."[11] Likewise, a noted educator concludes:

> We might as well face the likelihood that teaching may not consist of standard best ways to do particular things. Being a good teacher, like being a good statesman or a good mother, may involve infinite possible human excellences and appropriate behaviors, no one much more a guarantor of success than the others.[12]

One needs to come to terms with the fact that there is no one right way in teaching or in mothering, that the right way evolves as one applies a good dose of personality, intuition, common sense, past experience, and values along with the accumulated knowledge and skill offered by professionals.

Besides putting professional advice in context, you also learn to deal with the well-intentioned, often conflicting and sometimes hurtful advice of relatives, parents, friends, and colleagues. And despite disagreements, you learn to exploit the experiences of other mothers and teachers in acquiring those important tricks of the trade—how to get gum out of hair, how to get the most out of consumable workbooks.

Learning how to utilize expert and "not so expert" knowledge is critical because one's preparation prior to actually taking on the new role can never be adequate. Not only would it be impossible to prepare totally for the myriad of new situations, but advice and knowledge take on a new meaning when one is actually confronting the phenomenon—being a teacher, being a mother.

While there is much truth in the common belief that one "learns to be a teacher (mother) by being a teacher (mother)," and that one learns from how one was handled as a child by mother and teacher, the preparation provided in student teaching programs, childbirth classes, magazines, books, and just talking with experienced practitioners and parents helps the neophyte to cope better with the new demands, helps eliminate some trial-and-error stumblings, counteracts the potential for misleading and miseducative lessons from experience, and helps one more efficiently and effectively meet personal and professional goals.

As mothering and teaching evolve, that which is learned from reflective experience reinforces the advice from professionals and shares some striking similarities. For example:

—You learn to establish and reinforce rules and routines, which requires clarifying your expectations and priorities. You learn how to say no, while stressing the positive and possible. And you learn how difficult it is to change patterns once they are set—asserting yourself and dealing with initial crying and complaints is far preferable to becoming a long-term nag about behavior patterns that should never have been allowed to become established in the first place.

—In matters of management, you learn, as Dr. Spock suggests, that "a strictness that comes from harsh feelings or a permissiveness that is timid or vacillating can each lead to poor results."[13] Moderation combined with a preventative rather than punitive approach seems to work best. You also acquire eyes in the back of your head, extra antennae, the ability to read subtle messages, and a repertoire of nonverbal desists and encouragements. You learn how to handle tantrums and being tested in a world that is considerably more out of your control than that previously experienced. And you learn the importance of not taking things too personally but also expressing anger when appropriate.

—You learn to deal with constant interruptions and juggling several balls at once. You learn when to intervene and when not to intervene and how to take advantage of "teachable moments." You learn how to separate the important from the trivial, to respond or not to respond. And you learn the importance of pacing, the timing of motivation, redirection, and variation. Getting your charges to help takes direction, patience, and some lessons from Tom Sawyer. And you learn to delegate to husband and assistants, to baby-sitters and substitutes.

—You learn to deal with several dilemmas concerning your goals. For example, the more you encourage a child to explore, be independent, be creative, to write and do science projects, the more work you make for yourself. Allowing children to "mess about" with materials or ideas and letting them try things you can do better demands compromises with orderliness, schedules, efficiency, and control.

—You also begin to see elements of the environment in a new light—the often-passed playground, the previously discarded margarine tubs, the taken-for-granted community services all become valuable resources. You become a hoarder of potentially useful material (e.g., catalogs, toilet paper rolls) and ideas (e.g., socks that stay on, nontoxic washable markers, good spontaneous activities). You learn your way around forgotten closets and storage rooms, around toy stores and new sections of department stores.

And you are introduced to another world—a world where birds are huge and grouches live in garbage pails; a world where mention of "baseball" sends a class of twelve-year-olds into uncontrollable laughter. While parts of this world are new, other parts are wonderfully familiar reminders of worlds left behind years ago.

Entering the world of teaching and that of mothering also involves coming to terms with the conditions of the work place and the public image of the mother and the teacher. Literature on teaching and child care speaks about the physical isolation of mothering/teaching, which can lead to social isolation.[14] Being underpaid and having little contact with other adults, mothers and teachers seek their rewards from themselves and their child/children. Without a doubt these intrinsic rewards can be incredibly satisfying. Yet it can be demoralizing "to realize how little the world values a mother's job"[15] or in Lortie's words how the "real regard" for teachers never matches the "professed regard."[16] The messages are conflicting, however.[17] Although the work is not held important, if anything goes wrong, it is the fault of the teacher or mother. This responsibility can generate guilt and frustration as well as be a source of satisfaction and pride. The incongruities between societal importance and status ascribed to mothering and teaching are dilemmas faced by the neophyte at a time when the job seems much more demanding than the beginner ever realized and certainly more demanding than others imagine. Coping with the "just a teacher"/"just a mother" response of others is not easy at a time when friends in nine-to-five jobs and friends without children seem to have it much easier. It is easy to become envious of their free evenings and weekends, their more carefree life-style and their greater financial freedom. For new teachers and mothers, coming to terms with one's status demands a recommitment to one's choice and a confidence in one's ability to do a good job and to grow personally and professionally in a socially valuable, but undervalued, role.

NEW TEACHERS, NEW MOTHERS: DIFFERENCES

In many ways the differences between new teachers and new mothers suggest that new teachers have a more complex task facing them than do new mothers. Although there are also unique tasks facing new mothers, I will focus on unique difficulties facing beginning teachers in light of my desire to draw implications for the induction of new teachers.

As "Labor Day" draws to a close, a long-anticipated event brings immediate change in the lives of new mothers and teachers. Although the experience is still tiring and awesome, nature has eased the transition for the new mother by simplifying her immediate tasks. Sleeping and eating are the primary preoccupations of her new little one. Her initial focus revolves around fulfilling the baby's basic needs for sleep, drink, cleanliness, warmth, and love. Slowly, as the baby develops, the complexity of the new mother's task increases. In contrast, most new teachers are asked to assume all the responsibilities of experienced teachers from the first day of employment. It is not only that the concrete tasks required of new teachers and experienced teachers are indistinguishable, but that the dilemmas of teaching confront the neophyte from the start. New mothers have eighteen months before facing the challenging dilemmas of the "terrible twos"; new teachers face their equivalent almost immediately. New teachers are asked to adjust to their roles in full-blown fashion while nature has provided a more gradual unfolding for the new mother, which matches the growth of her newborn.

Another difference between the experiences of new mothers and new teachers is related to the baby's continuing growth, which confronts the new mother with a gradually changing set of demands and the comforting knowledge that difficult periods in development (e.g., sleepless nights, early evening fuzziness) will soon pass. It almost seems that once a feeding schedule or set of diversionary techniques becomes comfortable, the developing infant and the evolving new demands force the mother to adjust once again. The forced changes in patterned ways of interacting facing the new mother (e.g., coping with the newly mobile infant) almost preclude the stagnation that often follows when the new teacher finds something that works. Much of the literature on teacher induction speaks about the teacher's adopting expedient survival mechanisms that become stultifying permanent teaching strategies. As McDonald argues:

> The beginning teacher focuses on what is necessary to "get the job done" —manage the class, prepare lessons, grade papers, teach each lesson. Effectiveness means doing these things reasonably well, without getting into touble; it means being accepted, even liked by the students. The teaching practices which seem to produce these ends merge into a style, which—whatever its other merits—works for the beginner. This is his style, and he will rationalize it and ignore its limitations.[18]

Given the immediate assumption of full-blown responsibility, which encourages a survival style, and the fact that the teacher sees only a slice of the developmental life of a child (often making difficult times seem permanent and eliminating the need for continual changes), it is not surprising that "stagnation" is a concept often found in the literature on teacher development.[19]

Some have said that a mother of a twenty-year-old has had twenty different years of experience while a teacher with twenty years experience has had one year twenty times.[20] While definitely an exaggeration, it does remind us that it takes much more effort to keep the new teacher growing—an effort that must occur during the induction years because it is less likely to happen later.

In addition, the new mother may be in a safer environment for nonevaluative problem solving, analysis, and reflection—necessary ingredients for growth. Most new mothers are not fearful about asking for help; such a request does not reflect negatively on their basic competency nor does it have anything to do with whether they will be rehired! Asking advice of a pediatrician does not carry the imagined (and sometimes real) consequences of asking help from a principal. Their differential power over the advice seeker affects the way their knowledge and skills are utilized.

The structure of interaction also accentuates this difference. While in the hospital, the new mother talks with her pediatrician daily. The checkup visits are scheduled at regular intervals, and other visits are scheduled as problems arise. In contrast, most new teachers after their interview and orientation meetings have one-on-one conversations with their principal only when the one or two formal evaluative visits are scheduled or when problems arise. As Feiman-Nemser comments, "Under such circumstances, it is hard to separate judgments of competence from discussions of practice."[21]

Support from others also differs for new mother and new teacher. For nine months, the mother-to-be is the center of much attention. Few question her choice, most share her joy and excitement. The arrival of motherhood is cause for celebration. In contrast, the teacher-to-be faces the questioning doubts of relatives, friends, and self about this choice of profession. The arrival of teacherhood is not cause for celebration, but rather a "nonevent" for almost everyone but the new teacher. Mostly the new teacher is ignored by peers[22] and subjected to their "burned-out" commentary in the teacher lounge. The missing "new father" counterpart heightens the isolation of the new teacher.

Colleagues and other mothers can be sources of both support and competition for the neophyte. Brazelton speaks about

> the subtle ways American mothers compete with each other. Each is ready to help another feel inadequate as a mother, to see her baby's behavior as inadequate. . . . The speed with which each child takes steps to grow up seems to be equated with success in mothering.[23]

While there is definitely a competitive flavor to some mother-to-mother interaction, there is also much sharing of ideas, tricks, problems, outgrown clothes, and equipment. Unfortunately, "many new teachers feel cut off and isolated from those people who could help them the most: experienced teachers."[24] The corresponding lack of sharing among teachers may relate to the fact that teachers, unlike mothers, do not often get to view each other "in action," that time for informal interchanges is limited, and that the natural personal competition is augmented by public competition—teachers are constantly being judged and compared by administrators, colleagues, parents, and students. And these comparisons and judgments, unlike those of mothers in the playground—which can be just as hurtful—can have consequences in terms of employment.

The tasks involved in the job that is being judged are also quite different. Teaching, unlike mothering, is concurrently:

management of individual learning;
coordination of several groups working on different tasks;

the social organization of the classroom as a collective enterprise;
planning and implementation of curriculum as the allocation of time
and resources to activities;
the struggle for power with administrators, students and community
members over the control of classroom activities and emphases.[25]

Held particularly accountable for specific cognitive and affective outcomes,
teachers are responsible for designing and implementing an appropriate
curriculum. In providing effective learning environments, the teacher, unlike
the mother, faces a variety of content decisions:

1. How much time will be devoted to a subject (e.g., economics) or goal
   (e.g., social problem-solving).
2. How different subjects/goals will be related.
3. What topics/objectives will be taught.
4. To whom the topics/objectives will be taught.
5. When and how long each topic/objective will be taught.
6. In what order and how each topic/objective will be taught.
7. How well the topics/objectives are to be learned.[26]

The "answers" are neither found in textbooks nor immutable once discovered. The teacher's continuing dilemma is to find a balance between such
factors as:

high and moderate success rate
whole class, small group, individual instruction
time allocated to different subject matter goals
cognitive and affective concerns
coverage and mastery
teacher decisions, joint decisions, child decisions
absolute attention and realistic inattention
standardized criteria of evaluation and idiosyncratic criteria
needs of individuals v. needs of group
needs of teacher v. needs of students
maximizing v. minimizing individual differences.[27]

While the desirable outcomes may be equally clear to the new mother and
the new teacher, the goals are more diffuse and limitless for the new mother.[28]
The kinds of specific outcomes the new teacher is asked to achieve within the
first ten months on the job for 20 to 240 different learners place very concrete
demands on the new teacher for which she is to be held accountable.
Unfortunately, progress is often not as visible as it is to the new mother, who is
watching the most rapid period of human growth. The new teacher wonders
whether her students are really learning as fast and as well as they should be.
As Lortie describes it, evaluating progress produces a

torrent of feeling and frustration; one finds self-blame, a sense of inadequacy, the bitter taste of failure, anger at the students, despair and
other dark emotions. The freedom to assess one's own work is no occasion
for joy, the conscience remains unsatisfied as ambiguity, uncertainty, and
little apparent change impede the flow of reassurance. Teaching demands, it seems, the capacity to work for protracted periods without sure
knowledge that one is having any positive effect on students. Some find
it difficult to maintain their self-esteem.[29]

Unlike the new mother, who literally just has to watch rather than directly
orchestrate much of the learning process, new teachers know that students'
progress is largely dependent on their efforts.

Although the teacher does not have the twenty-four-hour, twenty-one-year
responsibility of the new mother, having to focus on the development and
education of more than one child at a time definitely affects the character and
complexity of the tasks involved. While both new mother and new teacher
must maintain control, order priorities and activities, and arouse and sustain
the child's interest,[30] the new teacher must accomplish all of these tasks within
a group context. Not only does the group context complicate the actual tasks
involved, but it may also be the source of problems for the child-oriented new
teacher.

Even though mothering and teaching generate similar feelings, the roles
demand different responses because of the teachers' responsibility to a group
of students rather than to an individual child. As Katz has outlined it, mothers
respond with high affect, high attachment, irrationality, spontaneity, and
partiality. In contrast, new teachers, who typically have entered teaching
because of their enjoyment of children, are now asked to demonstrate low
affect, detachment, rationality, intentionality, and impartiality as they
manage and instruct a group of children.[31] New mothers can play out all their
feelings as a child's primary advocate, while new teachers, to survive, must
contain some of their very natural impulses when interacting with a class of
children.

Besides adapting to the particular group of learners with their varied
learning rates, knowledge, experience, and different ethnic, racial, cultural,
and social backgrounds, the new teacher is also faced with adjusting to the
social system of the school.[32] This adjustment involves not only coping with a
myriad of administrative policies and procedures, but also figuring out and
appropriately responding to the values, norms, and politics of the adult
school community. While the social systems in which the new mother exists
are basically familiar (i.e., family, neighborhood) or may be ignored (i.e.,
mothers at the playground), the new teacher's very livelihood is dependent on
coping not only in her classroom, but also in the larger context of the school's
social system. Although interacting primarily with youngsters, the new
teacher is very much enmeshed in a new, oftentimes not very friendly or open,
adult world.

Outside the school, the new teacher often is faced with the demands of beginning adulthood as well—a first apartment, a new marriage, a new community, a first car. Being on one's own for the first time involves all kinds of nonteaching adjustments, which for many new graduates are taking place simultaneously with assuming the role of teacher. As women are delaying motherhood, more new mothers are lessening the effects of simultaneous adjustment to adulthood and marriage. But for most new teachers, having just completed teacher education programs, teaching is their entry to adulthood.

Besides the logistics of living one often has to cope with the fact that "being on one's own" is not what one expected. Added to these potential emotional strains is the fact that

for some, the setbacks experienced in teaching are the first serious ones of their lives. They expected teaching to be satisfying, yet it does not seem to be. They had all sorts of expectations and plans but few of them are working out.[33]

Obviously, the new teacher does have an option that the new mother does not have—that is, the option of leaving. Hence, an additional agenda faces the new teacher. Did I make the right decision? Is teaching for me? For how long? Is the problem this particular job? Or are there other things I would prefer to be doing? The new mother may question her decision, but most realize that their choice is not retractable. While the new mother is faced with the finality of her choice, the new teacher is faced with continually reassessing her choice. In exchange for freedom comes the burden of choice.

IMPLICATIONS FOR TEACHER INDUCTION

Exploring similarities and differences in the experiences of beginning mothers and beginning teachers provokes many thoughts about the induction of new teachers. Besides increasing awareness of the first-year experience, it also illustrates the appropriateness of a particular conception of teaching and teacher education, and suggests certain changes in school culture to support learning from teaching and changes in society to support teachers.

The discussion of similarities and differences highlights for the new teacher some important aspects of the first-year experience for which one is rarely adequately prepared. Awareness of anticipated experiences cannot take the place of actually experiencing, but it should help the new teacher face the struggles of the first year more realistically. For instance, to understand that coping, struggling, and experimenting are the norm—something that is a desirable stance of a growing adult rather than a sign of personal failure or an indication of inadequate preparation—might provide a different perspective for the first-year teacher. The numerous comparisons cited in the first two sections not only provide the beginning teacher with a more realistic perspective, but serve to remind teacher educators, staff developers, administrators, and colleagues—most of whose first-year memories have been reshaped by years of experience—about the particular needs, interests, and concerns of the beginning teacher.

The similarities between beginning mothering and teaching illustrate dramatically that teaching is more than a repertoire of knowledge, skills, and attitudes that the teacher brings to bear in an effort to create certain changes in learners. This technological view of teaching, underlying many competency-based teacher education programs, fails to capture the educational dynamics and demands that face the new teacher. A more inclusive view sees teaching, like mothering, as a dynamic, deliberative process. Teaching entails applying the basic tools of the trade—one's experience, intuition, and understanding of particular learners, context, and subject matter—in what is essentially a fast-paced, continuous, complex, problem-solving, and decision-making process.[34] Some of these decisions, representing Schön's "knowing-in-action," appear spontaneous. Other, more conscious decisions involve "reflecting-in-action" and "reflecting-on-action" by the thoughtful practitioner.[35] The similarities between beginning teaching and beginning mothering accentuate the value of a deliberative rather than a technological orientation toward teaching. Teaching and mothering involve much more than "application of scientific theory and technique to instrumental problems of practice."[36]

But exploration of the differences between mothering and teaching also provides insight for those working with beginning teachers. The analogy highlights the additional pedagogical knowledge needed by the beginning teacher, the importance of providing teachers with the same impetus toward growth forced on mothers by the changing child, the needed changes in the school culture that would support the learning teacher and more profound changes in the way society views teachers.

Given the different roles mothers and teachers are expected to perform, the challenging demands of their jobs should evoke qualitatively different responses. But the similarities—the isolation, the constant need for experimenting, the multiple choices and decisions, the physical exhaustion, the rewards from interacting with children—have a tendency to evoke similar responses. As McDonald has said, "In the aloneness—of personal struggle—evolves an individualistic, self-sufficient approach to teaching."[37] Lortie talks about what teachers learn about teaching as being "'intuitive and imitative' rather than 'explicit' and 'analytical'; it is based on individual personalities rather than pedagogical principles."[38] "Socialization into teaching is largely self-socialization; one's personal predispositions are not only relevant but, in fact, stand at the core of becoming a teacher."[39]

While such an orientation is likely to persist and in itself may be one of the main attractions of teaching, there is a danger of "excessive realism"—the danger of accepting the kind of teaching that one has observed as the "upper and outer limits of the possible."[40] In making one's decisions—consciously and unconsciously—one may be trapped by habit and tradition. The teacher with knowledge is more truly free to choose.[41] To make intelligent decisions about the dilemmas facing the teacher charged with the education of twenty-five to thirty-five children (e.g., whole group versus small group versus individual instruction, cognitive versus affective goals), one needs more than accumulated experience, intuition, and personal values. One also needs to rely on "accumulated knowledge of how children develop and learn, and what is appropriate pedagogy for children of a given age range and experiential background."[42] There are curricular, instructional, organizational, and management skills that facilitate the task of teaching groups of children within a given period of time with limited resources in a particular social context. Given the specific role and social responsibilities expected of a new teacher in contrast with those of a new mother, it is clear that knowledge—let's call it pedagogical knowledge—plays a more critical role for the beginning teacher than for the beginning mother. Relying on parents' natural self-interest to curb extremes, society can more afford "individualistic, self-sufficient approaches" to parenting than to teaching. While most parents rely on various sources of knowledge, it is the obligation of teachers to have acquired a common pedagogical knowledge base that underlies their unique teaching styles and personalities. This knowledge—the mark of a professional—is a critical element informing the deliberative process central to teaching.

While this knowledge base for teaching certainly includes some of the traditionally identified areas (e.g., child development, teaching methods), this content perspective of pedagogical knowledge has helped create a misperception that one can learn how to teach by mastering specified bodies of knowledge. Given the nature of teaching, an equally important perspective is helping the beginning teacher to use this knowledge along with intuition, experience, and values in the deliberation process. The knowledge does not point to the "one right way" but awareness of it helps one decide which are the "better ways" in certain circumstances given certain goals. And it is a knowledge of ends as well as means, for both means and ends are "defined interactively as [the teacher] frames a problematic situation."[43]

Acquiring pedagogical knowledge is not enough; learning how to use it in the practical world of teaching is essential. Too often beginning teachers see no relation between what they learned in the college classroom (with the exception of student teaching) and what they do on the job. One might attribute some of this sentiment to lack of experience—not enough familiarity with the phenomena to realize what is and is not useful—but some of it is related to an emphasis on learning how to teach rather than learning from teaching in preparatory programs.[44]

Besides being a more appropriate stance in view of the deliberative nature of teaching, an emphasis on learning from teaching provides the new teacher with the mother's "developing child." Instead of stagnating with coping mechanisms of the survival stage, the new teacher receives impetus from self-analysis and reflection. Learning from teaching ensures a continual process of self-growth and change. Ever-changing, long-time challenges are delivered with a new baby, but they are there only for new teachers who have learned to see teaching as a complex mixture of rational decision making and value judgments rather than the static application of a body of knowledge.

With beginning teachers who have been taught how to learn from teaching rather than beginning teachers who have just learned how to teach, the focus for the school becomes one of supporting their learning rather than eliminating their problems. As Feiman-Nemser has noted, "alternatives of boredom and burnout or growth in effectiveness are less a function of individual characteristics and more a reflection of the opportunities and expectations that surround teachers in their work."[45]

Helping teachers to continue to learn from their own teaching would be facilitated if the experience of new teachers were more like that of new mothers: a more gradual assumption of full responsibilities, a safer environment for risk taking and experimentation, and nonjudgmental assistance.

The British experimentation with a reduced workload is worth exploring. The teaching load for beginners is reduced by up to 25 percent.[46] With their released time, these neophytes meet with experienced teachers, attend special noncredit, nontuition college courses designed for them, become involved in teacher center activities or curriculum development projects. These experimental programs combine a more gradual transition into teaching with nonjudgmental colleague support—from both peers and experienced teachers.

The pediatrician role from the new-mother analogy might be performed by a principal, a supervisor, or an experienced master teacher given released time to work formally and informally with the new teacher. The idea of periodic "well-baby" checkups might help replace the present problem-oriented seeking of assistance with the idea that all can benefit from professional dialogue about "what's happening in the classroom." Rather than being a sign of weakness, participation in such interchanges could be seen as indication of the professionalism of the beginning teacher. These frequent dialogues could also help new teachers put their performance in more realistic perspective by helping visualize the progress that is so often elusive to the newcomer wishing to immediately emulate the "masters"—the ideal, as well as the real. Forced to confront one's behavior, it is less likely that "survival tactics" will become engrained habits. Such dialogue could increase awareness of choices, as well as model the desired stance of reflective inquiry.

Fortunate is the new teacher who resembles the new mother in finding a playground full of supportive, largely noncompetitive, mothers or constructively involved relatives. The assistance offered during induction is likely to mean more if it takes place in a school where, formally and informally, all teachers view their own professional development as part of the job. Little refers to two powerful norms that characterize such schools. "The 'norm of collegiality' refers to the expectation that improving one's teaching is a collective undertaking. The norm of 'continuous improvement' refers to expectations that analysis, evaluation and experimentation are tools of the profession that can help teachers be more effective."[47]

While the above changes in school culture may seem at the same time obvious but difficult to achieve, they would be greatly facilitated by an equally obvious and monumental change in the way society views teachers and teaching. The status and financial compensation accorded teachers do not match their importance. Children and society have always deserved more, but the crisis in quality is particularly critical now. Schools are finding increased competition from hospitals, courts, and corporations as talented women decide to make their contributions through the more lucrative and prestigious M.D., LL.B. and M.B.A. routes.

While new mothers face the same status/pay discrepancy, the choice of motherhood remains a female prerogative that is not a negative reflection of intelligence or success, does not preclude other vocational pursuits, and does not present one with the constant option of leaving. Whether to stay in teaching or not is one of the many puzzles facing new teachers. The first few years should be a time when beginning teachers are helped to make a realistic assessment about their future as teachers—in the particular school and in general. And it should be a time when we actively try to retain the services of those who bring something special to teaching. Teachers who receive support while they learn are more likely to stay positively committed to teaching. Undoubtedly, there are people who might still be in teaching if the struggling of their early years had taken place in a more supportive environment and if society truly recognized the importance of their contribution.

Declining test scores and fewer college students seeking teaching credentials indicate that the problem is more than keeping potentially good teachers from getting prematurely discouraged and outstanding experienced teachers from burning out. The problem is attracting quality candidates to a low-paid, low-status but vitally important profession at a time when neither avoidance of war nor commitments to relevance and social responsibility are adding to its attractiveness. It is highly unlikely that tougher admission standards, federal loan deferments, or token financial incentives will be able to turn the tide. Rather, "a broad national attack on the pervasive problems of the 'prestige, power, pay, and preparation' of America's schoolteachers"[48] is necessary. According to a report in *Education Week*, forty university presidents and thirty-eight state education chiefs participating at a conference called to discuss solutions to the crises in teaching agreed that "a climate now exists" to mount such an effort.

Unfortunately, the Band-Aid nature of most proposed remedies limits their effectiveness. Either they are not powerful enough to impact on the status issue or they do not involve a restructuring of the teaching profession. Two exceptions are the master teacher concept and the national service proposals.

Master teacher plans provide incentives for teachers by recognizing them financially, by title and by job description. Monetary rewards are tied to increased or differentiated responsibilities within the school. With or without a career ladder structure, there are many responsibilities teachers could take on, if desired and qualified. These might include responsibilities as curriculum developers, staff developers, supervisors, administrators, action researchers, subject matter or learner specialists, and school board or community liaisons. For those who want to remain full-time teachers, their additional responsibilities might be to serve as demonstration teachers, to try out new curricula, or to serve in other capacities at times that would not interfere with their teaching duties (e.g., during the summer months). Besides providing concrete evidence of recognition through money and title, these proposals have the potential of providing teachers with the ever-changing challenges of the "growing child." Even for teachers who know how to learn from their own teaching, sometimes an external change in demands is a necessary impetus for continued professional growth.

A more radical response might involve the establishment of two years of national service for all Americans eighteen to thirty years of age. Those wishing to meet their national service requirement in the public schools would have to meet rigorous academic standards to become a part of this selective, elite corps of national service teachers. If prepared to teach, they would have to pass a performance test to enter. If not prepared to teach, their first year would involve a subsidized graduate program. The first year in teaching for both groups would be paid internships as regular classroom teachers, with a reduced load, under the supervision of a master teacher. The second year of teaching would be full-time. During the two to three years of service, rigorous deselection techniques reminiscent of the early Peace Corps would be in effect. At the end of two years of successful teaching, the graduates would form a cadre of first-step master teachers, publicly recognized and financially compensated. As at the end of any national service term, some would elect to stay in for a few more years or for a career. Others would go on to other things but with a better understanding of the dimensions and difficulties of distinguished service in teaching.

Whether master teacher or national service plans are needed yet and whether they would have the desired effects are still open questions. But the crisis facing the nation is here. Mothers may be having fewer children, but America does not face a critical shortage of children nor are good mothers likely to become an endangered species. But our children and their parents will soon face a crisis in teaching that spreads beyond the present shortage of qualified math and science teachers. Too many competent adults are seeking personal and professional satisfaction elsewhere. If quality education is really valued, some rather fundamental changes in the prestige, power, pay, and preparation of teachers is demanded. Attention to the beginning years of teaching is critical. As the nation begins its response to the teacher crisis, let us remember that "In the beginning is my end. . . ."[49]

Notes

1   Kevin Ryan, "Toward Understanding the Problem: At the Threshold of the Profession," in *Toward Meeting the Needs of the Beginning Teacher*, ed. Kenneth R. Howey and Richard H. Bents (Minneapolis: Midwest Teacher Corps Network and University of Minnesota/St. Paul Schools Teacher Corps Project, 1979), p. 35.

2   Karen Kepler, "BTES: Implications for Perservice Education of Teachers," in *Time to Learn*, ed. C. Denham and A. Lieberman (Washington, D.C.: National Institute of Education, May 1980), p. 146.

3   Benjamin Spock, *Baby and Child Care* (New York: Pocket Books, 1976), p. 1.

4   Barbara Sills and Jeanne Henry, *Mother to Mother Baby Care Book* (New York: Avon Books, 1980), p. 439.

5   Sharon Feiman-Nemser, "Learning to Teach," in *Handbook on Teaching and Policy*, ed. Lee Shulman and Gary Sykes (New York: Longman, 1983), p. 158.

6   Ryan, "Toward Understanding the Problem," p. 45.

7   Frances F. Fuller and Oliver Brown, "Becoming a Teacher," in *Teacher Education, Seventy-fourth Yearbook of the National Society for the Study of Education*, Part 2, ed. Kevin Ryan (Chicago: University of Chicago Press, 1975), p. 48.

8   Spock, *Baby and Child Care*, p. 20.

9   T. Berry Brazelton, *Infants and Mothers: Differences in Development* (New York: Delta, 1969), p. xviii.

10   Lilian G. Katz, "Mothering and Teaching—Some Significant Distinctions," in *Current Topics in Early Childhood Education*, vol. 3, ed. L. G. Katz et al. (Norwood, N.J.: ABLEX, 1980), p. 56.

11   Brazelton, *Infants and Mothers*, p. xviii.

12   Herbert Kliebard, "The Question in Teacher Education," in *New Perspectives on Teacher Education*, ed. Donald J. McCarty (San Francisco: Jossey-Bass, 1973), p. 23.

13   Spock, *Baby and Child Care*, p. 8.

14   Dan Lortie, *Schoolteacher* (Chicago: The University of Chicago Press, 1975); and Sills and Henry, *The Mother to Mother Baby Care Book*.

15   Sills and Henry, *Mother to Mother Baby Care Book*, p. 439.

16   Lortie, *Schoolteacher*, p. 10.

17   Sills and Henry, *Mother to Mother Baby Care Book*, p. 456.

18   Fred McDonald, "The Problems of Beginning Teachers: A Crisis in Training," in *Study of Induction Programs for Beginning Teachers*, vol. 2 (Princeton: Educational Testing Service, 1980), as quoted in Feiman-Nemser, "Learning to Teach," p. 161.

19   While some women believe that motherhood is "stagnating," the comment refers to the personal and professional growth of a woman who has devoted all her energies to child care, not stagnation in her role as mother, which changes as the child grows. In contrast, the concept in the teacher-development literature refers to stagnation in the role as teacher, which may or may not affect personal and other aspects of professional growth.

20   Ryan, "Toward Understanding the Problem," p. 45.

21   Feiman-Nemser, "Learning to Teach," p. 160.

22   Kevin Ryan, *Biting the Apple: Accounts of First Teachers* (New York: Longman, 1980).

23   Brazelton, *Infants and Mothers*, p. 208.

24   Kevin Ryan, "Why Bother with Induction," in *Beginning Teacher Induction—Five Dilemmas* (Austin, Tex.: Research and Development Center for Teacher Education, University of Texas, 1982), p. 20.

25   "An Overview of the Institute for Research on Teaching," (Michigan State University, October 1982), p. A-5.

26   Adapted from "An Overview of the Institute for Research on Teaching," p. C3.6.

27   Kepler, "BTES," p. 154.

28   Katz, "Mothering and Teaching," p. 49.

29   Lortie, *Schoolteacher*, p. 144.

30   Ibid., p. 152.

31   Katz, "Mothering and Teaching," p. 49.

32   Fred McDonald, quoted in J. T. Sandifur, "What Happens to the Teacher during Induction," in *Beginning Teacher Induction*, p. 38.

33   Ryan, *Biting the Apple*, p. 8.

34   Karen Zumwalt, "Research on Teaching: Policy Implications for Teacher Education," in *Policy Making in Education, Eighty-first Yearbook of the National Society for the Study of Education, Part I*, ed. Ann Lieberman and Milbrey Wallin McLaughlin (Chicago: University of Chicago Press, 1982), p. 224.

35   Donald A. Schön, *The Reflective Practitioner: How Professionals Think in Action* (New York: Basic Books, 1983).

36   Ibid., p. 30.

37   Fred McDonald, quoted in Sandifur, "What Happens to the Teacher during Induction?" p. 39.

38   Lortie, *Schoolteacher*, p. 62.

39   Ibid., p. 79.

40   Lilian G. Katz, "Issues and Problems in Teacher Education," in *Teacher Education: Of the Teacher, by the Teacher, for the Child*, ed. B. Spodek (Washington, D.C.: NAEYC, 1974), as quoted in Feiman-Nemser, "Learning to Teach," p. 155.

41   "An Overview of the Institute for Research on Teaching," p. A-26.

42   Katz, "Mothering and Teaching," p. 55.

43   Schön, *The Reflective Practitioner*, p. 68.

44   Feiman-Nemser, "Learning to Teach."

45   Ibid., p. 163.

46   Ibid., p. 160.

47   Judith W. Little, quoted in Feiman-Nemser, "Learning to Teach," p. 165.

48   Sheppard Ranbom, "Educators Seek Solutions to 'Crisis' in Teaching," *Education Week*, March 2, 1983, p. 1.

49   T. S. Eliot, quoted in Ryan, "Toward Understanding the Problems," p. 38.

Images of Schools

PHILLIP C. SCHLECHTY
University of North Carolina, Chapel Hill

ANNE WALKER JOSLIN
Charlotte-Mecklenburg Schools, North Carolina

Metaphors not only reveal how one thinks and defines problems; metaphors also shape actual behavior.[1] Thus, it should be possible to learn much about the nature of the current debate over school quality and school reform through careful attention to the metaphorical images that implicitly and explicitly inform this debate.

The purpose of the present article is to consider how some commonly used metaphors shape the way school problems are defined and how the implicit and explicit acceptance of these metaphors leads to—or supports—particular reform proposals and calls for action. The basic thesis to be presented is that the metaphors that are commonly used in arguments about education are not adequate to the task. Rather than liberating thinking about educational problems, these metaphors focus attention on solutions that are at best piecemeal and at worst misguided.

Metaphors should not, however, be rejected as useful tools for framing educational arguments. Indeed, metaphors are often the fundamental scaffolding surrounding serious efforts at developing comprehensive descriptions, explanations, and predictions. In a word, well chosen metaphors are useful beginning points for educational theorizing or indeed for theorizing in any field. However, the argument presented here is that the metaphors now used in educational debate are not well-chosen. In the last half of this article (after a discussion of some of the more commonly used metaphors), the metaphor of the school as a knowledge work organization will be advanced. This metaphor, we believe, has the potential of bringing together the positive strengths of some of the more commonly used metaphors, without presenting researchers and theoreticians with the limitations of these more commonly used images of schools.

The specific metaphors to be discussed are:

the school as a factory
the school as a hospital
the school as a log in a pastoral setting with Mark Hopkins on one end and a
    motivated or able student on the other end
the school as a family
the school as a war zone

147

THE SCHOOL AS A FACTORY

As Callahan has shown, the idea of a school as a factory is deeply embedded in educational thought and practice.[2] What is important is that the implicit use of the factory metaphor gives rise to a variety of reform recommendations that are quite consistent with the notions of mass production, assembly line techniques, and quality control. Some examples of these recommendations are:

1. Careful attention should be given to the development of sophisticated and reliable instruments to support inspection and quality-control efforts.
2. Tight supervision and detailed task analysis are the best ways to improve or maintain performance (e.g., direct instruction for children and tight supervision for teachers).
3. The best way to improve instruction is through detailed descriptions of student tasks and teacher tasks (e.g., detailed descriptions of classroom behavior systems and time-on-task research).
4. Rationalization, differentiation, and specialization are necessary to effective schools (e.g., strengthening teacher certification requirements, making sure that teachers do not teach out of field, developing clear job descriptions).
5. Individual workers (teachers) should be provided individual incentives for productivity (e.g., merit pay, bonuses for reduced absenteeism).

Not only does the factory metaphor shape the way problems and solutions are defined, it also shapes perceptions about how roles and relationships should be defined in schools. For example, the factory metaphor can be used to support the argument that principals should be viewed as managers, teachers as workers, and students as products. The factory image also suggests that human relationships should be characterized by dominance/submission, superordination/subordination, and passivity. Taken to its logical extreme, the factory metaphor suggests that students are nothing more than raw materials to be worked on, manipulated, and modified. Students (as raw material) are to be shaped, molded, and modified (behaviorally, of course) into useful products. In the most efficient school, the direction this "shaping" takes is predetermined and known. Furthermore, whether or not a product (student) is acceptable should be determined by quantifiable measures and assessed against known tolerance limits.

One should not assume that the factory model necessarily requires that one be insensitive or inhumane to differences among students. Indeed, one can as well justify individualized instruction on the basis of highly variable raw material as by other less dehumanizing perspectives. However, the tendency of the factory model to suggest that students are *things* can lead to callous disregard for human and aesthetic values. Indeed, those who embrace the factory model, especially at the secondary level and certainly at the college level, could certainly argue that one of the ways to decrease low-quality products is to take in only raw material of high quality. Furthermore, defective products that wind up on the scrap heap of society can be justified as the necessary cost of quality control.

THE SCHOOL AS A HOSPITAL

Having frequently attempted to use medical metaphors in describing teaching, especially teacher education, we are well aware that many teachers resent being compared with physicians. There are, obviously, many explanations for this resistance and resentment, not the least of which may be status envy. Yet, many programs and reform recommendations in the field of education assume that schools are or should be analogous to hospitals. For example:

1. It is often recommended, especially by teacher leaders, that management decisions and professional decisions should be clearly distinguished and that the professionals (i.e., teachers) should have autonomy in making professional decisions. The managers (i.e., principals and central office personnel) should have their decision-making authority limited to scheduling, purchasing, and coordinating. Many specific curriculum proposals and reform efforts, especially those directed toward children with special needs, are quite explicitly based on hospital models (e.g., diagnostic-prescriptive teaching, individual education plans).

2. The emphasis on individualized instruction, especially when connected to the more clinical aspects of schooling, clearly embraces the medical/ hospital model. School psychology, with its penchant for giving batteries of tests, clearly parallels the burgeoning testing movement in medicine. (Family physicians, like many school teachers, are concerned that the threat of litigation and the availability of sophisticated tests compels them to prescribe tests that may be harmful to the overall well-being of the patient. However, in a litigious society, such tests must be given "just in case.")

Since the hospital metaphor is less consistent with the realities of school than is the factory metaphor, those who view schools as hospitals are likely to be viewed as more radical reformers than are their more industrially minded counterparts. For example, if the medical/hospital metaphor were to come to dominate educational thought, it would cause fundamental reform in the power structure of schools. Those who now enjoy privilege and authority (e.g., administrators and specialists) would be subordinate to teachers. Salary structures would be modified to reflect this new condition. Class size, of course, would need to be reduced dramatically since the hospital/medical model assumes a one-on-one relationship between the client and his or her professional(s).

THE SCHOOL AS A LOG

One need only read the Paideia Proposal[3] or Theodore Sizer's[4] recent proposals for reform in schools to understand that the Mark Hopkins image continues to flourish as a source of educational criticism and recommendation. The reforms called for are, metaphorically speaking, clearing the brush from around the log so that the student and teacher can see each other. In more specific terms, the Hopkinsites recommend such things as:

1. Returning to a classic form of education in which the classics (or basics) are emphasized.
2. Giving teachers the high honor and status they deserve.
3. Selecting teachers from the brightest and best of college graduates and providing them with the materials, resources, and time to teach.
4. Removing discipline problems from the classroom posthaste.

(Indeed, some Hopkinsites argue for abolition of compulsory education so that those who are in schools are only those who "really want to learn.")

It should not go unnoticed that the Mark Hopkins model is more frequently used by those who address the problems of secondary schools than by those who address the problems of the elementary schools. Furthermore, many of the most outstanding proponents of the propriety of this model are themselves products of or employed by elite institutions of higher education. The metaphors used to define realities are, after all, products of the culture from which they derive.

THE SCHOOL AS A FAMILY

The metaphor of the school and/or class as a family is not commonly used in the public debate (i.e., the debate that occurs in the professional journals, newspapers, and mass media), but it is often used in the conversations in teachers' lounges and school corridors, especially in the lounges and corridors of elementary schools. Phrases like "my children," "individual differences," and "unique potential" are nearly as commonplace in some elementary schools as they are among concerned parents. And, like parents, elementary teachers resist and resent programs that destroy the integrity of the "family" (e.g., pull-out programs). One of the common complaints of elementary teachers is that "they are always taking my children away from me." Furthermore, when asked what specific recommendations for reform they might have, elementary teachers frequently make recommendations that are family-like. For example:

1. Children should be treated as unique individuals, each with his or her own capacities and limitations. The whole child should be taught.
2. Children should not be pushed to perform before they are ready.
3. Classroom teachers should be given time with their children, for the

relationship between teacher and children is the most important relationship in the school.

4. Teachers should not be taken away from their children for in-service. (Substitute teachers cannot do any more than baby-sit.)

THE SCHOOL AS A WAR ZONE

Among teachers, especially junior and senior high school teachers, the metaphorical expressions used frequently suggest a battlefield imagery. Few education professors have escaped the criticism that "you people in the ivory tower have been out of the trenches so long that . . ." Who has not heard the expression that "there is no substitute for frontline experience"? The combative imagery is sometimes expressed by teachers when they leave the teachers' lounge in phrases like "well, back to the wars" or "back to the trenches."

The battlefield imagery is sometimes used to convey the notion that students are "troops to be commanded and armies to be deployed." At other times, the suggestion is that students (and parents) are enemies to be conquered, that classes are battles to be won, and that lesson plans are matters of strategy and tactics.

Regardless of the specific forms the imagery takes, the battlefield metaphor generally conveys a sense that conflict, hostility, and aggressive action are a normal and expected part of school and classroom life. Winning and losing take on special meanings in such a context and cooperation and accommodation take on strange meanings. (Young teachers who get too friendly with students are often viewed by their more senior colleagues as persons who "collaborate with the enemy." Faculties must present a "united front.") Even the way the term *burnout* is used in education is vaguely reminiscent of the term "battle fatigue."

Some of the recommendations that logically derive from the battlefield metaphor are:

1. Actions should be taken to establish or reestablish the authority of teachers.
2. Corporal punishment should be viewed as a legitimate form of discipline.
3. Disruptive students should be expelled from schools and classrooms.
4. Administrators and teachers should present a united front. (An effective principal always backs his or her teachers.)
5. Teachers who teach in undesirable locations should receive "combat pay."

A BRIEF CRITIQUE

We will never have a proper grasp of schools and the schooling process until we are able to describe and analyze schools in terms that reflect the unique characteristics of the schooling enterprise. Schools are schools. Schools are not factories, hospitals, or even families. It is unfortunately the case that we still do not have an adequate enough grasp of schools to describe them in their own terms. Consequently, those who discuss school matters rely heavily on metaphors.

Given the preceding discussion of some of the prevailing metaphorical frames that are used in the current educational debate and given the general knowledge of the content of that debate, it should be clear that most who engage in the debate over educational quality mix the metaphors they use freely and probably without conscious thought. Mixing metaphors can cause or signify sloppy thinking. Clearly, the debate over educational quality is not free from sloppy thinking, but such thinking may not be the only reason for mixing metaphors in educational arguments. It may be, and we think it is, the case that the reason mixed metaphors are used in educational debate is that the metaphors commonly used are not adequate to the task. For example, ordinary language clearly indicates that schools are places of work. Educators, parents, and students talk about homework, class work, seat work, and busy work. Thus, there is an intuitive appeal to the notion of the school as a place of work. Fortunately or unfortunately, the most salient work place in our society, at least until recent years, has been the factory. Thus, the factory metaphor has appeal.

Yet, schools are not, or should not be, factory-like. Ideas do not develop on a prearranged schedule. Indeed, children do not develop on a prearranged schedule. Certainty, prediction, and control, all of which are essential to the manufacturing process, simply do not exist in the public school environment. Indeed, the more one attempts to impose certainty and control, the more one is likely to produce curricula and outcomes that are antithetical to other desired outcomes (e.g., creativity and critical thought).

Just as the factory or work-place metaphor has intuitive appeal, so does the hospital or medical metaphor. For example, we know that in the end what happens in school is what happens to individual children. Thus, the unique needs of the individual must be taken into account and teachers must be given latitude in deciding how to respond to those needs just as a physician must render professional judgments and decisions. Yet the reality of schools overwhelms the hospital/medical metaphor. As Lortie,[5] Dreeben,[6] and others have observed, unlike doctors, teachers have not been socialized as professionals. Indeed, teachers do not even possess a common language to describe their actions. Without such a common language, practice cannot be submitted to critical evaluation. What is more, teachers seldom deal with individual children. Rather, teachers deal with classes, groups, collectivities, and aggregates. Mass psychology and mob psychology may be as important to the teacher as is clinical psychology—or so it can be argued. Teacher as actor and student as audience may be as useful an analytic tool as is teacher as professional and student as client. Thus, the hospital/medical metaphor model breaks down in the face of other realities of school.

Mark Hopkins and the log is an ideologically compelling metaphor precisely because most of those who are concerned with schools, especially secondary schools, are products of the *academy,* from which the metaphor arises. In addition, classroom teachers and building administrators seem to enjoy the reveries of the pastoral scenes created by the Mark Hopkins imagery. Nostalgic conversations of by-gone days (which probably never were) can perhaps help relieve the tension of weary teachers and harried administrators. But in the reality of schools where some students are bright and highly motivated and other students are barely functional, where street noises invade the classroom and jet aircraft drown out the teacher's voice, the pastoral scenes stirred up by the image of Mark Hopkins and the log become nothing more than a pleasant reverie. Indeed, this pleasant daydream can make reality appear, by contrast, quite nightmarish.

For persons who enter teaching (as many teachers do) to help others and to nurture the young, the image of the school and the school class as a family also has appeal. Given the crushing power of bureaucracy and the debilitating effects of depersonalized and mechanistic approaches to teaching, clinging to the family imagery undoubtedly bolsters many teachers' feelings of worth in systems where students and teachers are victimized. However, the family metaphor does little to suggest how schools can or should be organized, for there are vast differences between families and schools and school classes. Among other things, there are simply too many children and too few adults. Patterns of age segregation and subject-matter specialization vary markedly from the realities of family life. As Harry Broudy notes, the intimacy of knowledge that would be required of teachers to deal with the whole child (as parents should do) is beyond the capacity of schoolteachers.[7] Not only do teachers have too many children to know, they know students far too short a time. In the life of a child, a semester or even a year is a short period of time. Even the most detailed record keeping cannot make up for the tacit understandings gained from living with a child.

School as war, while ideologically repugnant to some, often serves as an expressive metaphor for teachers who feel beseiged and threatened. Certainly, popular accounts of life in classrooms, including accounts provided by persons in high political office, would lead one to believe that schools are battlefields where casualties are taken every day.

Unfortunately, wars always have losers and some wars never have winners. Indeed, war signifies a fundamental breakdown in human rationality and a disruption of national discourse between and among the warring parties. Wars seldom solve problems and wars are seldom solutions though wars do dislocate problems and create the need for solutions.

Thus, the metaphor of the school as war holds little prospect for development of long-term solutions. What the persistent and widespread use of the warfare metaphor might suggest is the need for a new way to frame the educational debate.

THE SCHOOL AS A KNOWLEDGE WORK ORGANIZATION:
A SYNTHESIZING METAPHOR

The purpose of school is to provide youth with those experiences that adults believe will foster the ability to master, articulate, and use the dominant symbol systems of the culture. The existence of some of these symbol systems are apparent to all (e.g., language systems, number systems). There are, however, other symbols as well (e.g., stories and modes of explanation— clusters of symbols) that convey the dominant values of the culture or suggest culturally approved standards of beauty, truth, and justice. Symbols are shared ways of expressing ideas and concepts. One of the symbols used to stand for ideas and systems of ideas is the word *knowledge.* Thus, it can be argued that, broadly conceived, the purpose of schooling is to motivate, instruct, and support children in doing tasks that will foster the ability to use knowledge. Hence, it can be argued that the purpose of schools is to get children to do knowledge work.

In preindustrial and industrial societies, schools and institutions of higher education were the dominant knowledge work organizations in society. Thus, if schools could not be understood in their own terms (i.e., without the benefit of metaphors), there were few sources of metaphorical analysis available in the larger culture. With the emergence of the postindustrial society, however, knowledge work organizations have emerged as one of the most important organizational phenomena in our culture. Indeed, as Drucker[8] and others have pointed out, in the twenty-first century, knowledge work will be the dominant occupation of most of those who graduate from our schools.

EMERGING LITERATURE

Students of education have frequently pointed out that the general literature in the field of management and organizational theory is of limited usefulness in the study of schools. The reason this is so, these critics suggest, is that most of the literature on management and organizational theory is based on models of factories, hospitals, and military organizations, all of which are unlike schools. However, beginning in the early 1960s, management theorists (e.g., Dreeben[9]) began to seriously address issues related to managing managers and managing professionals. Implicit and explicit in this literature is the assumption that the kinds of management styles and organizational styles that are appropriate to motivating, instructing, and evaluating persons who manipulate symbols and who manage people is fundamentally different from the organizational forms appropriate for dealing with persons who manipulate and produce physical objects. Unfortunately, few of the ideas contained in this literature have, until quite recently, been seriously considered by educators. Even more unfortunately, those ideas that were considered were often misunderstood and misapplied. For example, the idea of results-oriented management and management by objectives was crudely adopted by some educators, but in its educational manifestation, results-oriented management became measurement-dominated management and management by objectives became management by behavioral objectives. Few educators understood the subtle differences between management results and results of management. Even fewer seemed to grasp the differences between efficiency and effectiveness.[10]

In recent years, a number of popular books have caught the attention of educators. Among the more frequently cited are W. G. Ouchi's *Theory Z*, *The Art of Japanese Management* by Richard Tanner Pascale and Anthony G. Athos, *In Search of Excellence* by Thomas J. Peters and Robert H. Waterman, and *High Output Management* by Andrew F. Grove.[11] It is our view that one of the reasons this literature has intuitive appeal to educators is that these authors have identified the school-like qualities of knowledge work organizations. We think educational thought could be advanced considerably if educational researchers would center their attention more directly on the knowledge work qualities of schools. The remainder of this article is intended to illustrate some of the ideas about schools that the knowledge work metaphor seems to suggest.

STUDENTS AS KNOWLEDGE WORKERS

As has been noted elsewhere, educational theorists have generally been ambivalent about the social position of students in the school.[12] Sometimes students are viewed as members (i.e., inside the school), sometimes they are viewed as products, and sometimes as clients. The knowledge work metaphor resolves this issue. Students are insiders for they are the primary workers. Thus, the immediate determinant of productivity in the schools is dependent on the work done by students. Such a view squares with the lament of teachers that much of the effect of what they do is dependent on the characteristics of the students they teach. (As will be seen shortly, however, the knowledge work metaphor does not relieve teachers of accountability for productivity of students. It does refocus attention on those elements related to student productivity for which the teacher can and should be held accountable.)

The power of the idea of the student as knowledge worker is perhaps best revealed in the suggestion the knowledge work metaphor provides for interpreting and explaining some of the results of recent research on effective teaching. There is a striking parallel between what the effective-teaching literature has shown to be effective with children and what the management literature has shown to be effective with unskilled workers. Tight supervision, clearly defined tasks, immediate corrective feedback, and careful inspection of how the task is done are all recommended strategies in the supervision of unskilled workers.[13] The parallels between these recommended strategies and the strategies growing out of the effective-teaching literature (e.g., careful monitoring, immediate corrective feedback, and the provision of clear tasks with a high probable success rate) are to us, at least, not surprising. After all, a great deal of the research on effective teaching has been done in relation to unskilled knowledge workers (i.e., young children and children from impoverished backgrounds). Furthermore, the dependent variables for most of this research (gain scores on basic skills tests in language and mathematics) are themselves measures of low-level products that one would expect unskilled workers to produce with the right kind of supervision. Where the effective teaching literature falls short is in providing direction in how to supervise (i.e., teach) children as they move from being unskilled knowledge workers to being skilled knowledge workers or as they move from being skilled knowledge workers to being professional knowledge workers. The effective-teaching literature is almost totally devoid of suggestions for teaching higher-order skills and abilities. If the knowledge work metaphor has any power, one might expect that as children become skilled knowledge workers, the appropriate teaching strategies would be totally different from those used to teach unskilled knowledge workers. Literature in management and supervision suggests that skilled knowledge workers function better when they have considerable control over the conditions of their work and when evaluative feedback is based on the products produced rather than on the way one produces the products. Similarly, there is growing evidence that professional knowledge workers are more productive when they have considerable control over both the conditions of work and the types of products to be produced.[14]

In summary, it is being suggested that the management and teaching styles in the secondary schools could be improved if some lessons were taken from the management and teaching styles used at IBM and Hewlett-Packard. In a view of students as knowledge workers, an entire new literature is open to educational researchers and theoreticians and that is the literature related to the management of unskilled, skilled, and professional knowledge workers. This literature might well provide useful recommendations to the theoretical knowledge about effective teaching and also provide provocative hypotheses for future research. Certainly, there are differences between Public School 109 and IBM, but the differences are not nearly so great as the differences between Public School 109 and Bethlehem Steel.

THE TEACHER AS EXECUTIVE/MANAGER

In a recent article, David Berliner argues for the proposition that it might be well to conceive of the role of teacher as executive.[15] He goes on to describe how closely the functions of executives parallel the functions of teachers. Berliner's argument will not be summarized here. Rather, it will be asserted that by viewing the student as worker, one is compelled to reconceptualize the role of teacher. The logical reconceptualization moves the teacher from the role of worker (as in the factory model) to the role of first-line supervisor or executive. As Berliner's article illustrates, such a conceptualization causes one to apply theories and propositions to teaching that have heretofore escaped the attention of most who do research on teachers and teaching. Equally important, such a conceptualization has the effect of enhancing the status of teachers and contains the possibility that the authority relationships in which teachers commonly find themselves could be redesigned.

As will be seen in the section that immediately follows, this conceptualization could satisfy many of the conditions suggested by the medical/hospital model without violating the realities of the school. The chief reality that the hospital/medical metaphor violates is that in the reality of schools, teacher success depends on the ability to motivate, direct, and instruct large groups of youngsters to do work that, it is assumed, will lead to learning. Seldom do teachers teach individuals.

THE PRINCIPAL AS MANAGER OF MANAGERS

If the teacher is an executive/manager, then the principal is no longer a manager of production workers. Neither is the principal similar to a hospital administrator, where it is assumed that there are necessary antagonisms between bureaucrats and professionals. Finally, the principal is not some unnecessary vegetation blocking the view of Mark Hopkins from his students. Rather, the principal, much like the director of a research-and-development component or the plant manager of a semi-autonomous branch of 3M Corporation, is a manager of managers. Principals would know, or should know, that many who work for them and many whose work they are asked to evaluate know more about their work than do the principals. They would know, or should know, that by virtue of the office occupied, they have position power. However, by virtue of personal expertise and hands-on experience, those they manage probably understand better than others what is needed to assure maximum productivity of the work force for which they are responsible. Such a view of the role of principal would certainly refocus debates surrounding teacher evaluation. Among other things, it would cause school systems to view teacher evaluation as something more than the scientific checklist and behavioral indicators that so warm Tayloresque hearts. Results-oriented management would probably replace management by behavioral objectives. It would probably become commmonplace that evaluative conferences would center on goal setting, timelines to be met, products to be presented, and mutually agreed upon criteria for evaluating the merit and worth of these products. These goal-setting conferences would probably be a time when the teacher/manager could indicate the resources he or she would need if the timelines were to be met and the products to be forthcoming.

In summary, it is being suggested that if the knowledge work metaphor were consistently applied in thinking about the organization of schools, many of the debates and questions that are now raised would be refocused. For example, the evaluation system of knowledge work organizations assumes a developmental stance. Outcomes cannot always be predicted and controlled, but once outcomes emerge, they can be measured and assigned some worth. Short-term, sporadic evaluations would be abandoned and continuous evaluation would take their place. Feelings of mutualism and collegial support would be enhanced. Evaluation and staff development would no longer be separated since staff development would be a part of evaluation. In knowledge work organizations, evaluations are viewed as the primary means by which the organization communicates to its members what the expectations are and should be, and as any good staff developer knows, clear expectations are essential to improved performance.

THE ORGANIZATION OF SCHOOL SYSTEMS

Just as the knowledge work metaphor does not lose its power when one moves beyond the classroom, it does not lose its power when one moves beyond the schoolhouse door. This is especially true if one conceives of knowledge work organizations as organizations that commit a substantial portion of their energy to creating novel responses to market conditions and are successful at this endeavor.[16] Given such a definition, the knowledge work metaphor can shed considerable light, or at least shed some provocative light, on the management of school systems as well as of school buildings. For example, one of the most perplexing problems in educational theory, research, and practice is the problem of centralization/decentralization. Some people argue for decentralization if for no other reason than that the empirical realities of schools suggest such a strategy to be appropriate. The effective-schools literature clearly suggests, for example, that the building-level units and characteristics of the principal are critical determinants of school effectiveness. This being the case, some argue that school policy should be developed to foster the inventive genius of building-level units.[17] On the surface, such an argument has appeal. Yet the idea of a school system suggests that there should be some unifying quality among the school buildings that are a part of that system. Concepts of equity would suggest that the quality of education received by children should not be determined by the luck of the draw or the unique characteristics of the faculty and principal of the school to which they are assigned. What Peters and Waterman suggest is that the dichotomy between centralization and decentralization is a false one.[18] Depending on conditions, some functions should be decentralized and others should not. There are two elements that should never be decentralized and one that cannot be decentralized. The establishment and articulation of superordinate goals and binding myths is necessarily a function of the top administration of the organization. Articulation of the unique values and commitments and reinforcement of these values and commitments in behavior as well as words must flow from the top. What the school system is about, where the school system is going, and what problems must be given priority must be preached from the superintendent's office. Many kinds of authority can be delegated, but the moral authority to articulate the school system's way, its values and commitments, must reside with the chief executive officer. Thus, the selection of the superintendent must involve more than choosing a technically competent and academically well-prepared administrator. The superintendent is or should be the chief teacher in the school system—the person who defines problems and inspires others to solve them. Leadership, then, is more important than managerial skill, though managerial skill is not to be discounted.

A second responsibility that cannot be delegated is responsibility for bottom-line results. In the end, the quality of performance of the work force in schools as well as the quality of the work force at IBM is the responsibility of the chief executive officer. As one large city school system superintendent put the matter, "Test scores and other measures of student achievement are like profits in a large corporation. You don't hold first line supervisors [i.e., teachers] accountable for profits at IBM. You hold the CEO accountable. What the first line supervisor is accountable for is doing those things that top management believes will produce profits. If first line supervisors do those things well, they should be rewarded. If these things do not lead to profit and growth in the long run, the CEO should be fired, not the first line supervisor."

The one element that cannot be centralized regardless of strenuous effort to do so is problem-solving capacity. Problems cannot be solved from the top down. They must be solved from the bottom up. But the problems that are to be solved and are worth being solved can only be decided from the top with, of course, suggestions, directions, and advocacy for this or that problem as a priority item coming from the bottom to the top. Championing problems and championing solutions should be just as much encouraged in schools as it is in America's best-run companies.

In summary, one of the lessons that the knowledge work metaphor might teach us about school administration, especially in large school systems, is that the function of the central office is problem identification, not problem solving. Problem solving is best left to those whose hands-on experience and expertise provide them with the advanced knowledge to invent novel solutions.

A FINAL COMMENT

Other implications for the use of the knowledge work metaphor have not been developed here because of space limitations. For example, ways in which the knowledge work metaphor might inform decisions about curriculum and curriculum design have not been discussed. In addition, implications of the knowledge work metaphor in regard to the need for long-term planning and work-place and marketplace embedded research and development activity have not been discussed. What we have tried to do is to suggest that the prevailing metaphors we use in our debates about schools limit our vision. Worse, they are based on institutional forms whose vitality and importance in modern society are presently in doubt. The very term *postindustrial society* suggests that the factory metaphor is a historical relic.

The status, authority, and power of traditional professions like medicine and law are now undergoing serious challenge and even a nonfuturist might suspect that what is now understood as professionalism and the professional models that support it will soon undergo fundamental alteration. The pastoral scene suggested by the Mark Hopkins metaphor perhaps never existed even in great universities, but if it did, it no longer does. Indeed, even the most elite universities are experiencing considerable difficulty in competing with the knowledge work organizations, especially in competing for personnel with the qualities of mind suggested by Mark Hopkins. One need only visit some of the major corporations to recognize that the leisure of the theory class is shifting from the university to the corporate world. Given this view, we have suggested that it might help to inform our debate if the metaphors selected were drawn from emerging organizational forms rather than those of a bygone era. Not only might such metaphors drag and push schools and educational research into the twenty-first century; such metaphors might also be more consistent with the realities of schools. Schools are, after all, places where children and youth are brought together to work on knowledge. Whether they learn to work well or poorly may well determine whether America will lead or follow in the search for excellence in the postindustrial society.

Notes

1   Ernest House, "How We Think about Evaluation," in his *Philosophy of Evaluation: New Directions for Program Evaluation* (San Francisco: Jossey-Bass, 1983).

2   R. E. Callahan, *Education and the Cult of Efficiency* (Chicago: University of Chicago Press, 1962).

3   Mortimer Adler, *The Paideia Proposal: An Educational Manifesto* (New York: Macmillan, 1983).

4   Theodore R. Sizer and Thomas F. Koermer, *Perspectives: A Review and Comment on National Studies* (Reston, Va.: National Association of Secondary School Principals, 1983).

5   Dan C. Lortie, *Schoolteacher* (Chicago: University of Chicago Press, 1975).

6   Robert S. Dreeben, *The Nature of Teaching* (Glenview, Ill.: Scott Foresman, 1970).

7   Harry S. Broudy, *The Real World of the Public Schools* (San Diego: Harcourt Brace Jovanovich, 1972).

8   Peter Drucker, *Management: Tasks, Responsibilities, Practices* (New York: Harper & Row, 1973).

9   Dreeben, *The Nature of Teaching.*

10   Having suggested the significance of these distinctions, we should perhaps spend time in a discussion of the nature of these differences. Given space limitations, we cannot provide such a discussion. The reader who finds these distinctions of interest is advised to read (or reread) Drucker's *Management* and Andrew Grove's *High Output Management* (New York: Random House, 1983). To us it is not altogether clear how it came to be that results-oriented management, which Drucker called management by objectives, came to be distorted by educators to the point that when teachers and administrators hear the term *management by objectives* they immediately think of behavioral objectives. We think this is unfortunate, for such books as *The Art of Japanese Management* by Richard Tanner Pascale and Anthony G. Athos (New York: Simon & Schuster, 1981) and *In Search of Excellence* by Thomas L. Peters and Robert H. Waterman (New York: Harper & Row, 1982) clearly show that there is not a necessary antagonism between management that focuses on reasonable results and innovativeness, creativity, and a sense of being in control of one's own work life. Yet, when teachers and administrators hear the terms *results-oriented management* and *management by objectives,* the image they have is of a stifling bureaucracy in which it is more important to do things efficiently than to do them effectively.

11   W. G. Ouchi, *Theory Z* (Reading, Mass.: Addison-Wesley, 1981); Pascale and Athos, *The Art of Japanese Management;* Peters and Waterman, *In Search of Excellence;* and Grove, *High Output Management.*

12   Phillip C. Schlechty, *Teaching Social Behavior: Toward an Organizational Theory of Instruction* (Boston: Allyn and Bacon, 1976).

13   See, for example, Robert Dubin, *Human Relations in Administration, with Readings,* 3rd ed. (Englewood Cliffs, N.J.: Prentice-Hall, 1968).

14   The idea of students' having control over the conditions of work and the products to be produced might strike the reader as reminiscent of the past, when the cry was to let the student do his or her own thing at his or her own pace. A return to the lack of direction of the past is not being suggested here. What is being suggested is that if schools, particularly secondary schools, have clear and distinct goals, and if the teaching and management styles in those schools are properly oriented, the skilled and professional work force in the secondary schools (i.e., the students) could conceivably be brought to pursue excellence in the achievement of individuals goals that are consistent with the overall goals of the school.

15   David Berliner, "Executive Functions of Teaching," *Instructor,* September 1983, pp. 18–33, 36, 38, 40.

16   Peters and Waterman, *In Search of Excellence.*

17   See, for example, John I. Goodlad, "The School as Workplace," in *Staff Development: Eighty-second Yearbook of the National Society for the Study of Education,* ed. Gary A. Griffin (Chicago: University of Chicago Press, 1983).

18   Peters and Waterman, *In Search of Excellence.*

Teacher Evaluation and School Improvement

MILBREY WALLIN MCLAUGHLIN
Stanford University

Policymakers at all levels of government are pressured to respond to critical conclusions about the status of American education[1] and to escalating public demand to "do something" about the schools. Questions of education quality, consequently, are on the agenda of most state legislatures and local school boards[2] and the debate about "solutions" is heated. Teacher evaluation, this article argues, can be a powerful strategy for achieving these school-improvement goals.

Practitioners may find this position surprising if not wrong-headed. Many doubt that teacher evaluation can serve both accountability objectives and improvement concerns. Indeed, many practitioners have divorced improvement and assessment purposes in teacher evaluation so that staff-development activities will not be seen as punitive. But it is also true that few districts have actively pursued links between teacher evaluation and improvement. Most educators see current teacher evaluation practice as a waste of time and resources. In a majority of school districts, teacher evaluation constitutes an uneven, desultory ritual that contributes little to school improvement but much to teacher anxiety and administrator burden.[3]

As teacher evaluation typically is conceived and practiced, it could be little more. Most teacher evaluations comprise standard checklists completed by the principal after a brief classroom observation. Principals usually base ratings on their own sense of good practice; not surprisingly, assessments based in the "I know what I like" school of evaluation can vary among schools and classrooms. Evaluation in this instance reflects a principal's individual preferences rather than a consistent set of criteria to inform either accountability or improvement.

However, principal inconstancy is less problematic than it might be because most teachers receive "satisfactory" or "outstanding" ratings; "needs improvement" or "unsatisfactory" findings are rare. Administrators explain the preponderance of these salutory assessments in terms of the political and bureaucratic problems associated with teacher evaluation. Low ratings risk conflict with the teachers' organization; evaluators do not have the skills to confidently do more; support from "downtown" is often not forthcoming in the event of a negative or controversial appraisal; insufficient time and resources are available to respond to less than satisfactory ratings anyway.

Teachers are no happier with the current state of assessment practice. Strong teachers complain that this system does not acknowledge excellence, provides feedback too general to be useful, and fails to document incompetence. Weaker teachers are also dissatisfied. They express resentment that hoped-for diagnosis and assistance is not a result of their evaluation and that their satisfactory marks are meaningless.

Teachers assert that a checklist approach to evaluation, especially one grounded in a process-product model that assumes specific teacher behaviors lead to particular learner outcomes, is an irrelevant and inappropriate evaluation tool. A number of serious concerns are raised about this deterministic approach to teacher evaluation. Among them:

1. Learner outcomes are cumulative; it is difficult to isolate the effect of any one teacher on student performance.

2. Teacher behaviors and activities interact with numerous factors to affect student performance. Student socioeconomic status, school climate, pupil abilities, previous instructional treatment, are but a few of the many factors that determine teacher effectiveness for any given student.[4] Teacher "effectiveness," however defined, is highly contextual and conditional.

3. Teachers vary enormously in the practices that work for them and the problems they confront in their particular classrooms.[5] As Good, a longtime student of teacher effectiveness, put it: "One myth that has been discredited by classroom observation is that schooling is a constant experience with teachers behaving in similar ways and pursuing similar goals with a common curriculum."[6] No single instructional program works for all teachers or all students; effectiveness depends on the classroom context. Thus there can be "no single, simple method of evaluating teacher effectiveness because there is no single concept of what the teacher should be undertaking in the classroom."[7]

4. Teachers' effectiveness varies depending on the goals defined for the student or the class. Not only are the objectives described for students multiple and substantively diverse (e.g., academic, emotional, or social outcomes) but the strategies successful in achieving one goal (memorization of facts, for example) are often counterproductive for other instructional objectives (e.g., higher-order problem-solving skills).[8] Further, the effectiveness of particular teacher practices may be curvilinear: Too much of a good thing can depress outcomes.[9]

Yet most teacher evaluation activities, with their closed-ended checklists, prescriptive categories, and ambiguous standards, disregard this complexity. The incompetence of principals as teacher evaluators compounds instrumentation problems. Teachers seldom respect principals as experts on classroom practice or as skilled classroom observers,[10] and in the absence of principal credibility, teachers consider the evaluation illegitimate comment on their performance and ignore its findings. Given the state of teacher evaluation practices in most districts, then, misgivings about the ability of teacher evaluation to contribute to school improvement are unsurprising. As an essentially bureaucratic mechanism, present teacher evaluation practices can inform neither practice nor policy in a meaningful way.

But theory and experience suggest that teacher evaluation of another stripe can support teacher growth and development, strengthen the role of the principal, and contribute significantly to the vitality and coherence of the school.[11] A number of school districts have adopted teacher evaluation practices based in principals' strengthened supervisory, diagnostic, and prescriptive skills. In districts that are moving away from the deterministic, process-product model of teacher evaluation, principals are trained to observe classroom practices, assess teacher solutions to classroom problems, gauge the quality of teacher-student interactions, and analyze the structure of instructional processes. Principal training framed in this model acknowledges the conditional nature of teacher effectiveness and focuses on individual teacher judgments and choices within broad and widely held categories for effective teaching.[12]

TEACHER EVALUATION AND IMPROVEMENT

Experience shows that teacher evaluation based in this process perspective supports the formal authority of the principal as evaluator with *functional* authority based in technical knowledge, evaluation skills, and shared language. Teacher evaluation grounded in this design is a potent tool for school improvement because it can affect factors that are fundamental to how teachers and principals go about their jobs and how well they carry out their responsibilities for instruction and management.[13] Most important are:

> teacher motivation and sense of efficacy
> effective communication and shared goals
> principal's instructional leadership
> teacher learning and development

TEACHER MOTIVATION AND SENSE OF EFFICACY

It is axiomatic that teachers' motivation and their sense of professional effectiveness are central to school-improvement efforts and to maintaining high-quality classroom practices. Teachers' sense of efficacy is tied to an educator's primary source of satisfaction, the intrinsic rewards associated with the teaching role—service to youngsters or transmitting knowledge associated with a particular discipline.[14] The extrinsic rewards attached to a teaching career are low; the ancillary benefits (with the exception of a long summer vacation) are effectively nonexistent.

Yet it is difficult for teachers to collect the intrinsic rewards that motivate them and provide satisfaction. The greatest obstacle to teacher sense of efficacy, ironically, is lack of feedback about their performance—credible information about how well they are carrying out their responsibilities. To this point, significant and recurrent doubt about the worth of their work with students is a consistent teacher characteristic.[15] Efficacy, as this suggests, is not entirely an internal construct; it relies on environmental response that acknowledges good performance.[16] A number of factors frustrate teacher participation in what Lortie calls "craft pride" or efficacy.[17] The structure of the profession itself makes it difficult for teachers to experience professional accomplishment. Most professions ideally are characterized by explicit career progress, not by a static position of competent practice.[18] Teaching, however, is a relatively "flat" occupation, with few of the stages or plateaus that mark accomplishment and success in other professions—medicine or law, for example. Thus there is little in the structure of the profession to tell teachers they are doing a good job.

Another impediment to teacher sense of efficacy is inherent in the teaching task. Unlike other areas of professional or semiprofessional activity, there is no agreed-upon technical core of knowledge or unambiguous set of guidelines for successful practice.[19] Furthermore, "outcomes" for teachers are relatively complex, ambiguous, indeterminate, and long-run. A lawyer can judge success by case outcome; an agronomist can measure achievement by the number and type of new agricultural techniques in place. Teachers, however, have no such unequivocal or unitary measure. Student achievement scores, the outcome measure favored by school boards, citizens, and policymakers, are not seen as adequate measures of effectiveness by teachers.[20] Classroom effectiveness, in the teachers' view, rests in the successful diagnosis of classroom problems and the selection of strategies to meet them and in producing long-term changes in youngsters' attitudes and capacity. As one particularly acid commentator on the process-product school of teacher effectiveness research put it: "Teachers are not hired to cram information into students' heads to be retained just long enough to enable them to pass objective tests. Teachers are hired to educate children, to produce important, lasting changes in their behavior, not short-term changes in test scores."[21] Successful teaching outcomes, in this view, are as indeterminate as the practice itself.

Ironically, then, while self-reflection lies at the heart of professionalism,[22] self-monitoring and assessment are difficult for teachers to carry out. There is no template for success that teachers can lay beside their performance and assess the extent to which they have achieved their personal and professional goals. And long-term outcomes may never be evident to teachers. Consequently, teachers must rely on the reflection and feedback of others to gauge their effectiveness and support professional pride. For this feedback to be credible, it must come from individuals who teachers believe can make authoritative judgments about their performance.

The norms and the process of schooling preclude those individuals most able to provide that feedback—fellow teachers—from doing so. The cellular structure of the school and the isolation of teachers in their classrooms is much remarked upon.[23] Teachers have little opportunity to observe their peers, to compare classroom practices, or to comment on collegial practices. Instead, time spent with colleagues during the school day typically is perceived as "stolen."[24] But even if opportunities for peer observation were increased, the norms dominant in most school settings prohibit collegial assessment. Conventions of teacher autonomy join with norms of collegial support to make peer criticism unprofessional. So strong is this ideology of noninterference that even when teachers know about "bad" practices, they will make no move either to assist a colleague or inform responsible adminstrators.[25]

The principal, in his or her role as evaluator, thus has a crucial role to play in providing the credible feedback essential to a teacher's sense of efficacy. Regular classroom observations, based in principal-evaluator classroom expertise and observational skills, can provide the review and diagnosis essential to teacher satisfaction, efficacy, and growth. Far from perceiving visits from a competent principal-evaluator as a "threat" or a waste of time, teachers view them as professionally and personally rewarding. To this point, districts studied as part of the preliminary research for Rand's teacher evaluation study provide strong evidence of teacher support for this principal role. A teacher in one New Jersey district, inadvertently excluded from evaluation visits on two occasions, somewhat playfully filed a grievance for being overlooked. Teachers in a Minnesota district with a strong, diagnostically based teacher evaluation system voted to continue funds for teacher evaluation as a high priority when the district's budget was trimmed. In Washington state, teachers amended their collective bargaining agreement to include more and unannounced principal visits; they felt that principals were not seeing what was "really going on" and so the feedback to teachers—positive and negative—was less useful than it might be. In districts such as these, teachers have come to value their evaluations as an important source of information about their performance and primary support for their sense of efficacy and so for their professionalism.

COMMUNICATION AND SHARED GOALS

Open, frequent, and candid communication among teachers and school administrators is characteristic of effective schools[26] and a factor in successful planned change activities.[27] Effective communication is two-way and includes significant emphasis on instructional, not just administrative, matters.

Communication of this nature is not easy to achieve and is not part of the normal character of information transmission within school buildings. Bureaucratic pressures encourage one-way telegraphic communication rather than conversation between teachers and administrators. Even when the occasion for exchange presents itself, communication is less effective than it might be because teachers and administrators lack common language. An important result of principal training in clinical supervision is acquisition of this common language.[28] Such training permits principal-evaluators to speak clearly, precisely, and very specifically to teachers about their performance, to interpret classroom events, and to analyze teaching practices. Principals are thus able to move beyond global statements about teacher performance ("Keep up the good work!" "More discipline is needed during seat work.") to discuss particular concepts of classroom practice and provide teachers concrete examples gathered by observation (e.g., pointing out that a teacher spends most of her time teaching to the right side of the classroom). As one teacher, commenting on her principals' supervisory and evaluation expertise, put it: "It puts words on problems as well as strengths. I have a clear notion of what needs to be improved and [concerning her own documented improvement] I really don't think all of this would have been possible without evaluation."[29]

Providing principals with the skills to make classroom observations of this diagnostic nature and communicate findings in ways that teachers can relate directly to classroom practice supports communication in the other direction as well. Teaching staff in schools where principals possess this expertise report that they talk much more with principals about classroom issues because shared language makes such a conversation possible. Judith Warren Little noted this phenomenon in her study of school success and staff development: "[Only administrator observation of classroom practices] and feedback can provide the *shared referents* for the shared language of teaching, and both demand and provide the precision and concreteness which makes talk about teaching useful."[30] Teacher evaluation rooted in administrator observation and diagnostic skill, in short, provides both the language and the content of the communication associated with effective schools and improved practice—concrete talk about instruction and strategies for improvement.

This kind of evaluation allows principals to inform teachers regularly about school-wide goals and to assess teacher performance in terms of these goals. Thus teacher evaluation can support the mutual understanding between teachers and administrators that is necessary to combat the segmented and sometimes incompatible practices seen in many schools. At the same time, it can provide the information to enable teachers and administrators to align instructional content, classroom activities, and instructional goals. This strategy thus moves both knowledge and practice of a school's professional staff toward the shared goals crucial to school improvement and effectiveness.[31]

PRINCIPAL LEADERSHIP

The central and essential function of the principal in school improvement and school effectiveness as "instructional leader" or "gatekeeper of change" has become a truism. A substantial body of research focuses on the activities associated with this pivotal role—for example, identifying and supporting good classroom practices, integrating school-wide instructional activities, and keeping activities of the professional staff apace of changing school needs, district priorities, and knowledge about more effective practice.[32] Teacher evaluation can be the key to principal leadership because it provides the occasion, structure, and information that support these activities, namely, regular teacher observation, discussion about teacher work problems, and assistance to teachers through regular feedback and analysis.[33]

Teacher evaluation also allows principals to exercise effective control over the quality of classroom practice because it appeals to teacher incentives for improvement and growth and assists in the "counseling out" of less effective teachers. Schools are normative organizations and teaching is a craft in which excellence relies heavily on commitment, enthusiasm, and the desire to do one's best. Coercion and punitive oversight are not effective strategies for promoting excellence in teaching or school improvement broadly defined.[34] Indeed, experience suggests that heavy-handed accountability measures can actually make things worse in the classroom because teachers do not see the outcome measures typically employed—namely, student achievement scores—as legitimate or the process sufficiently sensitive to the complex process of teaching. The result, too often, is bitterness at "the system," frustration, and decisions to give up goals of excellence and instead do just enough to "get by." However, a teacher evaluation system that furnishes specific, detailed, and believable information about classroom performance can engage teacher commitment to growth and enthusiasm for learning new skills.

The same information that motivates teachers to grow professionally can also increase the quality of educational services in a school through the counseling out of teachers who appear ill-suited to teaching and unlikely to profit from in-service education opportunities. In the face of detailed, concrete information that points to performance problems, and given adequate remediation opportunities, most teachers who continue to have difficulty in the classroom are amenable to suggestions that they seek another vocation. The same norm of service that encourages teachers to gain new skills in the light of documented problems, it appears, supports decisions to resign when personal lack of fit with the profession can be demonstrated. To this point, one Lake Washington, Washington, principal who counseled out seven teachers in the past five years commented that "with only one exception, they all left with a smile."[35]

TEACHER LEARNING AND DEVELOPMENT

Teacher evaluation that describes and diagnoses teacher practices in specific, concrete terms can provide the most effective and legitimate means of "quality control" because it appeals to internalized norms of professionalism and points the way to do better. Teacher evaluation of this stripe relies on the *normative* power of legitimate authority and informed feedback to stimulate teacher development and change.

Such teacher evaluation not only is compatible with notions of effective authority in the school organization, but is also compatible with what we know about how adults learn. Unlike children, adults seldom learn simply because someone tells them to. Indeed, demands to learn new skills, particularly where they involve replacement of existing routine, threaten an adult's already well-organized self-concept and established level of accomplishment. Adult motivation to learn new things must come from within. Teacher evaluation has an important role to play in stimulating this internal motivation. To this point, Brundage concluded on the basis of a comprehensive review of adult learning that "what seems most clear in discussions on motivation is that the tendencies which are labeled 'motives' arise from within the learner. These are not something added on by an external agent. . . . The behavior of the external agent must be viewed as contributing either to feedback or to reinforcement and by this route indirectly to further motivation."[36] Similarly, Knowles says that adults are motivated to learn as they experience needs and interests that learning will satisfy.[37] Concrete information about areas in which teaching practice can be improved furnishes precisely the most powerful kind of motivation for teachers—authoritative and legitimate feedback on ways to be a more effective teacher.

The salience of teacher evaluation in this role is amplified by what we know about how teachers learn to teach. Teachers learn to teach primarily in two ways, as students and on the job; preservice teacher education programs play a weak role in teacher development.[38] Teacher learning requirements are developmental. As Nemser details, first-year teachers engage in formative skill development; it is only after teachers master fundamental teaching skills that they begin to concentrate on the relationship between what they do and student behavior.[39] This means that on-the-job learning is most significant to teacher performance and that support of this learning, as well as assessment of performance, must be keyed to a teacher's developmental stage. Experience has shown that unitary or uniform staff-development activities too often are too little too late. A strong teacher evaluation program is essential to the identification of differentiated strategies of diagnosis and assistance that can support teacher development. Given the centrality of on-the-job learning for teachers, teacher evaluation may be one of the most potent teacher development strategies available.

CONDITIONS NECESSARY TO
EFFECTIVE TEACHER EVALUATION

Teacher evaluation is not something most school principals like to do. For one thing, they have little confidence in their ability to carry out fair, consistent, and meaningful evaluation of teachers' classroom performance. Second, teacher evaluation and the associated anxiety threaten the stability in the school and encapsulate the tension school administrators feel between their roles as instructional leader and building manager. Nowhere is the potential incompatibility between these two roles more apparent than in teacher evaluation. Principals tend to minimize conflict in this area by minimizing teacher evaluation.

Finally, teacher evaluation is but one of the multiple demands on a building administrator's time and energy. Indeed, in terms of urgency, two broad classes of concerns eclipse teacher evaluation and performance issues: relations with parents and the community and student discipline. Until these issues central to administrator control are resolved, administrators are not inclined to turn to questions of classroom quality and teacher performance.[40] Given all of these factors, it is not surprising that principals tend to spend little time on evaluation (approximately 5 percent of their time) and that the assessment of teacher performance is largely pro forma and cursory. Teacher evaluation, in short, is an activity that most principals have little interest in or capacity to carry out.

"Business as usual" conditions cannot promote and support teacher evaluation practices of the type discussed here. Rand's teacher evaluation study points to at least five conditions essential to a teacher evaluation program that can contribute substantially to school improvement:

extensive and regular training for principals
resources for evaluators
teacher participation in program design
explicit central office support and involvement
integration with other district management activities[41]

TRAINING FOR PRINCIPALS

In most districts, principals receive little if any training related to their teacher evaluation responsibilities. For teacher evaluation of the type assumed here, principal training is substantial and ongoing. A weekend workshop as the program is getting underway is insufficient to give principals the requisite clinical, diagnostic, and staff-development skills.

Training of this sort requires substantial initial investment; equally as important, there must be continued attention to refreshing, refining, and building on the diagnostic skills of principals. In Lake Washington, for example, district administrators attend a two-week workshop each August. Teacher evaluation and teaching processes are always a focus of these workshops. Through simulation, role-modeling, videotapes, and other devices, administrators receive extensive and increasingly sophisticated training in clinical observation, notetaking, reporting, and conference skills. In addition to these yearly training retreats, follow-up administrator development seminars are held at least once a month. Training principals to carry out this role, in short, is not something that is "finished"; rather it is an ongoing, iterative activity.

EVALUATOR RESOURCES

In most school districts, principals have *responsibility* for evaluation but do not have the *authority* or the *resources* to act on their findings. This lack of effective responsibility both undercuts building principals and undermines the credibility of the evaluation activity. When principals lack the authority or resources to respond to problems identified in the process of evaluation, the activity becomes little more than a time-consuming but empty exercise. Further, the teacher frustration and alienation that can be expected to result from evaluation without appropriate follow-up may be counterproductive to improvement goals.

Resources for principals to use in response to evaluation findings are crucial if principals are to take teacher evaluation seriously and if evaluation is to support teacher improvement. For one thing, evaluators must be able to respond quickly in order to make the tie between evaluation and improvement an effective one. Teacher motivation to respond to evaluator assessment will be highest immediately following an evaluation session and the nature of improvement concerns will be freshly defined. Resources for evaluator use are also important from the perspective of the most effective support for teacher learning because evaluators can "tailor" a teacher-development prescription.

Districts handle this requirement for decentralized and nonstandardized resources in different ways. In Lake Washington, for example, each school has a discretionary fund that principals can use to support the in-service education activities suggested by a teacher's evaluation—special workshops, a course at the nearby university, enrollment in a district in-service activity, released time for observation in another setting, and so on. Salt Lake City has a remediation team composed of central office specialists and especially identified consultants who work with teachers identified as having difficulty. Other districts use mentor teachers or teachers on special assignment to respond individually and immediately to principals' request for assistance in a classroom. Evaluator resources such as these are necessary to a teacher evaluation effort that serves school improvement rather than merely accountability rituals.

TEACHER PARTICIPATION

The effective teacher evaluation practices examined in the Rand study included teachers in the development of district teacher evaluation practices.[42] Teachers and administrators agreed that teacher participation was a necessary ingredient in the success of the program. Teacher involvement is important for a number of reasons. One of the most salient is the fact that teachers can maximize the transitive rewards of teaching only if they have played a role in specifying the criteria and strategies used in assessing their performance and that of their students.[43]

The Rand study found that teacher participation was important to building the trust between administrators and teachers necessary for the system to work;

it also provides concrete evidence that the district did not intend to implement a "gotcha" system of teacher assessment and that improvement is a mutual goal.[44] If an evaluation system is to serve teacher-improvement objectives, it is essential that teachers see it as equitable and relevant. Teacher participation is a necessary means to that end. Finally, teacher participation in design is crucial to teacher commitment to do something about evaluation outcomes.

EXPLICIT DISTRICT-LEVEL SUPPORT

Teacher evaluation is not something to which building administrators would devote substantial time or attention, all other things being equal. It conflicts with their facilitative and supportive role; it consumes already inadequate time. Express district-level commitment is essential to a strong and consequential teacher evaluation program. Principals and teachers must see teacher evaluation as a district priority and something that is taken seriously by the superintendent and central office staff. Without this support, evaluation will remain a pro forma, bureaucratic responsibility.

Central office support can be shown in a number of ways. Support will be evident, of course, in the resources made available for principals to respond to teacher performance assessment. Less tangible elements of support are required as well. Active central office oversight of principals' evaluation activities conveys a strong signal about the priority afforded evaluation and the attention it should receive. To this end, some districts review principals' evaluation reports for care and comprehensiveness. Indeed, in many districts where teacher evaluation is unusually effective, principals are evaluated on the quality of their evaluation. Some districts even attach sanctions to teacher evaluations in an effort to focus principals' attention on the issue and halt what one teacher called "the dance of the lemons." In one California district, for example, principals are penalized at salary time if a teacher they rated as competent proves incompetent when transferred to another school.[45]

Political support from "downtown" is critical. Sometimes principals will not act on observed teacher problems because they fear the political fallout. Decisions about teacher probation are inherently political; in making this recommendation, a principal risks problems with the teachers' organization as well as parent or community members who may believe that a teacher has been judged wrongly. And many principals have found little if any support from downtown if a probationary placement became a heated issue. Principal confidence that the superintendent and central office staff will be supportive on tough decisions and will not, as one principal put it, "leave us out on a limb while they back off for political reasons" is essential to a strong teacher evaluation system.[46]

In short, if a district wants a strong teacher evaluation system that can contribute to improvement goals, it must demand it, support it with multiple resources, and give it the political and bureaucratic backing it requires.

INTEGRATION WITH DISTRICT MANAGEMENT ACTIVITIES

A strong and meaningful teacher evaluation system demonstrates substantive integration and strategic consistency with other district management activities. The development of technical knowledge is relatively useless in the absence of organizational structures and processes to use it. In most districts, teacher evaluation is rendered effectively inconsequential by its isolation from other district management activities. For example, Rand's preliminary assessment of teacher evaluation practices across the country found that these activities typically had no connection with district planning, staff development, curriculum development, or program evaluation activities. Where teacher evaluation was effective as a school-improvement strategy, however, there were explicit interrelationships among these district activities—each informing and reinforcing the other through common goals, expectations, and processes. In this way, teacher evaluation is a *central* part of an administrator's responsibilities, not just a categorical and ancillary requirement.

The necessity of substantive and strategic consistency with district management practices draws attention to the fact that there is no "best model" of teacher evaluation. To this point, the unusually effective teacher evaluation systems examined as part of the Rand study differed along every possible "design" dimension—the role of the teacher, the role of the principal, the timing and nature of the evaluation process, the resources available to evaluators, and the criteria established for teacher performance. While each of these four systems offers important lessons to inform choices in other districts, their effectiveness reflects the fact that they fit the district's particular management style and tenor.

In summary, teacher evaluation can be a potent school-improvement tool not because it puts a floor under classroom practices—the goal of accountability-based evaluation models—but because it addresses the incentives central to individual development and the teacher's sense of professionalism. Evaluation when seen in this light cannot be subjected to the quick fix, but requires the interaction of a host of factors that build on the norms and values central to the teaching profession.

Notes

1 J. L. Griesemer and C. Butler, *Education Under Study: An Analysis of Recent Major Reports on Education*, 2nd. ed. (Chelmsford, Mass.: The Northeast Regional Exchange, 1983).

2 United States Department of Education, *Meeting the Challenges: Recent Efforts to Improve Education across the Nation* (Washington, D.C.: U.S. Department of Education, November 15, 1983).

3 In preparation for identifying case study sites and developing an analytical framework, Rand analysts conducted an extensive literature review and national search for promising teacher evaluation practices. This preliminary work, which provided an overview of current theory and

practice, is reported in L. Darling-Hammond, A. E. Wise, and S. R. Pease, "Teacher Evaluation in the Organizational Context: A Review of the Literature," *Review of Educational Research* 53, no. 3 (Fall 1983): 285–328; and A. Wise et al., *Teacher Evaluation* (Santa Monica, Calif.: The Rand Corporation, 1984).

4   L. J. Cronbach, "Beyond the Two Disciplines of Scientific Psychology," *American Psychologist*, February 1975, pp. 116-27; and B. H. McKenna, "Context/Environment Effects in Teacher Evaluation," in *Handbook of Teacher Evaluation*, ed. J. Millman (Beverly Hills: Sage Publications, 1981), pp. 23-37.

5   D. Armor et al., *Analysis of the School Preferred Reading Program in Selected Los Angeles Minority Schools* (Santa Monica, Calif.: The Rand Corporation, 1977); and T. Good, "Research on Classroom Teaching," in *Handbook of Teaching and Policy*, ed. L. Shulman and G. Sykes (New York: Longman, 1983), pp. 42-80.

6   T. Good, "Teacher Expectations and Student Perceptions: A Decade of Research," *Educational Leadership* 38, no. 5 (February 1981): 418.

7   R. M. W. Travers, "Criteria of Good Teaching," in Millman, ed., *Handbook of Teacher Evaluation*, p. 22.

8   N. Bennett, *Teaching Styles and Pupil Progress* (London: Open Books, 1976); and J. A. Centra and D. A. Potter, "School and Teacher Effects: An Interrelational Model," *Review of Educational Research* 50, no. 2 (Summer 1980): 273-91.

9   Darling-Hammond, Wise, and Pease, "Teacher Evaluation in the Organizational Context."

10   S. Feiman-Nemser and R. E. Floden, "The Cultures of Teaching" (draft manuscript, Michigan State University, 1984), p. 46.

11   W. C. Jacobson, "We Brought Teachers Up to Snuff, and So Can You," *The Executive Educator*, February 1984, p. 41; R. P. Manatt, K. L. Palmer, and E. Hidlebaugh, "Evaluating Teacher Performance with Improved Rating Scales," *NASSP Bulletin* 60, no. 401 (1976): 21-23; Millman, *Handbook of Teacher Evaluation*; G. B. Redfern, *Evaluating Teachers and Administrators* (Boulder, Colo.: Westview Press, 1980); and Wise et al., *Teacher Evaluation*.

12   Good, "Research on Classroom Teaching." Detailed description of the various approaches to practices that fit within these broad parameters is beyond the scope of this paper. For details see the work of Madeline Hunter, Richard Manatt, and George Redfern as well as the case studies reported in Wise et al., *Teacher Evaluation*.

13   See, for example, M. Cohen, "Instructional, Management, and Social Conditions in Effective Schools," in *School Finance and School Improvement*, A. Odden and L. D. Webb (Cambridge, Mass.: Ballinger Publishing, 1983).

14   D. C. Lortie, "The Balance of Control and Autonony in Elementary School Teaching," in *The Semiprofessions and Their Organization*, ed. A. Etzioni (New York: The Free Press, 1969); idem, *Schoolteacher* (Chicago: The University of Chicago Press, 1975); and G. H. McPherson, *Small Town Teacher* (Cambridge: Harvard University Press, 1972).

15   Lortie, *Schoolteacher*; P. T. Ashton, R. B. Webb, and N. Doda, *A Study of Teachers Sense of Efficacy* (University of Florida, Foundations of Education) nd; P. W. Jackson, *Life in Classrooms* (New York: Holt, Rinehart & Winston, 1968).

16   A. Bandura, "Self-Efficacy Mechanisms in Human Agency," *American Psychologist* 37, no. 2 (1982): 40; and B. Fuller et al., "The Organizational Context of Individual Efficacy," *Review of Educational Research* 52, no. 1 (Spring 1982): 7-30.

17   Lortie, *Schoolteacher*, p. 121.

18   W. Moore, *The Professions* (New York: Russell Sage Foundation, 1970), p. 80.

19   Lortie, "The Balance of Control and Autonomy in Elementary School Teaching"; idem, *Schoolteacher*; Ashton, Webb, and Doda, *A Study of Teachers Sense of Efficacy*; Jackson, *Life in Classrooms*; and S. Sarason, *The Culture of the School and the Problem of Change*, 2nd ed. (Boston: Allyn and Bacon, 1982).

20   Jackson, *Life in Classrooms*; Ashton, Webb, and Doda, *A Study of Teachers Sense of Efficacy*; G. D. Fenstermacher, "A Philosophical Consideration of Recent Research on Teacher

Effectiveness," in *Review of Research in Education*, vol. 6, ed. L. S. Shulman (Itasca, Ill.: F. E. Peacock, 1978).

21   D. M. Medley, "The Effectiveness of Teachers," in *Research on Teaching: Concepts, Findings and Implications*, ed. P. L. P. Peterson and H. J. Walberg (Berkeley: McCutchan Publishing, 1979), p. 17.

22   D. A. Schon, *The Reflective Practitioner: How Professionals Think in Action* (New York: Basic Books, 1983).

23   S. L. Lightfoot, *The Good High School* (New York: Basic Books, 1983); Jackson, *Life in Classrooms*; Lortie, *Schoolteacher*; E. L. Boyer, *High School: A Report on Secondary Education in America* (New York: Harper & Row, 1983); M. Fullan, *The Meaning of Educational Change* (New York: Teachers College Press, 1982); and McPherson, *Small Town Teacher*.

24   McPherson, *Small Town Teacher*, p. 51.

25   Ashton, Webb, and Doda, *A Study of Teachers Sense of Efficacy*, p. 240.

26   Cohen, "Management and Social Conditions in Effective Schools."

27   P. Berman and M. W. McLaughlin, *Federal Programs Supporting Educational Change, Vol. VIII: Implementing and Sustaining Innovations* (Santa Monica, Calif.: The Rand Corporation, 1978): and J. W. Little, *School Success and Staff Development: The Role of Staff Development in Urban Desegregated Schools* (Boulder, Colo.: Center for Action Research, 1981).

28   Jacobson, "We Brought Teachers Up To Snuff, and So Can You"; and Wise et al., *Teacher Evaluation*.

29   See the Lake Washington case in Wise et al., *Teacher Evaluation*.

30   Little, *School Success and Staff Development*, pp. 102-03.

31   Cohen, "Instructional, Management, and Social Conditions in Effective Schools."

32   A. Blumberg and W. Greenfield, *The Effective Principal: Perspectives on School Leadership* (Boston: Allyn and Bacon, 1980).

33   J. B. Wellish et al., "School Management and Organization in Successful Schools," *Sociology of Education* 51 (1978): 211-26.

34   Etzioni, *The Semiprofessions and Their Organization;* and R. E. Elmore and M. W. McLaughlin, "Strategic Choice for Federal Education Policy: The Compliance-Assistance Trade-Off," in *The 81st Yearbook of the National Society for the Study of Education*, ed. A. Lieberman and M. W. McLaughlin (Chicago: The University of Chicago Press, 1982).

35   Wise et al., *Teacher Evaluation*.

36   D. H. Brundage, *Adult Learning Principles and Their Application to Professional Planning* (Toronto: Ministry of Education, Ontario, 1980), p. 40.

37   M. Knowles, *The Adult Learner: A Neglected Species* (Houston: Gulf, 1978), p. 31.

38   S. F. Nemser, "Learning to Teach," in Shulman and Sykes ed., *Handbook of Teaching and Policy*, pp. 150-70.

39   Ibid., p. 162.

40   Blumberg and Greenfield, *The Effective Principal*.

41   Wise et al., *Teacher Evaluation*. These conditions are consistent with the "organizational approach" for managing teacher incompetence developed by E. M. Bridges, *The Identification, Remediation and Dismissal of Incompetent Teachers* (Burlingame, Calif.: Association of California School Administrators, 1984). In particular, Bridges stresses the importance of tight interrelationships among district policies and the need to support evaluators and administrators with information and resources for remediation.

42   Wise et al., *Teacher Evaluation*.

43   Lortie, "The Balance of Control and Autonomy in Elementary School Teaching," p. 36.

44   Wise et al., *Teacher Evaluation*.

45   Bridges, *The Identification, Remediation and Dismissal of Incompetent Teachers*.

46   Wise et al., *Teacher Evaluation*.

Interactive Research and Development— Partners in Craft

JOANN JACULLO-NOTO
Teachers College, Columbia University

"Teachers want to be consulted in the planning of staff development programs and district curriculum projects, but, when it comes to implementation, doing the hard work, that's when they back off."

In conversations with school superintendents and principals, this theme, or variations on it, is heard more and more frequently. What does it tell us about job satisfaction and teachers' attitudes toward their own growth, and what are the implications for staff development?

INTERACTIVE RESEARCH AND DEVELOPMENT—THE STRATEGY

GROWTH VERSUS ROUTINIZATION

Educational leaders today are struggling to find ways to help teachers continue to grow, intellectually and emotionally, despite school environments that tend to routinize and regularize. The very nature of teaching and the organization of our educational system often seem to mitigate against creativity. Too often teachers remain in the same school district, at the same grade level, and even in the same classroom for twenty to twenty-five years. On a broader level the problem has been exacerbated by the "graying of the faculty," that is, the increased average age of classroom teachers and the inability of most districts to hire new teachers who may be younger and more recent graduates of teacher education programs. Concern is now being expressed that ramifications of this problem are and will continue to be a negative force in efforts to improve student achievement in the classroom. Research has shown that teachers who remain challenged and satisfied in the classroom are perhaps the pivotal force in education, certainly the key to a dynamic school. Unlocking the factors that encourage job satisfaction may therefore be the first step toward creating staff-development programs that are welcomed by experienced teachers and provide genuine opportunities for intellectual, social, and emotional growth.

One program, Interactive Research and Development on Schooling (IR&DS), a model that seems to work in a variety of settings, is collaborative research, a strategy that involves researchers and practitioners in an interactive

R&D process. The notion of collaborative research dates back to the 1940s and the action research of Corey's era,[1] which emphasized and encouraged the cooperative study of problems by practitioners and researchers. Prior to this, Lewin[2] and Lippitt[3] had created a useful set of terms and definitions concerning cooperative study, which Corey used to develop an action research strategy. Ward, in her analysis of collaborative research, notes that although Corey and others focused on curriculum, and more recent collaborative research focuses on teaching (Interactive Research and Development on Teaching) and schooling (Interactive Research and Development on Schooling), the underlying premises are the same.[4] The essential features of IR&D are:

1. *R&D team composition:* Each team is composed of a researcher, a developer, and several teachers.
2. *Collaboration:* Decisions regarding research questions, data collection procedures, material development, etc., are researched collaboratively. A work *with* rather than work *on* approach is emphasized.
3. *Problem-solving focus:* The problem to be studied comes from the school situation.
4. *Interactive R&D:* R&D occur concurrently during the process.
5. *Maintaining the integrity of the setting:* The integrity of the classroom is preserved during the research process.
6. *IR&D as an intervention strategy:* The R&D process is a staff development strategy. Rigorous and useful research is conducted as part of the R&D process.[5]

ANTECEDENTS TO IR&DS

RESEARCH AND DEVELOPMENT

There are several important reasons for conceiving of research and development as concurrent processes involving both researchers and practitioners. One is to increase the relevance of the research to the real problems and concerns of the teachers involved. So often traditional or linear research focused on questions or problems identified by researchers outside the school setting. Not only did the problems often have little relevance to classroom life as teachers viewed it, but teachers found the reports of these research efforts difficult to read. The language used was that of university researchers and not that of teachers. Compounding the situation was the time lag of approximately eight years between the conducting of the research and the dissemination of the research findings. Schools, classrooms, and children change, sometimes rapidly, to meet changing social conditions. This time lag between the completion of research and its development often mitigated against the usefulness of the research to school practitioners.

A second important reason for conceiving of research and development as concurrent processes is to enable teachers to develop their problem-solving capacity using research methodology. The concept of in-service teacher education dates back to the turn of the century and the teacher institute. During the twentieth century, in-service teacher education moved through several phases, from the teacher institute to summer school to the notion of teacher improvement as an administrative and supervisory function. It was not until the mid-1920s, when teacher education colleges developed, that a trend occurred shifting in-service teacher improvement away from administrative controls back to the hands of the teacher. By the 1940s some were advocating in-service education for the entire school staff. It was no longer assumed by some that the positive direction set by an outside expert constitutes the most effective means of improving the performance of teachers.[6] Individuals also began to question the aims and training procedures of in-service education. The 1956 NSSE Yearbook focuses on the advent of an action research approach, which was used by Corey and others as a vehicle for the development of teachers' ability to apply a systematic problem-solving strategy to educational problems they observed. These writers, commenting on the usefulness of the strategy to teachers, note that there are many similarities between action research and research conducted by research specialists. The two primary differences, however, are that the problems for study identified in action research are often ones that defy the controlling of many variables in the complicated settings of classrooms. In addition, if teachers conduct the research, the problem of communicating the results of research to teachers does not occur.

Parker, in this same NSSE Yearbook, builds a convincing case for action research as a powerful staff-development strategy. He sees in-service education as dependent on people working on problems that are significant to them. To do so, individuals need assistance with the content of the instructional problem under study and with human relations and cooperative group process skills as well as a problem-solving methodology. Parker believes that as people work in groups to solve problems there are greater resources at their disposal from the multiple group members as well as partial objectivity, which may result from the very nature of several working together and cross-checking each other. If one believes that group decisions help individuals achieve behavior change and that schools need continuity and stability, then it makes sense to reach decisions by group consensus. As Parker comments, "Each member of a group is superior to the others in some respect. The resources of *all* are richer than those of any one member."[7] In research methodology the relationship between procedures and goals is critical to the outcome. Teachers engaged in an action research endeavor soon come to know this on their own. Such realizations greatly sharpen their problem-solving capacity. The recent IR&DS study documents the usefulness of the collaborative R&D strategy as a staff-development tool. A look at the outcomes of that study may encourage those of us seeking new ways to achieve teacher growth.

IR&D—PARTICIPANTS AND SITES

THE THREE TEAMS

The IR&DS project was conceived by principal investigators Gary Griffin and Ann Lieberman with several purposes in mind. One goal of the project was to determine the degree of success with which individuals with different backgrounds and professional orientations could fill the roles of developer and researcher. Over a twenty-two-month period three teams, each composed of a researcher, a developer, and four to six teachers, worked together on a research question that emanated from the teachers' own school setting. One team was made up of staff from a single suburban school district (SD). Another team consisted of teacher center specialists (TC) from the United Federation of Teachers (UFT). The third team, located in an intermediate agency (IA), consisted of individuals in a variety of positions in a vocational education high school. The role of staff developer on each team was filled by professionals with different backgrounds and work situations. The staff developer on the teacher center team was a consultant with extensive experience in teacher development. The assistant superintendent of the district served as the developer on the school district team, while a principal in the vocational high school filled the developer role on the intermediate agency team. On two teams the researchers were full-time university professors, while a classroom teacher with a doctorate in education served as the researcher on the school district team. The project office was located at the university (IHE). The project staff housed there provided technical assistance to the teams when it was requested and documented team progress through the twenty-two-month cycle.

Another goal was to analyze the professional growth that occurred in the teacher participants as a result of the experience. If five or more years of practice is used as a yardstick to indicate an "experienced teacher," then eleven of the twelve practitioners were experienced. Specifically, their teaching careers ranged from two years to twenty-six years. These teachers all regularly read a number of professional periodicals and had participated in many types of staff-development programs in the past, both in and outside of their districts. Several had served on district curriculum planning committees and those on the teacher center team had taken leadership roles in teacher training. On the whole, these individuals were representative of the kinds of teachers school superintendents hope and expect will remain active and involved in their professional work in schools.

THE THREE CONTEXTS

The differences in the contexts in which each of the three teams worked were quite dramatic. The SD team worked in a suburban upper-middle-class community where teacher development was talked about and supported in many concrete ways. The entire team believed in teachers' being involved in research. The teacher participants had been working on a districtwide writing committee so they knew each other and had worked together. Everything seemed ready for them to engage in interactive research.

The TC team members worked in a large urban area with an abrasive culture. Stereotypes of what this harsh environment does to people immediately come to mind. Team members had all been teachers before they were selected to be teacher specialists. Their job was to provide and facilitate professional development for teachers. They worked in three geographically dispersed areas of the city. Each was responsible for a full-time Teacher Center, either in an elementary or a secondary school. The TC team was in its second year of a two-year federally funded project when the IR&DS project began.

The IA team was composed of teachers from two separate campuses. Two of the team members were counselors, one was a teacher of auto mechanics, and one a teacher of cosmetology. The school was a regional collaborative vocational education school where students were based for half of their school day. Although team members had little or no knowledge of research or research procedures, it was thought that due to the collaborative nature of this agency, teachers might well be ready to engage in this type of strategy.

IR&D—PROCESS AND OUTCOMES

DEFINING THE PROBLEM

During the twenty-two month period of the project, each team identified an issue of concern to themselves and their colleagues. The issue was stated as a research question and they then developed a research design to study that question. Because research and development were to be conducted concurrently, frequent contact with other teachers in their schools and school districts was essential to the success of the project.

The SD team decided to study elementary-school children's writing. Their study was entitled "The Qualities of Good Writing: How They Are Perceived, Acquired, and Applied by Children." The TC team studied teacher job satisfaction in a large urban setting. Their research question was, "What are the factors that enable some teachers to maintain positive attitudes about their jobs?" The IA team decided to focus on the disruptive student in the classroom, a problem that has always existed but appeared more prominent with the advent of mainstreaming. Their research question was, "How can the frequency or severity of disruptive behavior in the classroom be reduced?" The team proposed to try out and evaluate interventions designed to reduce classroom disruptions.

CONFLICT, COMMITMENT, COLLABORATION

As researchers studying the individuals engaged in collaborative R&D, we were able to identify several themes concerning adult development across teams and contexts. The themes of conflict, commitment, and collaboration emerged from our study of the process as well as from the participant's self-reports or "logs." The data sources through which this valuable information was collected included pre- and post-interviews, audiotape recordings of all meetings, and pre- and post-questionnaires, participant contact reports, and the aforementioned logs. We were able to follow and analyze how participants on each team coped with conflict, commitment, and collaboration. Sometimes the conflict emerged as team members took on new roles, roles that clashed with the responsibilities of current professional roles.

Conflict emerged in all three teams in different ways.[8] For the SD team, conflict developed over the formulation of the research question. The team could not decide whether they wanted to study the children or the teacher and whether they wanted to do an experimental design or a case study. On the surface these decisions appear simple; they were, however, complex for the team since each team member had a great investment in his or her views of these issues. Through a series of meetings, during which one team member openly considered leaving the team, the decision was made to use a case-study approach with teachers studying students in their own classes. This team experienced conflict over the substance of the task on several occasions. As part of this pattern, when conflict arose they would confront it over the course of several meetings until the problem was resolved. Interpersonal relations were open and quite positive.

The TC team's conflict pattern differed from that of the SD team. Their episodes of conflict were slow starting, continuous and complex. This team's conflict occurred over a range of issues, including problems of group process, lack of trust, differing norms of work behavior, logistics for arranging meetings, and different definitions of the meaning of parity and collaboration. They agreed quickly on the research problem, since their interests were clear and similar. Despite recurring conflict over the issues mentioned, this team worked successfully through the IR&D process. Interpersonal relations were never strong, so the team was often off task. Their work world was made up of factors that often caused dissension. Therefore disagreements and fragmentation were not new to them. In this IR&D team situation, the logistics of meeting arrangements, the stress of involvement in a project, and the lack of experience and patience for research for some team members over unequal contributions to the effort all added to the conflict.

The IA team's conflict was not over substance, as in the SD team, nor over group process matters, as for the TC team. This team's pattern of conflict centered on the difference between the researcher's view of IR&D and the team's view. The teachers and the developer were interested in solutions to school problems. The researcher wanted to do a research study to explore the issue of disruptive students in class while the teachers wanted to solve the problem of student disruptiveness. This conflict persisted throughout the project, surfacing only at one or two critical points in the process.

The personal and professional outcomes for teachers were greatly affected as teachers took on leadership roles and researchers and developers became less of a pivotal force on each team. Questions of commitment were raised because of the amount of time and energy required by what was, for most of these practitioners, a first R&D experience. For example, on the SD team, the teachers conducted lunchtime presentations in other elementary schools in the district and at town civic group meetings to explain the project. They became spokespersons for the project and consequently for some of the district's work in the teaching of writing. On the SD team, the teachers said at the completion of the project that in the second year they did all the work on their own. In fact, the developer, the assistant superintendent in the district, had participated less frequently in year two. In addition, the team rarely used the consultant that year. During this period the teachers and the researchers (a classroom teacher) devoted more time to the project than in year one and at several points, when pressured by other professional and personal commitments, questioned who they were doing the work for. Their perceived lack of support caused them to question what benefits they were deriving from this effort, which demanded so much time and energy. On the TC team, the teacher specialists were very much aware of time devoted to team meetings as time away from their Teacher Center jobs. No substitutes could be secured to do their work while at meetings because of the nature of the work itself. These team members questioned the time they devoted to meetings, especially when, following the meeting, they would return to their jobs at 3:00 P.M. with several hours of work still to be done.

Almost as a byproduct, the project identified some of the sticky matters that surface when institutions with different time schedules, reward structures, and purposes come together for the mutual good of both. For instance, when time schedules had to be adjusted, in many cases it was the university project staff who revised the timeline and due dates of deliverables as requested by the teachers. Negotiations between the institutions and people involved centered on who could afford to bend on a particular issue. Throughout the two years, questions continued to be raised about how schools and universities could continue to collaborate on research projects.

REINFORCEMENT, RECOGNITION, AND RESPECT

For the university researchers, the question studied by the Teacher Center team had far-ranging significance. Anyone concerned with long-range staff development has probably attempted to identify those rewards, or incentives, to which teachers respond most positively. The Teacher Center team was able to identify what came to be called the 3R's of job satisfaction: reinforcement, recognition, and respect. Results of this team's research indicated that reinforcement from adults (and from students) and particularly recognition and respect from fellow teachers, administrators, and parents are essential if teachers are to remain positive about their jobs.

What was most interesting to the university researchers was the discovery, in fact the statement by the very team that studied this question, that the opportunity to participate on an IR&D team over an extended period of time enabled them to experience the reinforcement, recognition, and respect all teachers need. For example, speaking at faculty meetings, as well as at parent association meetings and even at national conferences, gave these teacher researchers the recognition and respect they needed and deserved. Members of both the school district and Teacher Center teams reported that this project had been "an unmatched growth opportunity for all of us." Quantitative and qualitative data revealed the extent of professional growth. Teachers on the SD team reported that they had become researchers. Those on the TC team stressed the pride they felt in completing interactive R&D. On the IA team, the practitioners/researchers reported a powerful understanding of a problem-solving stance and a new appreciation of the concept of teaching and learning from one's peers.

CROSS-SITE COMPARISONS

DIFFERENCES IN CONTEXT—R&D AS A LEARNING DEVICE

More specific short- and long-term rewards differed for the three teams. Initially, the SD team was very enthusiastic about working with the IHE and expected to lean heavily on the university to learn how to do rigorous research. In the end, however, it was actually the teachers who designed the research, collected the data, and wrote the final report. Their rewards emanated from their own new sense of power and authority as a result of doing research. One teacher reported, "We now feel we can speak with authority not only on research, but about teaching, about how children learn and also about being professional."

The project gave the teacher specialists on the Teacher Center team a new status among their union peers. More important, they came to see the process and product of their work to be of prime benefit to Teacher Centers, to the union association, and to themselves. Research became an important tool to them in their work with teachers.

For the IA team, although the vocabulary and the systematic research process was of some benefit to the team members, the most powerful rewards came through a development opportunity. They ended the two-year project with a greater sense of confidence in their own abilities both to solve problems and to engage their peers in a similar process.

All team members were questioned, at the beginning and end of the project, about their own and their colleagues' interest in various types of staff-development activities. One result of participation on the interactive research and development team seemed to be a much stronger interest on the part of the teachers in an exchange of ideas with colleagues at other schools and in professional conferences. One interesting change, over the two years, was that the participating teachers seemed to feel that their colleagues were far less interested in in-service activities than they were. These teachers saw themselves as highly professional, in part as a result of this experience. At the end of the project they spoke of plans for their own professional growth, and in several cases were quite explicit about their futures in the field of education.

LEARNING ABOUT RESEARCH

Most of the IR&DS teacher participants entered the project with little knowledge of research methods or design and some doubts about how much they expected to be able to learn. At the end of the project, however, many had learned a great deal, and expressed pleasure and a new sense of confidence. A similar tale can be told about the development process. There is evidence that teacher participants on all three teams became more knowledgeable about development, particularly from the standpoint of unique and atypical ways of going about it. The TC team was able to set aside small amounts of money to replicate the process they had experienced with additional teams of teachers and principals in the urban school district. The IA team teachers served as staff developers for the district in a variety of capacities following the project. They believed they had credibility with other teachers in the district. Outside consultants, whom they viewed as ineffective in many instances, lacked this quality. Their realization that development can be process-oriented rather than product-oriented was the most dramatic outcome.

THE PROBLEM-SOLVING PROCESS

The sense of accomplishment that team members felt as a result of participation in this project was further enhanced because of the requirement that R&D be problem-solution oriented. Identifying and acting on a perceived problem provided a focus for the teacher-researchers' work in their school districts. The SD teachers reported a greater understanding of and sensitivity to student differences, teacher preferences, system rules and policies, parental expectations, and curricular demands. At the midway point in the project, the assistant superintendent announced to the team that the ten released-time days planned for year two would be reduced to five or less. The team struggled with this decision for several weeks. It was not until the completion of the project that several teachers on the team were able to accept this administrative decision. Although the team discussed parent complaints about the substitutes who had been secured to cover their classes while they attended team meetings and their own misgivings about these substitutes, it took months for them to understand this action in any terms other than lack of administrative support for the project. Both the SD and TC teams reported a new appreciation for the complexity of schools and school life. For the Teacher Center team, the interactive R&D strategy provided a stimulus and a means to act on a problem that they, as staff developers, had been aware of for some time. As they completed their research on teacher job satisfaction, they realized that they too were responding, as participants in the IR&DS project, to a new sense of recognition, reinforcement, and respect. The IA team teachers, who had entered with a more generalized view of the process than the members of the other two teams, developed increased awareness of institutional problems as a result of the project. For all, this had been a powerful learning experience.

IMPACT ON THE SCHOOL DISTRICT

There is evidence too that the three teams' R&D had an impact on their respective school district sites. The SD team developed a method of involving additional district teachers in the writing-process approach. Other teachers in the district have now created a research team to further the work on the study of children's writing. The TC team members created teams similar to their own in eleven other schools. It will be interesting and exciting to observe the impact that these new teams have on their schools. The changes that took place in the intermediate agency were, perhaps, the most dramatic. The teachers on that team had never before done any research, nor had they been exposed to the products of research. For them, staff development had always taken the form of an outside expert coming in to address an issue. This was becoming, for many, less and less tolerable. Now, with their newfound "expertise" and confidence, the IA team teachers were willing and eager to be reponsible for conducting their own problem-solving workshops and to be used as peer staff developers. They had, after all, tried out several interventions on a major problem that had been identified by both students and teachers. As a result they had had an opportunity to learn systematic problem solving and at the same time take on the role of developer.

CRAFT LEARNINGS

PRODUCT ORIENTATION

What have we learned about the problems and prospects of implementing an interactive research and development strategy in other settings? The learnings from the IR&DS project have been many concerning teachers, the university, and the task of collaboration. Regarding teachers, this project reaffirmed that teachers, working with curriculum plans of a week's or a month's duration and benchmarks for student achievement, quickly become product-oriented. IR&D requires methodological planning, reflective thinking, reevaluation, and adjustment of goals. All this activity takes time and delays the project. Research in fact promises no solution or product, which is problematic for teachers in a product-oriented setting. Refocusing on the process, rather than on the product, can be one of the most challenging aspects of the IR&D strategy.

TIME DEMANDS

The demands on teachers' time from a variety of sectors, including the school district, parents, and children, are also problematic. We learned that IR&D needs to be packaged so that teachers can find the time to become involved. By dividing work among team members, omitting the writing of lengthy reports, and carefully planning team work around the demanding school schedule, IR&D can become more manageable for teachers. In addition, IR&D projects can focus on school district curriculum-development and staff-development goals. Often districts set aside funds and time (released time, professional development days, summer workshops) for work on district goals. An IR&D strategy can provide the vehicle for work on these district goals while tapping district support structures already in place. The SD team selected a topic that was central to the district's curriculum-development efforts. This did give them access to a consultant already hired by the district to work in this area with teachers, which they might not have had if they selected another curriculum area. In addition, once the portion of the project supported by external funding was completed, the teachers were able to continue using the IR&D strategy in that curricular area since it was a targeted district goal. When both the district and the teachers benefit from an endeavor, time demands become somewhat less problematic.

SEARCH FOR PERFECTION

Another important learning concerning teachers is that they enter this experience wanting very much to "do it right." The teachers involved in IR&DS repeatedly looked to the university for direction. Deciding when to provide the direction and how much to provide was critical in this process. At the conclusion of the project, teachers said, "We went to the university for help and they didn't help us. They made us do it on our own and we learned so much." The need to do it right and the unfamiliarity with research procedures often led teachers into demanding more help than they really needed. Knowing when to provide help and when to encourage teachers to struggle with a problem on their own can greatly affect how much teachers learn from this experience.

INSTITUTIONALIZATION AS A PROBLEM

We realized at the conclusion of the project that a vital concern of the teachers was where does all this go from here. The dissemination of the IR&D strategy in their district and in other schools was important to teachers. They wanted to give greater meaning to their work and for them dissemination was important. Of the three sites involved, only one had the capacity to institutionalize the model. Teachers in the other sites have faced the letdown of the completion of the project with no mechanism for continuing the strategy in their schools or districts. In some ways, this gave IR&DS the same aura of projects that come and go in teachers' lives. The great investment of time, effort, and so forth, these teachers made to the project made the impact of failing to institutionalize the process all the greater. In this, perhaps, more than in other types of innovative projects, the high investment of self demands a specific dissemination plan.

COLLABORATION WITH THE UNIVERSITY AND THE FIELD

There were several learnings about the university that emerged from this project. In these times of shrinking resources, both human and material, can resources be made available to such a collaborative effort between the university and schools? Clearly, all research and development efforts come at some cost to the institution. Identifying carefully in advance the potential costs to the institution can be critical in building a positive experience for those university faculty participating in university/school linkages.

The time constraints experienced by teacher participants were also experienced by university faculty participants. What became clear as the project progressed was that the university schedule and work demands are as rigid as elementary and secondary schools schedules. Carefully orchestrating faculty time devoted to an interactive R&D effort is essential for a positive experience for the researcher and developer. For the university such a collaboration is uncharacteristic and goes against the norms of many university settings. Perhaps more so for the university than for the school, the careful shepherding of such a project through the institution will encourage a positive institutional response to collaborative work with schools. For example, informing the university dean and others in the hierarchy about the project initially and at set intervals may help to engender administrative support for those professors engaged in collaborative projects with teachers. Also, the inclusion of the project on department meeting agendas when research and development work is discussed can lead to greater faculty awareness of and interest in ways professors are working *with* teachers. For both the university and the schools, clarity about expected project outcomes is important. Whether the expectation is rigorous and useful R&D products or a positive staff-development experience, all those involved need to know and be reminded of what they are about.

Collaboration is difficult even under the best circumstances. When success abounds, all want the credit. Yet, who from which institutions bears the burden of the failures can quickly become an issue in any collaborative effort. Traditionally, when the university and the schools are involved in a project orchestrated by the university, the school people can easily blame the university when things go wrong. In traditional research efforts, all agreed the university faculty were supposed to have the answers. In an IR&D project, each participant brings a special expertise to the project. All enter the project as presumed equal partners. This does pose a problem when it comes time to share responsibility for the failures and problems that occur along the way. Deciding early on the areas where agreement between the sites can be reached and where issues must be negotiated may be helpful in dealing with both the successes and failures of any collaborative endeavor. Negotiation between individuals and institutions is the crux of the strategy. University faculty and project staff who are prepared to give up some of what they want in deadlines, procedures for project completion, and so forth, will find negotiations with teachers and administrators easier to handle. Historically, university faculty set the rules for R&D. Collaborative R&D means some of those rules are negotiable. This is a major adjustment in thinking and behavior for university faculty. For teachers who may expect university faculty to have limitless knowledge and information and time to devote to the effort there may be some disappointments as these fail to materialize. The limits of what each individual can give to the project are tested regularly in team meetings. The overriding question in these negotiations is, how flexible ought I be in this endeavor?

From firsthand experience in an IR&D project and the benefit of other applications of the strategy it appears that some settings are able to implement the strategy more effectively than others. School sites where staff development is a stated and observed goal and where school improvement is an ongoing process are likely to have greater success in an IR&D experience. Additionally, schools are likely to fare better with the model where teachers are seeking alternatives to traditional in-service courses and where there is a history of collaborative effort within the district, as well as a history of the positive use of outside resources. The presence of these bottom-line site characteristics can make the IR&D strategy more attainable in the complex setting of schools.

Universities differ widely in their approach to collaborative R&D with schools. Some institutions have a history of successful collaborative R&D efforts. It appears that universities with a service as well as research orientation to schools will have some flexibility to allocate resources to such a collaborative endeavor. A current linkage with schools sets the stage for the kind of partnership IR&D requires. Finally, a university faculty committed to building the capacity of school personnel to solve their own problems can make the critical difference in establishing parity in such an IR&D team effort.

There can be little doubt about the effectiveness of IR&D as a staff-development strategy for experienced teachers. It provides recognition, reinforcement, and respect for these professionals. Teachers, while they are learning to act in a new area—that of research and problem solving—at the same time can be receiving the positive feedback so important to their morale and sense of self. Yet IR&D is complex, in part because collaboration is a skill that is learned over time, through trial and error or success and failure. To understand the power of IR&D one needs only think of Lortie's description of teaching as an unstaged career, where the work assigned to a first-year teacher is identical to that assigned to a thirty-year veteran. A conflict arises because the veteran teacher, according to Lortie, feels depreciated if he or she teaches with about the same average level of effort as the first-year teacher.[9] The IR&D project gave teachers who saw themselves as a cut above average new skills and understandings, a platform from which to share these, and an opportunity to have their own positive view of themselves confirmed by others. This is an important factor in encouraging these teachers to operate above the average level of effort in their classrooms.

Waller long ago rejected salary increase as the solution for upgrading the teaching profession.[10] He considered the crux of the problem to be the drudgery of the work and the low social standing of the profession. I submit that Waller's description of teaching still holds true five decades later. What IR&D shows us is that teachers who are given the opportunity to participate in a systematic problem-solving experience can gain the favorable attention of peers, parents, and administrators. Furthermore, when these teachers see themselves as knowledgeable and valuable, others see them that way too.

Return now to the beginning of this article, to that plaintive cry of principals and superintendents. These teachers involved in IR&DS were not afraid of doing the hard work of R&D when they could see benefit to themselves and to their school districts. These twelve teachers, I believe, are representative of the many other teachers who want to continue doing a good job and are willing to take on the hard work. Lightfoot recommends that schools be considered "environments that not only inspire the learning and socialization of children but also encourage the development of adults. The intellectual and psychic growth of teachers will inevitably have repercussions on their confidence, risk-taking, and creativity in approaching pedagogical tasks."[11] IR&DS is a strategy that allows for creativity and risk and in the process builds confidence. Let us nurture the teachers along with the children.

Notes

1 Stephen M. Corey, *Action Research to Improve School Practice* (New York: Bureau of Publications, Teachers College, Columbia University, 1953).

2 Kurt Lewin, *Resolving Social Conflicts* (New York: Harper & Row, 1948).

3 Ronald Lippitt, *Training in Community Relations: A Research Exploration Toward New Group Skills* (New York: Harper & Row, 1949).

4 Beatrice A. Ward and William J. Tikunoff, "Collaborative Research" (Invited paper, The Implications of Research on Teaching for Practice Conference, February 25–27, 1982, sponsored by the National Institute of Education, U.S. Department of Education).

5 Ibid., p. 5.

6 Herman G. Rickey, "Growth of the Modern Conception of In-Service Education," in *In-Service Education for Teachers, Supervisors, and Administrators: The Fifty-Sixth Yearbook of*

the National Society for the Study of Education, ed. Nelson B. Henry (Champaign: University of Illinois Press, 1957). p. 59.

7   J. Cecil Parker, "Guidelines for In-Service Education," in ed. Henry, *In-Service Education for Teachers, Supervisors, and Administrators,* p. 106.

8   Ann Lieberman and Joann Jacullo-Noto, "The Power of the Context on Interactive Research and Development on Schooling: Themes and Variations" (Paper prepared for the Annual Meeting of the American Educational Research Association, Montreal, 1983).

9   Dan Lortie, *Schoolteacher* (Chicago: University of Chicago Press, 1975), p. 85.

10   Willard Waller, *The Sociology of Teaching* (New York: John Wiley, 1932).

11   Sarah Lawrence Lightfoot, "The Lives of Teachers," in the *Handbook of Teaching and Policy,* ed. Lee Schulman and Gary Sykes (New York: Longman, 1983), p. 258.

Teacher Directed In-Service:
A Model That Works

JUDITH SCHWARTZ
Scarsdale Teachers Institute

On most afternoons throughout the school year, teachers in Scarsdale gather in classrooms recently vacated by their students and become students themselves. In one classroom teachers are practicing programming with pocket computers. A physics teacher borrows a set of computers; this is the first time he is using computers in his classroom. In another building, elementary teachers are preparing for a field walk with a naturalist, using their schoolyard as a laboratory for their elementary children. Teachers from many disciplines are at work on a year-long program on writing across the curriculum. Others are attending an interdisciplinary seminar; still others are looking at political films and analyzing the ways in which artists create visual political messages.

The Scarsdale Teachers Institute (STI) exists to provide professional growth opportunities for teachers. The continued success of the institute results from teacher direction, community involvement, and financial support from the board of education. In 1982/1983, 55 percent of the staff, from novice to retiring teachers, participated in institute programs on their own time, with their own money, and usually not for salary credit.[1] What accounts for this consistently high rate of participation on the part of a highly skilled, well-educated staff, most of whom are already at the top of the salary scale? What accounts for the continuing involvement of teachers so that over a three-year period 80 percent participate in some institute activity?[2] Why, when asked about the impact of staff-development activities on classroom practices, do participants continue to state that the institute has had a greater impact on their professional lives than most university courses and most other staff-development activities? The institute exists because its philosophy and structure encourage teacher support and result in teacher "ownership."

The national attention focused on master teacher and merit pay plans as the answer to the loss of status and professionalism of teaching runs counter to existing research on effective staff development. Research indicates that teachers learn most from other teachers, and that practitioners working together effect change. The structure and organization of staff-development activities require teachers to be in charge.[3] Teachers need recognition of their worth through the structures of their institutions on a day-to-day basis, not just an occasional staff day or an occasional stipend. The vitality, energy, and growth of an educational institution make teachers feel that what they are doing has meaning, not just for themselves and their students, but for the total school community. The encouragement of a viable professional environment can come from enlightened central and school administrators, but it cannot be left to chance or only to administrative initiative. Such growth and development must be institutionalized and secured through teacher organizations, such as an in-service institute. Only when teachers have the real power to shape their futures can the professionalism of teaching flourish. The teachers in Scarsdale have developed and supported a program that provides staff development, professional growth, and improved school climate.

Although Scarsdale is privileged, it certainly is not immune to the difficulties facing other school districts; to wit, declining enrollment, a slowly changing population, and fewer young teachers. The average age of the teaching staff is about forty-five, a mature and seasoned staff. Most teachers have been in the district over the fifteen years necessary to reach maximum on the salary scale. Keeping the staff vital and providing continuing opportunities for growth are major concerns of the district. Like most upper-middle-class, highly motivated communities, Scarsdale supports its school system and maintains a constant vigil over the schools. Pressure from parents on teachers is not uncommon, and the need to meet performance standards both internal and external remains constant. Burnout might be a real problem for teachers if it were not for the institutional safeguards that protect professional autonomy and encourage teacher cooperation. The key elements in the success of the institute and the key elements in the important role it plays in the lives of the teachers and of the district are the relationships the institute has with the Scarsdale Teachers Association, the administration, the board of education, and the community.

Because it is a branch of the union, and is included in the negotiated teachers' contract, the institute has been able to weather community and school politics. The negotiating process has served as the keystone in its continued success. Questions of how to revitalize teaching and how to ensure teacher growth are answered in the structure of the institute. The remainder of this article will describe the history, structure, and workings of the STI in order to describe this model of in-service education.

HOW DID THE INSTITUTE START?

The Scarsdale Teachers Institute began offering courses in 1969/1970, after almost a year of planning by a small group of teachers. In order to establish a program that would provide teachers with the means to control their own professional growth, the Scarsdale Teachers Association initiated the program with the support of a grant from the National Education Association, the New York State Teachers Association, and the local board of education. At a time when teacher autonomy was an important issue and the growth of the union of great significance, the institute provided a clear avenue of exhibiting teachers' professional independence. According to the principles of the institute:

> The Scarsdale Teachers Association has sponsored the Institute in accordance with the principle of the professional autonomy affirmed by the New York State United Teachers and other educational groups. Scarsdale teachers have undertaken the Institute's organization, administration and course planning, thus assuming a large degree of responsibility for their professional growth.
>
> Scarsdale teachers also endorse the principle that cooperation among autonomous groups is fundamental to human survival and is no less essential to progress in education. They view the Institute as a laboratory for this principle. Here various groups of teachers, administrators and community leaders may work together for a valued purpose.[4]

Thus, the institute was founded to provide quality professional education to the staff of Scarsdale and to provide an independent and clearly autonomous mechanism for reinforcing teachers' professional status. Teachers in the school system endorsed the concept of the institute, and offered a wealth of suggestions for courses, speakers, and procedures. The executive board of the association then established a committee composed of teachers from the seven schools in the system to organize and operate the institute. Once the structure was in place, the leadership of the association negotiated the institute into the union contract.

Fifteen years later, STI still functions for teachers in the district. As a matter of fact, many of the same teachers are still taking courses there. With few modifications, the structure of the institute remains the same. A recent evaluation states:

> The Scarsdale Teachers Institute (STI) is a unique organization. It performs a valuable educational function for the Scarsdale Public Schools. Large numbers of teachers participate in the program. There is evidence of dedication and professional excitement. The leadership is cognizant of current educational trends and philosophies. Every effort is made to bring current educational expertise to the faculty at large. Teachers play a major role in the selection and teaching of the courses. Teachers perceive the STI as belonging to them. The STI offers scope, purpose and direction to the energies of a staff who would otherwise be restricted to the classroom. The STI offers a positive, constructive leadership role. From all points of view, teachers, administrators, and the Board of Education, the STI is perceived as a valuable asset to the district.[5]

The vision of the founders of the institute remains clear; the structure has remained basically unchanged. The most dramatic change over the years has been in the collaboration that has developed between the institute and the administration, and in the place the institute enjoys in the district. Because it has been held in place by the strength of the teachers' contract, STI has become institutionalized. It is a resource the district and the teachers can count on when doing their long- and short-range planning.

HOW DOES THE INSTITUTE WORK?

As evident from the organizational chart (see Figure 1), the staff is the source of strength for the institute. Members of the policy board are teachers; the director is a teacher chosen by the Scarsdale Teachers Association. The contract stipulates half-time release from teaching assignments for the director to administer the program (see Figure 2). This teacher is responsible to the committee, the association, and ultimately the staff. Since the program runs throughout the year, the development and implementation of programs are continuous.

The policy board is composed of teachers from each of the seven schools in the district. Although the term of office is not formally structured, most people tend to serve for a number of years. Serving on the Institute Committee is considered one of the more attractive voluntary assignments in the district. The organization of the committee tends to be governed by the informal power structure of the school, rather than the formal structure. Over the course of the fifteen years of the institute's existence there have been four directors, each serving for four to five years. The change in leadership took place informally when personnel decided they had served an adequate period of time. Since the staff is small (approximately 300 professional personnel) and the atmosphere positive, these informal procedures continue to work.

The major responsibility of the Institute Committee is to plan, implement, and evaluate the in-service program. Each committee member also assumes responsibility for representing the institute to his or her particular school and in bringing the views of the school to the committee. On a school level each committee member publicizes courses, distributes flyers, arranges luncheon meetings to discuss courses, sounds out teachers on their interests for programs, finds course leaders, and serves as the spokesperson for his or her school.

On the district or committee level, each committee person assumes responsibility for helping to develop the program for the year. This task involves in-depth interviews with teachers and principals during times of needs assessment, and in gathering suggestions for speakers, programs, courses, and course leaders. In addition to collecting data, committee members often serve as course coordinators, helping to organize and run particular programs. These members set policy and procedures for the institute that are not covered by contracts, and meet with the board of education to discuss future directions and present problems.

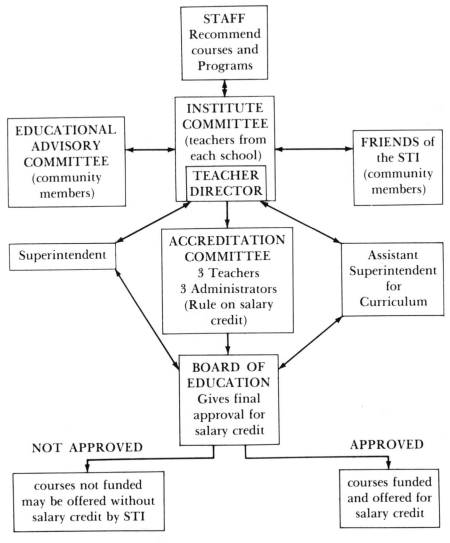

Figure 1. Scarsdale Teachers Institute
ORGANIZATIONAL CHART

Over the years, the committee has developed an elaborate planning process; the director and committee members meet with staff on building and department levels, with department chairpeople at the junior and senior high schools, with principals individually and in a group, and with members of the central administration. At the same time, the assistant superintendent for curriculum meets with the committee to set out the district's curriculum goals

1. The Board will provide for part-time (50%) leave for a teacher director of the Institute designated by the Association.
2. The Board will provide for suitable accommodations for Director's use as an Institute Center for all staff members.
3. An Accreditation Committee, composed of three administrators approved by the Association, shall review all Institute in-service course proposals. The Committee shall submit written proposals for recommendation to the Superintendent. Upon the recommendation of the Superintendent, the Board shall determine whether or not it will approve courses for salary credit, such courses may carry 1 to 3 units of credit. Requirements for study credit will be patterned in a manner generally consistent with university practices.
4. The option to offer a course without salary credit remains with the Institute.
5. In order to obtain salary credit a teacher must complete the requirements of the course. Teachers may earn up to 8 salary credits per year.
6. The Institute will prepare a yearly analysis of the nature and degree of success of Institute programs. The report shall provide a description of each course offered both for credit and non-credit and estimate the course's quality and effectiveness.
7. The Board will allocate $12,000 for the year 1983-84 for expenses of instructors and coordinators of in-service course approved for salary study credit and materials.

Figure 2. Major provisions of the contract of the Scarsdale Teachers Association and the Scarsdale Board of Education regarding the Scarsdale Teachers Institute.

for the following year. The committee also meets with the executive board of the association, and members of the Professional Development Committee (the district's grant-awarding group).[6] Once this elaborate needs assessment has taken place, the committee meets to develop the program for the following year (see Figure 3). The responsibility of implementing the program then rests with the director.

Once programs are developed, they are submitted to the Accreditation Committee, a group made up of three teachers appointed by the association and three administrators appointed by the superintendent (see Figure 2). The responsibility of the Accreditation Committee is to assess each course for salary credit. Usually the committee meets with the course planner or leader to discuss the need that led to the development of the course, the quality of each of the sessions, and the impact the course might have upon teachers' work with children. The institute has tried, over the years, to keep the notions of

Figure 3. Schedule of Program Development

March & April	Spring program begins. Institute Committee begins needs assessment. Institute Chairperson and Committee members meet with:

(a) Assistant Superintendent to assess District curriculum goals.

(b) Elementary Principals to assess building and District needs.

(c) Junior and Senior High Principals to assess building and District needs.

(d) Department Chairpersons at Junior and Senior High to assess department and school needs.

(e) Teachers to assess individual, school and District needs. Committee conducts in-depth interviews with individuals, as well as interviews with groups.

May	Formal questionnaire sent to staff including all recommendations from all levels of District. Institute Committee evaluates spring program, assesses the quality of each course and the full program for the year.
June	Institute Committee evaluates results of questionnaire, District goals and individual requests to determine fall program and select course leaders. Educational Advisory Committee meets to suggest speakers for fall program.
July	Institute Chairperson schedules program for fall and meets with course leaders for individual course planning. Institute Chairperson develops budget for the year.
August	Institute Chairperson writes and publishes catalogue. Course leaders prepare outlines for Accreditation Committee for recommendation to Board. Catalogue sent to printer at end of August.
September	Courses for fall presented to the Accreditation Committee at opening of school. Recommendations for course salary credit presented to the Board at the first study session in September. Institute Committee publicizes program in schools. Publicity goes to newspapers, in-house and local papers, other schools, community members, Friends of the Institute, and Educational Advisory Board for registration period prior to beginning of session in early October.
October	Institute Committee plans for winter programs. Coordinators write course descriptions for winter courses. Planning for spring program.
November	Accreditation Committee meets to assess courses for winter semester for recommendation to the Board. Educational Advisory Committee meets to make suggestions for spring program.

Figure 3. Schedule of Program Development (*continued*)

December   Institute Committee completes plans for the spring. Evaluation of fall program.

January   Accreditation Committee meets to assess courses for spring semester for recommendation to the Board. Winter courses begin. Institute Committee evaluates fall program.

February   Spring catalogue printed and distributed for registration period late February and early March. Institute Committee evaluates winter programs. Publicity for schools and community.

immediate applicability to classroom experience broad, since assessing what will have impact on the classroom is difficult. All experiences teachers have broaden and enrich their interaction with young people; for that reason, most courses are open to the entire school community. Often the Accreditation Committee requests changes in programs, asks that course descriptions be rewritten, and suggests alternatives to teachers. After the revisions process, the Accreditation Committee votes on a recommendation for credit for each course. Those courses recommended for salary credit are then submitted to the superintendent, who makes the final recommendation for credit approval to the board.

The board of education takes seriously its role in approving credit for institute courses. Often, the board will send back a course for revision or reevaluation. Usually, upon revision, the course will be approved. The Institute Committee meets with board members periodically to keep them informed and to enrich their understanding of adult education. If the board does not approve a course for salary credit, that is, for funding out of negotiated allocations (Figure 2), the institute retains the option of offering the course without salary credit and assuming the cost of the course itself.

The institute assumes that the salary credit for in-service credit requires some academic product; therefore, most courses require a paper or project. The time requirements for salary credit are linked to the New York State Department of Education regulations for graduate course credits, in particular twelve hours for one in-service credit. Thus, the model for in-service remains primarily an academic model. Since funding is tied to approval for credit by the board, this requirement has an important impact on the planning of the program.

The only additional source of funding for the institute comes from the teachers themselves, who pay approximately $30 for one credit. This money is used to maintain the institute, and to pay for printing costs, secretarial help, telephones, and refreshments.

STI draws on the community for support through two community groups, the Friends of the Institute and the Educational Advisory Committee. The

Friends of the Institute is a large group of residents in Scarsdale and neighboring communities who have expressed interest in the institute. They have taken courses, made inquiries, recommended speakers, or in some way made themselves known to it. These people receive all mailings and are invited to attend a lecture at one course free of charge each semester.

The second group plays an even more important role. The Educational Advisory Committee is a small group of community members who meet with the Institute Committee two or three times a year to provide support for program development. It is a rich resource of names, contacts, leads, and information. With its support, the institute develops programs that reflect the interests of the community as well as of the school. These members also serve as a public voice for the institute within the community, particularly important as new people move into the community and need to become acquainted with the schools.

Thus, the institute is structured, through the negotiations process, to provide maximum autonomy for teachers. With the exception of board approval of salary credit for courses, the administration, program selection, instruction, needs assessment, evaluation of programs, hiring and firing of consultants, committee selection, publicity, and public relations are all in the hands of the teachers—an admirable and often enviable position for the teachers of the district.

Yet, this responsibility can also have its limitations. The major difficulty facing the institute—and the major stumbling block in this model of in-service education—is that it requires a mature, interdependent relationship between the teachers and the administration. Inherent in this structure is the danger of developing a mentality that sets teachers and administrators apart. When teachers and administrators view each other as equals, partners in the same enterprise, albeit doing different jobs, this model of staff development enhances all aspects of a district. Administrators need to trust teachers' skills and be willing to share some power and teachers need to accept this responsibility and take charge of their own growth. Over the years, the institute has sought to develop avenues for cooperation with the administration and to integrate more activities with the planning of the district. This has required an effort on the part of the administration and the institute to work together in as cooperative a mode as possible. Teachers are better served through a cooperative mode; the effectiveness of in-service training is enhanced when it is reinforced through the resources of the entire district. Therefore, over the past few years the institute has developed closer ties to the administration through the continuous needs-assessment process, meetings with the board of education, revisions of the contract, district acknowledgement of the institute, and involvement of the Accreditation Committee at early stages of program planning (see Figure 3).

The two major problems inherent in effecting change—breaking down the isolation of the classroom and reinforcing new skills within the classroom by practice and coaching—cannot be done by the institute in isolation from the district. The district provides some workshops during the school day to meet specific curriculum goals, while the institute operates primarily after school. Also, teachers will not change their practices or the structure of their classrooms without the cooperation and support of the principals. Therefore, the goal of STI over the past few years has been to develop cooperative relationships with the administration based on mutual need and common purpose.

The institute offers a complete range of courses from noncredit programs serving the personal needs of teachers, such as exercise and gourmet cooking, to courses that meet needs of a particular department or group in the school. The programming usually covers the curriculum areas, methodology, and innovations in education. This past year, for example, courses included Film and Ideology, Environmental Studies, Sharing Literature with Children, Stress among Adolescents, Where Will the Workplace Be?, Strategies for Teaching Presidential Elections, and Effective Communication Skills. While these courses developed from teacher suggestions, board goals, and administrative concerns, each course primarily reflected teacher interest. Teachers who manage the courses hire outside consultants and members of the staff to teach. The results of these courses find their ways into the classroom in a variety of methods—some direct, some indirect—but in each case teachers have had the opportunity to work together and to share experiences that enrich them as people and as professionals. For most of these courses, it is entirely appropriate that the institute act independently and individually. Participants in the courses usually seek support from other staff members for recognition of their projects or their work in the classroom. Oftentimes courses at the institute will anticipate district curriculum work or introduce an idea that will need further exploration in other staff-development activities at the building level or in curriculum committees. Where Will the Workplace Be? touched on issues of career education, which the district is just beginning to examine, and Sharing Literature with Children is the second in a series of programs on literature in anticipation of the district's organization of a curriculum committee to examine the scope and sequence of literature in the elementary school.

These programs enhance the self-esteem of the teachers, increase their sense of themselves as professionals managing their own growth, and open new avenues for curriculum development, classroom practices, and interpersonal relations. The personal-needs courses provide teachers with an opportunity to relax together and enjoy one another's company, another important plus of the institute.

In areas where the board has a clearly articulated goal and a strong need for implementation, collaboration between the institute and the district becomes more useful and worthwhile. Writing provided one form of collaboration, and the need for computer literacy among the staff provided another, although with totally different models of interaction.

WRITING

Four years ago, as part of the ongoing curriculum review process, the district writing committee began looking at approaches to teaching writing in the elementary schools. As the same time, through the needs-assessment process, teachers asked the institute to offer a course in writing, emphasizing a closer look at the new work being done on the writing process. The coordinating teacher hired an outside consultant. That first course led to a collaboration between the curriculum office and the institute. The institute invited the consultant back to do a second course in writing, and the assistant superintendent for instruction hired her to work with the teachers taking the course during the day. The teacher who coordinated the course soon became the helping teacher in writing, a position created by the district to augment the writing program. That teacher is released from the classroom for the mornings to help teachers implement the writing program.

Once teachers had mastered the basics of the writing-process approach, they wanted continued work to refine their practices. The following year the institute offered A Writing Seminar for Scarsdale Teachers. The consultant returned on occasion, but the group functioned with a support system from within the staff. The course description states: "The group will meet in the evening, twice a month. Each meeting will involve clusters of teachers sharing drafts of current projects and discussing writing techniques."[7]

A group of teachers in one elementary school came to the institute to ask if they could work with the helping teacher in a course in which they would share what they were doing in their individual classes. The helping teacher was able to arrange time to meet with teachers in their classrooms during the day and then continue the work, bringing all the teachers in the project together after school. The credit course was so successful that the teachers became committed to understanding writing through more complex research. The helping teacher had been involved in an Interactive Research and Development on Schooling (IR&DS) research grant and was able to work with the course participants. They formed a research group, and again the institute was able to formulate a course, Writing Research or Classroom Research: The Place to Begin. The coordinator of the project writes:

> I had learned something about research from the IR&DS project; so I agreed to become a tentative guide, taking teachers through the research process. We were now teachers leading teachers, and had to develop our own support system. We did this through an in-service course sponsored by the Scarsdale Teachers Institute. We met for six two-hour sessions to study the nature of descriptive research.[8]

The teachers read research, investigated other teacher-researcher models, and began to collect data. They recorded much of what went on in their class-rooms, and searched for a problem or question on which they could focus a study. The result of the course was to be a proposal to the Professional Development Grant Committee for a summer grant to write up the results of the findings. The teachers received their grant, wrote and published their research, and presented their findings at a national conference. The teachers now consider their school "the writing school." This change in practices took four to five years to accomplish with the continuing support from the insti-tute, the curriculum office, the principal, and, of course, the teachers them-selves.

As the interest in writing grew, the institute began receiving requests from the junior and senior high to provide some program for them in writing. At a National Council of Teachers of English convention, a group of teachers attended a workshop on writing across the curriculum. Impressed by the project, the teachers asked the district to invite the coordinator of the project to Scarsdale to talk further about what he and his colleagues had been learning. The group met with teachers from all departments in the junior and senior high schools. The meetings were sponsored by the district and teachers were released from classes to attend. After the visit, teachers were interested enough in the idea of writing across the curriculum to ask the institute to develop a program for the next year. Coordinated by the helping teacher, this course, Writing across the Curriculum 7–12, was designed to meet monthly throughout the year so that teachers could work on writing projects in their classrooms, then bring them back to the class for discussion and analysis. The consultant made regular visits; he worked with teachers in their classrooms, or in free periods during the day, and then with the institute class in the afternoon. The cost of these visits was shared by the institute and the curriculum office. So, again, the collaboration between the district and the institute furthered the goals of the district and met the needs of the teachers.

SOCIAL HISTORY

Other collaborations have been initiated by teachers in a variety of ways. The junior high social studies department was awarded a professional develop-ment grant to bring in a consultant to work with them on using social history in the curriculum. The institute asked the consultant to prepare a three-day workshop for all teachers on integrating social history into the curriculum; the chairperson of the department coordinated the program.

COMPUTERS

When it became clear that the district would have to become more involved in computer education, the administration and the institute co-sponsored an introductory course on computer programming. The course was offered to the staff free of charge, after school and for credit. One hundred and twenty-five people registered for the course. This course, taught by an outside instructor, initiated formal computer education in the district. At this point, the board had limited and specific curriculum goals at the elementary schools, but teachers' interest in learning about computers was high. The district could not provide enough workshops during the school day to meet the demand, so the institute offered these programs. Institute programs were designed to meet the needs and interests of teachers, not to meet the specific curriculum goals of the district. For example, LOGO was offered to all teachers, not just the third- and fourth-grade teachers who were responsible for teaching LOGO in the classroom and were being serviced to some extent by the curriculum office. To maintain and increase the interest of the staff in computer programming, the institute offered courses in BASIC taught by members of the staff.

Over the past four years, STI has offered eleven courses in computers, including BASIC, LOGO, PASCAL, Computer Uses, Microcomputer Uses in the Library, and Programming with Pocket Computers, thereby augmenting work that is done within the district and providing opportunities for teachers to expand their understanding of computers in ways the curriculum office could not afford and did not wish to sponsor. Although a formal, financial collaboration does not exist, there is a mutual educational interest. As one teacher remarked, "As far as I am concerned, if it had not been for the institute's foresight and professional approaches to learning computers, I really do not think I could have gotten started. The quality of the courses and the positive support have enabled me to be where I am today."[9]

INTERDISCIPLINARY STUDIES SEMINAR .

Another form of collaboration developed the Interdisciplinary Studies Seminar, a semester program for high school teachers. One of the changes recommended for graduation requirements included a half credit in interdisciplinary studies for second semester seniors. Unlike most of the other changes in graduation requirements, this was recommended rather than mandated. The board of education thought that it would be best to first have a pilot project. High school teachers were enthusiastic about working together to develop curriculum. In this case, the collaboration took place on a building level. The institute approached the high school principal to ask for joint sponsorship and cooperation in developing the program. The principal and the coordinators of the course, two teachers with experience in interdiscipli- nary work, met with staff during the day, at the joint invitation of the princi- pal and the institute, to explore the interest in the program. The principal sat in on some of the initial planning meetings for the design of the course and helped encourage registration. Faculty entered the program with assurance that their work in the seminar would be given careful attention and consideration. The central administration and the board of education were invited to attend the final session of the course so that they, too, could be informed of the curriculum development.

The benefits that accrue to the district from the institute are manifold, but most important is the role the institute plays in maintaining the vitality and independence of the staff. The administration and the institute must maintain a delicate balance to preserve their individual interests and still find methods of working together to serve the general needs. Through careful management and a desire for collaboration, this model of staff development offers small districts the opportunity to build staff morale, implement new curriculum, and improve teaching skills. The district further benefits by encouraging teacher growth through risk taking and experimentation in a protected and supportive environment. Teachers can test new waters free from the fears of failure or evaluation; they can form networks to support their efforts at change, and they can find colleagues to guide them through new teaching strategies. Teachers use the institute to meet their particular needs—for new technology, personal interest, reflection on their own teaching, new ideas, or areas of concern that are not addressed in any other place in the district. The staff regards the institute as the place where new ideas are generated, where they have a chance to work with their colleagues and practice what they learn.

The varied roles teachers assume at STI encourage their interest and support in the work of the district. The autonomy teachers feel through the institute structure and their freedom to create professional programs provide the impetus for their support. Teachers manage their own growth. They run the courses, hire the consultants, manage the budgets. They often teach the courses they have designed, while at another session, or course, the same teachers become students. Teachers create programs in which they are the experts helping their colleagues. Part of the satisfaction that teachers derive from their jobs comes from being able to mentor—to share and pass on the skills they have acquired over years. Some of the lack of opportunity for altered roles or mobility in teaching is offset in this way. The institute provides the place for master teachers to share their skills and help their colleagues. The place that breaks down the barriers of the classroom walls continues to be the institute. Over and over teachers remark that the opportunity to talk with colleagues from other buildings and work together to solve common problems remains the best parts of the institute experience.

The original plan of STI was to develop an autonomous organization that would promote the growth of teachers and the growth of the educational program of the district. The major impetus in promoting growth was to provide continuing opportunities for teachers to work in many roles, to extend the breadth and depth of their experience. For the most part, this model has held true to its original purpose. The fiscal constraints and changing educational climate have made cooperation and collaboration between the institute and the administration necessary and desirable. Through careful planning, desire for the endeavor to succeed, and a recognition that teacher independence can benefit the district, the institute has succeeded. This cooperation and collaboration has been possible because the negotiated contract mandates the institute as a reality for the administration and the teachers, and therefore allows the flexibility necessary for collaboration. When teachers have real, not putative, strength, staff development works. STI continues to serve as a model of in-service education that enriches education.

Notes

1   Judith Schwartz, "Fitness Is a State of Mind," Institute Report to the Board of Education, August 1984 (unpublished manuscript).

2   Judith Schwartz, "One to Grow On," Institute Report to the Board of Education, May 1984 (unpublished manuscript).

3   Compilation of staff development research, *Journal of Staff Development*, 1981–1983; and *Staff Development* (ASCD Handbook, 1982).

4   Principles of the Scarsdale Teachers Institute, *One to Grow On* (course catalogue, Fall 1983), p. 3.

5   Lawrence Finkel, "An Evaluation of the Scarsdale Teachers Institute," May 1983, p. 6 (unpublished manuscript).

6   The Professional Development Program is another negotiated program held in place by the contract, which provides a sum of money to be allocated by a joint interest or group interest. The Scarsdale Teachers Institute and the Professional Development Committee meet together to share information about projects that might be of interest and become courses for the institute—and of work in courses that might be expanded into further curriculum projects. Again, most of the impetus for this collaboration comes from the teachers, who wish further recognition for their work. The institute has sponsored seminars to publicize projects developed by the Professional Development Committee.

7   *Fill It Up* (Institute course catalogue, Fall 1981), p. 8.

8   Adele Fiderer, ed., *Children Write/Teachers Learn*, a collection of research reports on the writing processes of students, grades K-6, prepared by teachers in the Scarsdale Public Schools (Scarsdale Public Schools, 1984), p. 4.

9   Teacher responses to institute questionnaire on evaluation of courses (March 1984).

Beyond the Commission Reports:
Toward Meaningful School Improvement

A. HARRY PASSOW
Teachers College, Columbia University

In the Julius and Rosa Sachs Memorial Lectures that I delivered at Teachers College in 1976 entitled *Secondary Education Reform: Retrospect and Prospect,* I observed that America was once again being pressed to reform its secondary education, as it had regularly been since before the turn of the century.[1] At that time, there were nine reports that had been issued between 1973 and 1975, each of which indicated major shortcomings in our high schools, and each of which proposed major changes in the nature of secondary schooling and its delivery systems.[2]

In looking at secondary schooling reform retrospectively, I wrote:

> The publication of the report of the Committee of Ten on Secondary School Studies in 1893 is usually described in histories of education as the watershed in secondary education. In the eight decades since then, we have witnessed a parade of committees, groups, and individuals which have been critical of the purposes and practices of high schools and have consistently pressed for reforms — some major and some minor. Throughout this same period, the American high school has been described as unchanging, static, and unbending.[3]

Prior to the outpouring of reform reports in the 1970s, educators seemed to have had to deal with only one commission or committee report at a time, so that the discussion could be focused on the recommendations being offered. How influential these reports were in affecting change has been a matter of discussion and debate, the differences stemming at least in part from the criteria being used to assess change.

After tracing the history of secondary education reform by committee and commission reports through nine decades, I noted:

> Schools have changed since the Committee of Ten report, despite the rhetoric of the American high school as an unchanging and immutable institution. Schools changed slowly, sporadically, and quite unevenly. We have very few examples of dramatic reform — witness the "era of curriculum innovation" of the 1960s when millions of dollars were spent in reforming curriculum and teacher education.[4]

206

The launching of Russia's *Sputnik I* in October 1957 opened the floodgates of criticism of America's educational system, especially of the high schools. Although James B. Conant had begun his study of the high school before the sputnik launch, his report, *The American High School Today,* was not issued until 1959. Conant's response to the question as to whether the comprehensive high school could meet its responsibility "for providing good and appropriate education, both academic and vocational, for all young people within a democratic environment which the American people believes serves the principles they cherish"[5] was that "no radical alteration in the basic pattern of American education is necessary in order to improve our public high schools."[6] Conant did, however, propose some twenty-one recommendations that became "checklists for reform" for schools across the nation.

Almost concurrently, the post-*Sputnik* period ushered in significant efforts for reforming education "to catch up with and pass the Russians in space." The National Defense Education Act (NDEA) of 1958 provided significant funding to upgrade the teaching of science, mathematics, and foreign languages through curriculum development, instructional materials production, and the training and retraining of teachers. The act also provided for improved guidance and counseling, especially in the high schools. Subsequently, other subject areas and the teachers in those areas were included under the NDEA canopy. The National Science Foundation increased its support for projects to improve course content and teacher competence in science and mathematics. Various foundations invested heavily in projects to upgrade instruction. The 1960s, especially the early part of that decade, were marked by projects in practically all subject areas that produced new curricula, instructional resources, technologies, school organization plans, teacher training methods, and personnel deployment patterns.

How much impact the flurry of curriculum projects and teacher training and retraining programs of the 1960s had on America's high schools is being argued still. Charles Silberman observed that "the reform movement had produced innumerable changes, and yet the schools themselves remained largely unchanged."[7] Writing recently on the curriculum reform efforts of the 1950s and 1960s, John Goodlad observed:

> Early collaborations involved primarily university professors and secondary school teachers. Inclusion of experts in human development and learning was stimulated by Jerome Bruner's book *The Process of Education.* The central focus was on developing new materials to do a significant part of the teaching job. Many teachers were brought into inservice workshops both for refining and learning how to use the learning materials, but their involvement tended to decline with the passage of time. And reform neglected many

aspects of change. With some exceptions, reformers regarded administrators, especially school principals, as potential blocks to, rather than partners in, curricular reform. A major shortcoming was that the movement never became linked to the structures and institutions preparing and certifying teachers. Consequently, there was no stream of incoming teachers knowledgeable in the new programs to pick up the momentum lost when the inservice teacher education programs — never encompassing more than a fraction of the teachers — declined and ultimately ceased.[8]

There were literally dozens of curriculum reform projects initiated after *Sputnik,* each with its own acronym — PSCS, BSCS, CHEM, CBA, UICSM, SMSG, and ESSS, to name but a few — involving, eventually, almost every area of the curriculum. New curricula, new textbooks, new instructional packages — many of them designed to be "teacher proof" — were produced, but most observers of that period agree that the "era of curriculum reform" was only on the surface and was shortlived.

By 1970, Charles Silberman, who had viewed these efforts in 1966 as contributing to the total remaking of American education, devoted a chapter in *Crisis in the Classroom* to "The Failures of Educational Reform." Silberman asked: "What happened? Why did a movement that aroused such great hopes, and that enlisted so many distinguished educators, exert so little impact on the schools?"[9] Silberman's explanation comprised a number of reasons, including the naivete, innocence, and even arrogance of the reformers: "Because the reformers were university scholars with little contact with public schools or schools of education, moreover, and because they also neglected to study the earlier attempts at curriculum reform, they also tended to ignore the harsh realities of classroom and school organization."[10] Furthermore, Silberman saw these reform efforts doomed to failure because classroom teachers were in a good position to sabotage curricula they found offensive — "teachers are not likely to have a high regard for courses designed to bypass them," for courses designed as teacher-proof.[11] The new courses were more difficult to teach than those they replaced, yet the reformers, when they employed in-service teacher education at all, focused on teachers "knowing" the subject that they were teaching. Silberman noted that while subject matter knowledge was certainly crucial, experience with NDEA and other in-service programs "made it painfully clear that mastering the subject matter does not begin to solve the problem of how to teach it."[12] Finally, he noted, failure to involve classroom teachers "in the creation and modification of the new curricula . . . tended to destroy, or at least inhibit, the very spirit of inquiry the new courses were designed to create."[13]

There are observers and analysts who do not view the reform activities of the sixties as completely dismal failures, but there are very few who see that period — "The Era of Curriculum Innovation" — as one in which reform efforts realized the hopes of their proponents. Marvin Lazerson, Judith McLaughlin, and Bruce McPherson, in "New Curriculum, Old Issues," have commented:

> The educational reformers [of the fifties and sixties] did not realize their dreams. As they attempted to implement their ideas, they found the task more difficult than they had foreseen. The reformers encountered a host of conflicts in local communities, in the schools, in the academic community, and in their own thinking about education. What seemed clear — the pursuit of academic excellence — became less certain in the shifting sands of implementation and ideological assumptions.[14]

Almost at the same time that the post-*Sputnik* reform efforts were at their peak, the so-called "War on Poverty" and the associated civil rights movement began. Passage of the Elementary and Secondary Education Act of 1965 and implementation of desegregation-integration programs and activities focused the attention of educators on questions of quality education and equality of educational opportunity. While nominally directed toward increasing excellence, the post-*Sputnik* curriculum and teacher education and reeducation efforts were in reality focused on equity. Compensatory and remedial education programs were the target of reform efforts. New curricula, new instructional strategies, and new instructional materials were developed, and teacher education and reeducation programs were designed to provide the competencies, knowledge, and skills needed to teach the children of the poor and of various racial and ethnic groups who were not being adequately served by existing educational programs. Some urban education reformers aimed their efforts and their rhetoric at remaking schools, not just implementing a few changes. Again, changes did occur, but few educators would suggest that equity issues have been resolved.

In the early 1970s, a number of reports were issued that dealt with the shortcomings of the high schools, examined the nature and causes of the problems of educating and socializing adolescents, and proposed major policy and program changes not only in secondary schools but in other agencies serving youth. Most of these reports were what might be thought of as "national committee reports," being issued by committees with such titles as the National Commission on the Reform of Secondary Education, the Panel on Youth of the President's Science Advisory Committee, the National Panel on High Schools and Adolescent Education, the Phi Delta Kappa Task Force on Compulsory Education and Transitions for Youth, and the National Commission for Manpower Policy. These reports were published and distributed through the usual publishers and booksellers, not unlike most of the national reform reports of the 1980s.[15]

One report of that period — *The Rise Report* — differed in that it was prepared by a state committee, the California Commission for Reform of Intermediate and Secondary Education. The commission delivered the report to the then superintendent of Public Instruction, Wilson Riles, with the comment, "We respectfully submit our Commission's statements and findings to you for your use as a tool to focus resources (both human and material) and begin the task of reform."[16] In its foreword, the commission pointed out that it had "attempted numerous times throughout the report to emphasize that the education of youth cannot be equated with schooling" and that recommendations for change in schooling alone could not possibly solve the problems that the group thought cried out for change.[17] The report contained no fewer than twenty-six major recommendations that the commission felt should begin the discussion and debate that would result in the remaking of education and schooling in the state of California. *The RISE Report* did start such a debate, although the commission itself saw the task of determining "how its recommendations should be implemented in an organized, systematic fashion" — how the reform should be brought about — as "clearly the job of the California State Department of Education."[18] Genuine reform, the commission maintained, could only occur "and have a positive and lasting impact if the people of California willingly and actively support the reform effort."[19] Moreover, the commission cautioned: "It is vital that the education community not only recognize the inevitability of change but also be a leader in the process of change. Change is bound to occur, but without the involvement of the education community, the task of reforming education can never be accomplished."[20] Changes in the intermediate and secondary schools of California did indeed occur in the following years, but the commission's vision of drastic reforms was realized only very incompletely.

The reform reports of the 1970s were pretty much in agreement on what was wrong with the schools: they did not and could not provide a complete environment for youth education; they had failed to provide a comprehensive education; they served as "social aging vats," age-segregating youth and prolonging their dependence on adults; they had not provided effective education-work experiences, they could not provide adequate citizenship education or education in the arts; and so forth. The reforms advocated ranged from creating a variety of educational options and alternative programs, to lowering the school-leaving age and offering alternatives to the conventional twelve-year schooling pattern, to integrating the learning and teaching resources of the school and community, to designing secondary education as part of a lifetime continuum of education, and similar suggestions for redesigning secondary-level curriculum and delivery systems.[21]

The key operant words in the reform literature of the 1970s were *electives, options,* and *alternatives.* The National Commission on the Reform of Secondary Education, established by the Kettering Foundation, for instance, saw the variety of alternatives "limited only by the legitimate needs of adolescents and the vivacity of imagination of educational planners."[22] That commission recommended, "Every adolescent should, with proper guidance, be able to select those forms of schooling and learning most congenial to his basic learning style, philosophic orientation, and tastes."[23] The National Panel on High Schools and Adolescent Education suggested that alternatives might include, but should certainly not be limited to, "mini-schools, schools-without-walls, open schools, alternative schools, optimal programs, internships, parallel courses, independent study, free schools, and apprentice and action learning."[24] As did the RISE Commission, the Kettering Foundation's national commission suggested that schooling "must be not only 'where you find it,' but 'when you want it.' " Further, it urged that schools recognize that "authentic learning can take place in a wide variety of settings, many of them remote from the schoolhouse."[25]

The reform reports of the seventies saw the schools as lacking in relevance and humaneness and faulted them because they failed to provide curricula and instruction that evolved from students' needs, interests, and concerns. Their recommendations called for drastic and dramatic changes in curriculum, teaching, organization and functioning, climate, learning sites, and in the relationships between the workplace and schools and between schools and other educating agencies and institutions. The concensus, in retrospect, seems to be that while some changes did occur, schools seem to be as unchanging and intractable as the reports accused them of being. Certainly schools did not open up almost unlimited options and choices for students, did not make work experience a central component of adolescent education, did not combine the resources of the school and community to provide a comprehensive education for youth, and did not, beyond a very limited extent, move learning out of the classroom. A "new view of secondary education and schooling" was not implemented.

By the 1980s, the nation's educators and citizenry were discussing another spate of reports, well over a dozen having been issued between

1982 and 1984. Included were reports entitled *Action for Excellence, Academic Preparation for College, High School, A Place Called School, Meeting the Need for Quality, Horace's Compromise, The Paideia Proposal, Making the Grade,* and *Educating Americans for the 21st Century.*[26] It was the April 1984 report of the National Commission on Excellence in Education entitled *A Nation at Risk: The Imperative for Educational Reform,* however, that caught the interest of the widest audience. A year after publication, the U.S. Government Printing Office reported having sold over 70,000 copies, and it was estimated that "private groups have reprinted at least another 500,000 copies for their own constituencies," these, in addition to extensive excerpts in major newspapers.[27]

I analyzed a number of these most recent reports in *Reforming Schools in the 1980s: A Critical Review of the National Reports,*[28] discussing their common themes and their recommendations. In one way or another, the reports assert that American education is experiencing a serious crisis that will render the United States vulnerable to its industrial, commercial, and even military competitors unless reform is undertaken and their various recommendations are implemented forthwith. The attainment of excellence in American education is the goal of most of the reform reports. As I enumerated in an article for *Phi Delta Kappan,* their recommendations include, among other things, "raising standards (not always clearly defined); setting higher requirements for high school graduation and admission to college; eliminating 'soft' subjects and mandating a common core curriculum for all students; increasing requirements in mathematics, science, and foreign languages; testing achievement more regularly; lengthening the school day and the school year; and generally 'getting tough' with students, teachers, and even administrators."[29]

In May 1984, the Department of Education issued a 229-page report entitled *The Nation Responds: Recent Efforts to Improve Education,* which summarizes the reform efforts of states and local districts responding to *A Nation at Risk.* The report begins with the assertion that during 1983, "deep public concern about the Nation's future created a tidal wave of school reform which promises to renew American education."[30] It was the comprehensive nature of the reform activities and proposals that gave promise for "significant long-lasting change." As the report pointed out, the current efforts "are not narrow in origin, focus, support, or goals. The diversity of task forces at work on education around the country — task forces including citizens, parents, students, teachers, administrators, business and community leaders, and elected and appointed officials — is evidence of the scope."[31]

The Nation Responds points out the unprecedented activities at the state level on the part of governors, legislators, and state education departments. (For example, by April 1984, 275 state-level task forces working on education reform had been identified by the Education Commission of the States.[32]) The report saw "the confluence of these Spate and national activities explain[ing] in large part the success of the reform movement."[33] Examples of these state-level reforms (as cited in the report) included:

- Forty-eight are considering new high school graduation requirements. 35 have approved changes.
- Twenty-one report initiatives to improve textbooks and instructional materials.
- Eight have approved lengthening the school day, seven, lengthening the school year, and 18 have mandates affecting the time of instruction.
- Twenty-four are examining master teacher or career ladder programs, and six have begun statewide or pilot programs.
- Thirteen are considering changes in academic requirements for extracurricular and athletic programs, and five have already adopted more rigorous standards.[34]

As for local efforts, the report states:

No systematic survey exists of the prevalence or nature of local efforts, but the number and quality of changes being publicized suggest a powerful and broad-based movement. Many local boards created their own local commissions and task forces in response to the national attention and rated their own schools against checklists of the findings of national reports.[35]

The Nation Responds also reported "a quantum increase in the variety of public school activities involving leaders of the university, corporations, and foundation communities."[36] The activities were not easily categorized or described, but some illustrations were given of the diverse reform activities at the postsecondary level:

- Teacher education reforms emphasizing more academic content as well as more experience in classrooms, including internship programs.
- Statewide and local study groups working with individual schools and districts to define the skills and competencies required to improve the chances of making a successful transition to undergraduate education.
- Undergraduate scholarships, frequently offered in conjunction with

local employers, to encourage study in such fundamental areas as writing, mathematics, and science.

- Thirteen collaborative experiments supported by the College Entrance
  Examination Board to smooth the student's passage from high school
  to college.
- A joint statement from the Presidents of Harvard, Stanford, Michigan, Wisconsin, Chicago and Columbia defining ways in which major
  research universities could strengthen their ties with schools.[37]

The Nation Responds: Recent Efforts to Improve Education adds to
the earlier survey by the Department of Education, issued in December
1983, entitled *Meeting the Challenge*.[38] Reading those two surveys together with the accounts found in the media, both general and educational, there can be no question that reforms are taking place. Every
state has committees, commissions, panels, and task forces at work considering policy mandates, regulation changes, and legislation aimed at
bringing about changes and "school improvement." With so many and
such a diversity of activities, it is not difficult to understand the Department of Education's characterizations of "a tidal wave of school reform,"
"a powerful and broad-based [reform] movement," and "a quantum increase," to cite just a few.

The current crop of reports is relatively clear about curricular changes
Clearly there are many efforts to improve the quality of education, but
are the changes they involve meaningful? It is relatively easy to mandate
increases in graduation requirements, but unless one attends to curriculum, teaching, and learning climate, the likelihood of realizing actual
qualitative changes will be remote. State legislatures, state departments
of education, and local school districts may prescribe curricula, more
rigorous courses, a common core curriculum for all, but there is no
assurance that instructional outcomes will differ. Mandating that there
should be more rigorous selection on the basis of academic aptitude and
that preservice teachers should take more academic courses will not in-
sure that "better" persons will enter teaching nor that the quality of
teaching will be improved. These improvement efforts may be necessary,
but they are not sufficient to bring about meaningful change.

The current crop of reports is relatively clear about curricular changes
that need to be made. *A Nation at Risk* proposes "five new basics,"
specifying the number of years of English, mathematics, social studies,
science, and computer science that should be required in the high
school. Mortimer Adler's *Paideia Proposal* offers the same goals for all,
the same curriculum for all, kindergarten through grade 12. John
Goodlad reaffirms the curriculum of the Harvard report *General Education in a Free Society* with its "five fingers of knowledge and experience,"
and he suggests the proportion of instructional time that should be de-

voted to each area. In *High School*, Ernest Boyer gives priority to the mastery of English together with a core of common learning that he regards as basic for all students. The College Board's report on Project EQuality spells out what college-bound students should know and what they should be able to do. A report from the National Science Board Commission details a K–12 curriculum in mathematics, science, and technology. The Education Commission of the States report would strengthen the curriculum by eliminating soft, nonessential courses; encouraging mastery of skills beyond the basics; and enlivening and improving instruction in those subjects retained. Theodore Sizer would organize instruction into four areas or large departments: (1) Inquiry and Expression, (2) Mathematics and Science, (3) Literature and Arts, and (4) Philosophy and History.[39]

While the current reform reports give a good deal of attention to subjects to be studied and suggest limiting or eliminating choices, they, unlike the post-*Sputnik* school improvement efforts, with one or two exceptions, do not address the *what* and *how* questions of curriculum and instruction. Mandating four years of English or an additional year of mathematics says nothing about the nature of the English or mathematics to be studied nor how success can be achieved in teaching or learning. For school improvement to be meaningful, the nature and quality of learning and teaching must be addressed. For school improvement to be meaningful, issues, questions, and strategies for curriculum and staff development must be dealt with.

Writing about the generation of reports of the seventies, I observed:

> The reports do not deal with the prime residents of the schools — students, staff and parents. There is no attention to the life and climate of the school, the intricate networks of social interaction involving individuals and groups which comprise the school's social system. The classrooms are but one part of the school's social system — affected by the hierarchies and the exercise of power; by learning environments, structured and unstructured; and by the formal and informal transactions — all of which exercise considerable influence on learning and socialization. Students are maturing earlier; they are more knowledgeable about some aspects of life, having been exposed to television and other media. Insights about the professional staff and about teaching have raised questions about the existence of a sense of the community and professional colleagueship. Attention to the school climate could well affect curriculum and instruction — both in their formal and informal aspects. To the triad of learner, society and knowledge on which curriculum was to be based as propounded in the *Cardinal Principles of Secondary Education*, a fourth element needs now to be added —

the school as an institution with a life, a climate, and ongoing transactions of its own.[40]

Those observations stemmed from a conviction that our insights and understandings about the school improvement process had grown considerably as a result of research and development activities focused on the management of change and innovation. The articles in this book inform us about the complexities of the schools as human organizations and the requirements for bringing about not just change but meaningful change. As Lieberman and Miller observe, "whether we looked at local problem solving, research transformed into practice, action research, or networking, we were drawn to the teachers, their world, and their work as the starting points for improving the schools."[41] Huberman and Miles argue that school improvement is a "reachable objective, and that we are beginning to understand the conditions for reaching it."[42] They see the conditions for achieving school improvement as "stringent" — improvement, if it is to be meaningful, cannot be attained by mandate or fiat. The other contributors have also examined the nature and complexities of staff development and curriculum development from different perspectives. They tell us that recent efforts to improve education can use the impetus of the national reform reports to stimulate change but that meaningful school improvement must go beyond legislation and mandate — it must involve changes in the knowledge, skills, attitudes, understandings, and values of staff; in the organizational relationships of the school; in the climate and environment of the school; and in the transactions between teachers and learners. What is needed is nothing less than to apply these insights about the school improvement process and to build on the climate for reform generated by the national reports.

Notes

1 A. Harry Passow, *Secondary Education Reform: Retrospect and Prospect* (New York: Teachers College, Columbia University, 1976).

2 California Commission for Reform of Intermediate and Secondary Education, *The RISE Report* (Sacramento, Calif.: California Superintendent of Instruction, 1975); Carnegie Commission on Higher Education, *Continuity and Discontinuity: Higher Education and the Schools* (New York: McGraw-Hill, 1973); National Association of Secondary School Principals, *Conference Report on American Youth in the Mid-Seventies* (Reston, Va.: NASSP, 1972); National Commission on the Reform of Secondary Education, *The Reform of Secondary Education: A Report to the Public and the Profession* (New York: McGraw-Hill, 1973); National Panel on High Schools and Adolescent Education, *The Education of Adolescents* (Washington, D.C.: U.S. Government Printing Office, 1974); Panel on Youth of the President's Science Advisory Committee, *Youth: Transition to Adulthood* (Chicago: University of Chicago Press, 1974); B. Othanel Smith and Donald E. Orolosky, *Socialization and Schooling: Basics of Reform* (Bloomington, Ind.: Phi Delta Kappa, 1975); Ruth Weinstock, *The Greening of the High School* (New York: Educational Facilities Laboratories, 1973); and Willard Wirtz and the National Man-

power Institute, *The Boundless Resource: A Prospectus for an Education/Work Policy* (Washington, D.C.: New Republic Book Co., 1975).

3   Passow, *Secondary Education Reform*, p. 3.

4   Ibid., pp. 53-54.

5   James B. Conant, *The American High School Today* (New York: McGraw-Hill, 1959), p. x.

6   Ibid., p. 40.

7   Charles E. Silberman, *Crisis in the Classroom: The Remaking of American Education* (New York: Random House, 1970), p. 50.

8   John I. Goodlad, *A Place Called School: Prospects for the Future* (New York: McGraw-Hill, 1983), pp. 292-93.

9   Silberman, *Crisis in the Classroom*, p. 179.

10   Ibid., p. 180.

11   Ibid., p. 181.

12   Ibid., p. 182.

13   Ibid.

14   Marvin Lazerson, Judith Block McLaughlin, and Bruce McPherson, "New Curriculum, Old Issues," *Teachers College Record* 86, no. 1 (Fall 1984): 299-319.

15   See note 2.

16   California Commission, *The RISE Report*, p. vii.

17   Ibid.

18   Ibid., p. 35.

19   Ibid., p. 34.

20   Ibid., p. 35.

21   See note 2.

22   National Commission on the Reform of Secondary Education, *The Reform of Secondary Education*, p. 101.

23   Ibid., pp. 99-100.

24   National Panel on High Schools and Adolescent Education, *The Education of Adolescents*, p. 44.

25   National Commission on the Reform of Secondary Education, *The Reform of Secondary Education*, p. 75.

26   Mortimer J. Adler, *The Paideia Proposal: An Educational Manifesto* (New York: Macmillan, 1983); Ernest L. Boyer, *High School: A Report on Secondary Education* (New York: Harper and Row, 1983); Business-Higher Education Forum, *America's Competitive Challenge: The Need for a National Response* (Washington, D.C.: Business-Higher Education Forum, 1983); College Board Education EQuality Project, *Academic Preparation for College: What Students Need to Know and Be Able to Do* (New York: College Board, 1983); Education Commission of the States Task Force on Education for Economic Growth, *Action for Excellence* (Denver, Colo.: Education Commission of the States, 1983); Goodlad, *A Place Called School*; Herbert J. Klausmeier, Robert C. Kerlin, and Monica Zindler, *Improvements of Secondary Education Through Research: Five Longitudinal Case Studies* (Madison, Wis.: Wisconsin Center for Educational Research, 1983); Marvin Lazerson et al., *An Education of Value* (Cambridge, Mass.: Harvard University Graduate School of Education, 1983, Mimeographed); National Commission on Excellence in Education, *A Nation at Risk: The Imperative for Educational Reform* (Washington, D.C.: U.S. Government Printing Office, 1983); National Science Board Commission on Precollege Education in Mathematics, Science, and Technology, *Educating Americans for the 21st Century* (Washington, D.C.: National Science Board, 1983); Paul E. Peterson, *Making the Grade* (New York: Twentieth Century Fund Task Force on Federal Elementary and Secondary Education Policy, 1983); Theodore R. Sizer, *Horace's*

Compromise: The Dilemma of the American High School (Boston: Houghton Mifflin, 1984); Southern Regional Education Board Task Force on Higher Education, *Meeting the Need for Quality: Action in the South* (Atlanta, Ga.: Southern Regional Education Board, 1983); and Southern Regional Education Board Task Force on Higher Education, *The Need for Quality* (Atlanta, Ga.: Southern Regional Education Board, 1981).

27   National Commission on Excellence in Education, *A Nation at Risk.*

28   A. Harry Passow, *Reforming Schools in the 1980s: A Critical Review of the National Reports* (New York: ERIC Clearing House on Urban Education [ED 242 859], Teachers College, Columbia University, 1984).

29   A. Harry Passow, "Tackling the Reform Reports of the 1980s," *Phi Delta Kappan* 65, no. 10 (June 1984): 674-83.

30   U.S. Department of Education, *The Nation Responds: Recent Efforts to Improve Education* (Washington, D.C.: U.S. Government Printing Office, 1984), p. 11.

31   Ibid., p. 15.

32   Education Commission of the States, *Action for Excellence.*

33   U.S. Department of Education, *The Nation Responds,* p. 16.

34   Ibid.

35   Ibid.

36   Ibid., p. 17.

37   Ibid.

38   U.S. Department of Education, *Meeting the Challenge* (Washington, D.C.: U.S. Government Printing Office, 1983).

39   See note 26.

40   Passow, *Secondary Education Reform,* p. 49.

41   Ann Lieberman and Lynne Miller, "School Improvement: Themes and Variations," this volume, p. 108.

42   A. Michael Huberman and Matthew Miles, "Rethinking the Quest for School Improvement: Some Findings from the DESSI Study," this volume, p. 80.

Contributors

TOM BIRD is managing director of the Center of Action Research, Inc., Boulder, Colorado. With support from the National Institute of Education, he is conducting a study of instructional leadership in eight secondary schools.

TERRENCE E. DEAL is professor of education at Peabody College of Vanderbilt University, where he teaches organizational processes and theory, research for administrators, and symbolism in organizations. For the past ten years he has studied the role of myth, ritual and ceremony, and symbols in organizational settings.

DAVID C. DWYER, currently at Far West Laboratory for Educational Research and Development, San Francisco, directs a comparative ethnographic study of the roles of principals in instructional management. He received his Ph.D. in 1981 from Washington University in St. Louis.

MAXINE GREENE is the William F. Russell Professor in the Foundations of Education at Teachers College, Columbia University. She is now working on a book based on her John Dewey Lecture, which will be titled *The Dialectic of Freedom*.

A. MICHAEL HUBERMAN is professor of education at the University of Geneva. He is the author of six books and numerous chapters and articles in the areas of adult learning, dissemination and utilization of knowledge, and qualitative research methodologies. His most recent books, co-authored with Matthew Miles, are *Innovation Up Close: How School Improvement Works* (Plenum, 1984) and *Qualitative Data Analysis: A Sourcebook of New Methods* (Sage, 1984).

JOANN JACULLO-NOTO is assistant professor in the Department of Curriculum and Teaching and director of teacher education at Teachers College, Columbia University. Professor Jacullo-Noto has interests in the areas of staff development and teacher education. Her articles include: "Inside/Outside—Who are the Experts: Collaborative Staff Development" and she has co-authored works concerning collaborative research and development.

ANNE JOSLIN is an adjunct assistant professor of educational leadership and instruction at the University of North Carolina at Charlotte and is currently serving as research project coordinator for the Charlotte-Mecklenburg Schools Teacher Career Development Program.

PAUL F. KLEINE received his Ph.D. from Washington University in 1967 and has served on the faculty of the University of Chicago and as division chairman at the University of Wisconsin-Parkside. Currently, he serves as director of the Bureau of Educational Services at the University of Oklahoma.

ANN LIEBERMAN is chairperson and professor in the Department of Curriculum and Teaching and executive secretary of the Metropolitan School Study Council at Teachers College, Columbia University. Her primary interest has been in educational change and school improvement. She has, for the last decade, attempted to bridge the gap between those studying how to improve schools and those working in them.

JUDITH LITTLE is a senior staff member at the Far West Laboratory for Educational Research and Development, San Francisco, where she directs a program of applied research in teacher education and professional development. In recent years, her major emphasis has been on the school as a work place.

MILBREY WALLIN McLAUGHLIN is associate professor of education, associate director of the Institute for Research on Educational Finance and Governance, and chair of the Evaluation Training Program at Stanford University. Her current research interests focus on teacher incentives and intergovernmental relations in education.

MATTHEW B. MILES is senior research associate at the Center for Policy Research, New York. A social psychologist, his main interests have been in educational innovation and the assessment of planned change in groups and organizations. His current research focuses on the skills needed by change agents in urban school improvement programs.

LYNNE MILLER is assistant superintendent for curriculum, South Bend Community School Corporation, South Bend, Indiana. She has written numerous articles on staff development and school improvement and is coauthor with Ann Lieberman of *Teachers, Their World and Their Work: Implications for School Improvement* (ASCD, forthcoming).

A. HARRY PASSOW is the Jacob H. Schiff Professor of Education at Teachers College, Columbia University. His most recent publication is *Reforming Schools in the 1980s: A Critical Review of the National Reports.* He has published numerous books and articles on curriculum development, education of adolescents and youth, urban education and education of the disadvantaged, education of the gifted, and school improvement and educational reform. Many of his writings deal with comparative and international education. He has served as Visiting Professor of Education at Stockholm University in Sweden and at Tel-Aviv and Bar-Ilan universities in Israel.

JOHN J. PRUNTY is an instructional designer at Maritz Communications Company. He recently returned from Australia, where he lectured in educational administration at Deakin University. His background also includes public school teaching, and research with CEMREL and Washington University in St. Louis.

SEYMOUR SARASON is a professor of psychology at the Institute for Social and Policy Studies at Yale University. His latest book is *Caring and Compassion in Clinical Practice: Issues in the Selection, Training and Behavior of Helping Professionals.*

PHILLIP C. SCHLECHTY is a professor of education at the University of North Carolina at Chapel Hill and is currently serving as special assistant to the superintendent of Charlotte-Mecklenburg Schools, Charlotte, North Carolina.

JUDITH SCHWARTZ is director of the Scarsdale Teachers Institute and president of the Scarsdale Teachers Association. She has been an English teacher at Scarsdale High School since 1965 and has worked on curriculum-development projects. She was president of the Southern Westchester National Organization for Women, 1978–1980, and developed a woman's studies course.

LOUIS SMITH has his Ph.D. in psychology from the University of Minnesota (1955). He teaches educational psychology and educational anthropology in the Department of Education at Washington University, St. Louis, Missouri. *The Complexities of an Urban Classroom* (1968) and *Anatomy of Educational Innovation* (1971) resulted from earlier field work research.

DOROTHY S. STRICKLAND is professor of education at Teachers College, Columbia University. Her publications include *The Role of Literature in Reading Instruction; Listen Children: An Anthology of Black Literature;* and *Harcourts' Elementary Language Arts Program.* She holds elected office in the National Council of Teachers of English and is past president of the International Reading Association.

LESLIE R. WILLIAMS is associate professor of early childhood education at Teachers College, Columbia University. Her interests include the history of early childhood education, design of programs for children from birth to age eight, and multicultural approaches to teaching young children.

KAREN KEPLER ZUMWALT, associate professor of education, Teachers College, Columbia University, faced the beginning years of teaching in Cleveland and Glencoe, Illinois, and through her students at Smith and Teachers College. Motherhood began 3 1/2 years ago, with a new challenge arriving this past summer.

Index